The World of
ROGER TORY PETERSON

The World of

ROGER TORY PETERSON

An Authorized Biography

BY JOHN C. DEVLIN AND
GRACE NAISMITH

Foreword by Elliot Richardson

*Paintings and Illustrations by
Roger Tory Peterson*

NYT **Times** BOOKS

The publisher is grateful to Robert Lewin of Mill Pond Press, Venice, Florida, for the use of the reproductions of Roger Tory Peterson's color paintings in the book and on the jacket.

The black-and-white drawings by Roger Tory Peterson are used by the kind permission of the artist. Drawings on pages i, iii, 1, 3, 24, 32, 48, 53, 62, 69, 71, 80, 90, 101, 115, 130, 139, 149, 151, 169, 188, 199, 215, and 239 reprinted from *Wild America* by Roger Tory Peterson and James Fisher, Houghton Mifflin, © 1955 by Roger Tory Peterson; page 53, reprinted from *Audubon* magazine, November–December 1968; page 90, reprinted from *The Bird Watcher's Anthology*, Harcourt Brace, © 1957 by Roger Tory Peterson. Ruffed grouse painting: "Collection of The New Britain Museum of American Art, New Britain, Connecticut [Charles F. Smith Fund]"

Book design: Beth Tondreau

Library of Congress Cataloging in Publication Data

Devlin, John C.
  The world of Roger Tory Peterson.

  Includes index.
  1. Peterson, Roger Tory, 1908–   2. Ornithologists—United States—Biography. I. Naismith, Grace, joint author. II. Title.
QL31.P45D48   1977   598.2'092'4 [B]   77-5480
ISBN 0-8129-0694-2

Contents

Contents

Illustrations

Acknowledgments

WRITING this book has been an experience, as exciting and rewarding as any we have had in our lives. Although Roger was an old friend, getting to know him as intimately as we did while working on the book was exhilarating. A whole new world of birds and people and places opened up to expand our knowledge and pleasure in the growing field of nature.

It took more than three years to research and write the book. We have taped dozens of interviews with Roger, and read dozens of his unpublished memos. We read scores of books about birds and bird people, conservation, and wildlife painting. We taped interviews with more than a hundred of Roger's friends and relatives. Replaying these tapes now is like nostalgically reliving our trips—to Jamestown, New York, Roger's hometown; to Florida where Helen Cruickshank lives and the Buchheisters winter; to Connecticut to see Edwin Way Teale; to Maine where Mrs. Clarence Allen lives, and to Toronto to visit Terry Shortt at the Royal Ontario Museum. There have been other places, equally delightful.

The book could not have been done without the significant cooperation and contributions of these and other wonderful people, drawn together by their affection for the incredible Roger and by their love of nature. Among them are:

Evelyn Allen, John Allen, Katherine Allen, Dean Amadon, Robert Arbib, Dr. Elisha Atkins, Irston Barnes, Clarence Beal, Richard and "Brownie" Borden, Paul Brooks, Hal Borland, Carl and Harriet Buchheister, John Bull, Mildred Washington Busse, Charles Callison, Roger Caras, Alton Carlson, Betty Carnes, Edward and Margaret Chalif, Chester Chard, Howard Cleaves, Roland Clement, Guy Coheleach, William Conway, Helen Cruickshank, Lois Darling, John Henry Dick, John A. Diffily, Cornelia Eastland, Eugene Eisenmann, Francisco Erize, David Lloyd Garrison, Devin Garrity, Elaine Giambattista, William Gunn, Wil-

Acknowledgments

liam V. Guthrie, Carl Hammerstrom, Marcia Harty, Robert Hernandez, Joseph and Peggy Hickey, George Holton, Eric Hosking, Paul Griswold Howes, Philip Humphrey, Barbara Hurst, Allan Jones, Stanford Jones, Irving Kassoy, Joseph and Barbara Kastner, Stuart Keith, John Kieran, Russ and Jane Kinne, Richard Kuerzi, Anne LaBastille, Margaret Lager, David and Ellen Lank, Robert and Katie Lewin, Lars Lindblad, John A. Livingston, Tom Lovejoy, Fernando Maldonado, Al and Kappy Maley, Harold Mayfield, Harold Mitchell, M. Lorimer Moe, Guy Mountfort, Wesley and Peggy Nord, John "Tex" O'Reilly, Barbara Peterson, Lee Peterson, Tory Peterson, Virginia Peterson, Olin Sewall and Eleanor Pettingill, Richard Pough, Noble S. Proctor, Bayard Reed, Elliot Richardson, Alvah Sanborn, Sir Peter Scott, Dr. Roy Lyman Sexton, Keith Shackleton, Terry M. Shortt, W. J. L. Sladen, Paul Spitzer, Alexander "Sandy" Sprunt, Gardner and Clare Stout, George Sutton, Joseph Taylor, Edwin Way Teale, Allen M. Thomas, Jean Vasiloff, Gertrude Whiting, and Farida Wylie.

John C. Devlin and
Grace Naismith, 1977

Foreword

It has been said that my old friend and teacher, Roger Tory Peterson, has done more than any other person to make the field identification of birds a science. I am sure that is true. But it is fair to say that Roger Tory Peterson has also done more than any other man to make field identification a sport.

When I first knew Roger Peterson he was a young teacher at the Rivers School in Brookline, Massachusetts. When he wasn't teaching me and my fellow students how to draw and paint or imparting to us his own enthusiasm for birds and other wild creatures, he was working on the first edition of his *A Field Guide to the Birds*. Once in a while—partly for science and partly for fun—he would go off on what he called a "century day." Starting one midnight and ending at the stroke of the following midnight, he and another equally gifted field ornithologist would undertake to identify within a twenty-four-hour period as many species of birds as possible. They would set off in total darkness and total silence in the woods of Essex County north of Boston, waiting and listening for the sound of owls. And of course they could distinguish instantly the sound of one owl from that of another—the screech owl or great horned owl or barred owl, and one which I confess never having encountered, Richardson's owl.

From the Essex woods they would go to the marshes near Lynnfield and walk out over an abandoned railroad track before dawn and listen for the calls of the short-billed and long-billed marsh wrens, and the sora rail and the Virginia rail. The next stop was the Mount Auburn Cemetery in Cambridge. By this time the sun would be up, making it possible not only to hear and identify the warblers and other migrants by voice, but also to see them in the trees. The great advantage of Mount Auburn for this purpose is that you can walk under the trees: there is no underbrush, and it is easy enough to avoid the gravestones.

At least three dozen species of warblers traverse Massachusetts every year. Most people are unaware of them because they pass through in the thickets or high overhead in the trees. They are beautiful little birds, quick-moving and graceful—orange and black, slate blue and black, yellow with various patterns. Their annual arrival in the Mount Auburn Cemetery and in every other green and open space in New England symbolizes for me the most important thing I learned from Roger Tory Peterson: that there is a lot of life around us that we don't take in because we aren't looking, we aren't listening, we aren't paying attention.

Even though I never became the kind of bird watcher who keeps a life list which he adds to year by year, I still remember almost every occasion when I saw a bird for the first time. Even now, whenever I walk along the shore of a certain cove at the edge of the Nauset Marsh in Eastham on Cape Cod, I remember the March day in 1933 when Roger Tory Peterson spotted a seaside sparrow, a rare visitor. I have never seen a seaside sparrow since.

Roger Peterson was the only real teacher of drawing and painting I ever had. Starting me off with charcoal still lifes, he led me through the early stages of painting in oils to the year's climactic effort—a painting of a hooded merganser sitting on a dead limb in a forest pool. My model was a stuffed bird donated to the school by some unknown benefactor, and I wish I could say that the painting itself was as handsome as the bird.

I shall always be indebted to Roger for skills of eye, ear, and hand. Indeed, it may well be that through encouraging me to develop these skills he also gave me an even more precious asset: the ability to endure pressure and adapt to changes of circumstance. What could more quickly restore a sense of proportion than a few minutes spent watching a self-absorbed Carolina wren build a nest? What could more completely eclipse large concerns than the constraining effort to make hand and brush obey eye and brain?

What Roger gave me he has given in equal and even greater measure to countless others. He set out to be primarily a painter of birds. He watched birds in the field so that he could paint them perfectly. But he is one of those people who feel the need to give, who are filled with an enthusiasm which they long to share. Throughout his career as an artist and ornithologist, the compulsion to teach and the love of teaching keep breaking in.

Roger Tory Peterson's field guides and the other books which bear his name have instructed millions of people in the richness of the natural world. If we were to single out his most important contribution, would it be these remarkable books? His brilliantly life-like portraits of birds? His extraordinary effectiveness as a spokesman for conservation and the environment?

His greatest contribution, I believe, is the sum of these—our enlarged awareness.

ELLIOT RICHARDSON

Introduction

ROGER TORY PETERSON has been hailed by many as having contributed more to the worldwide appreciation of birds than even the famed artist-naturalist John James Audubon.

The Peterson *A Field Guide to the Birds*, first published in 1934, has sold about two million copies. Peterson has also written eight other nature books, illustrated six more, contributed articles on birds and conservation to natural history and popular magazines, written dozens of introductions to nature books written by others, supervised production of several nature films, broadcast on radio and television, and traveled to more than eighty countries, as well as to the Arctic and Antarctic many times.

As a director of many wildlife and conservation organizations, he has wielded a tremendous influence in environmental and ecological conservation. But it was that first field guide that opened the doors for countless people to the exotic world of nature. Guides on everything from bugs to wild flowers to sea shells followed in the Peterson Field Guide Series. A Roger Tory Peterson environmental center is being established in his native Jamestown, New York, to honor his achievements in nature and conservation.

At sixty-nine, when most persons have retired, Roger Tory Peterson, a handsome, virile, six-foot, 180-pound man, was well launched on a new career as a "gallery painter," fulfilling a youthful ambition that had been sidetracked by his field guides, travel, and other activities. His bird portraits, published by Robert Lewin of the Mill Pond Press, have already become collectors' items. Guy Mountfort, president of the British Ornithologists' Union and co-author with Roger and P. A. D. Hollom of *A Field Guide to the Birds of Britain and Europe*, believes that Roger's paintings "deserve to be ranked with the great masters." Many others agree. Roger has painted at least four thousand birds (not species) in his life, every bird in North America and every European species, mostly for the field guides and other publications.

Roger Tory Peterson, as an inveterate traveler, is a member of the Explorers Club. In 1974 alone, Roger traveled to five continents to photograph and study birds. On the tour ship the *Lindblad Explorer* he has been a nature lecturer since 1967. He has exposed 100,000 color transparencies in his lifetime, nearly 10,000 on penguins.

He has twenty-six awards, six honorary doctorates of science, and two doctorates of humanities.

Roger's obsession with birds has never waned since he was an eleven-year-old boy in Jamestown. He says he was an "incorrigible kid," which no doubt will surprise many of his admirers who think of him as staid and puritanical. "I might even have wound up in a reform school if I had not developed my interest in birds."

He says that his father "whaled the stuffing out of me with a razor strap for misbehaving," but lived to see and be proud of Roger's first field guide. Originally rejected by five publishers, the first printing sold out in three weeks. The book is now in its forty-seventh printing, selling a hundred thousand copies a year, and a complete revision is being prepared. As bird watching and public concern over the environment has zoomed, the field guide series has sold more than four million copies.

"It was Peterson who made field identification a science," said Dr. Josselyn Van Tyne, former president of the American Ornithologists' Union. "Peterson," he said, "gave order to what had previously been a haphazard procedure."

"My identification system," explains Roger, "is visual rather than phylogenetic; it uses shape, pattern, and field marks in a comparative way. The phylogenetic order, which is related to evolution, is not emphasized within families. Similar-appearing species are placed together on plates and the *critical distinctions* are pointed out with little arrows."

The Peterson System has reduced the time necessary to become efficient in identifying the birds of a region from half a lifetime to two or three years. First applied to birds, this visual system is now used in many other branches of natural history.

There are an estimated forty million people interested in birds and birding. The bird business—birdseed, binoculars, cameras, field guides, travel—reaches $500 million a year. Since the first Peterson field guide, interest in birds is said to have increased fortyfold, and it is certainly no accident that the environmental movement was sparked in large measure by serious birdwatchers.

Roger prefers to think of himself more "as a cross-the-board naturalist—an interpreter, an elucidator—of the natural scene." He says, however, "that birds have been my focus—or obsession, an obsession from which I have never freed myself."

Roger Tory Peterson lives, with his third wife, Virginia, at Old Lyme, Connecticut, an early American community on the east side of the Connecticut River. (His first wife was Mildred Washington; his second, for thirty-two years, Barbara Coulter.) Roger chose Old Lyme in 1954 because of its rural charm and convenient location, halfway between his field guide publishers, Houghton Mifflin Company in Boston, and the art centers of New York City.

The Petersons own about seventy-three acres. They call it "The Cedars." Across Route 156 where their road, Neck Road, breaks off sharply, there are many marshes that once had nesting ospreys —fish hawks—in which Roger is intensely interested. The osprey colony was virtually wiped out by overuse of pesticides and is only beginning to return to the environmentally improved area.

The house is French Huguenot in style, squarish, charming, attractively settled against a verdant hillside, heavily wooded, with ivy-covered stone walls to hold back the terraces behind the house. A steep, narrow driveway winds to the house.

The house has three fireplaces—two upstairs and one on the first floor. There a glass wall gives an open view to a colorful garden with several bird feeders. It was ideal when Roger and Barbara were raising their two sons—Tory, the older, a banker in North Carolina with a wife and small daughter; and Lee, who lives in Old Lyme. Lee has written a book on edible wild plants for the Peterson Field Guide series.

It is an informal and cheerful house where young people and others from the community run in and out, borrowing binoculars, checking something from a bird book, or perhaps bringing in a dead bird for identification. There are soft drinks in the refrigerator, along, perhaps, with the "skin" of a bird that the artist is painting.

Roger's paintings of birds fill the house. In the living room there is a long couch where Roger frequently stretches out casually while he chats with visitors. He is inclined to dress casually, too, in slacks and turtlenecks. He talks easily, articulately (and some say endlessly) in a rather low voice at times monotonously rhythmic.

Roger has his office some distance from the house in a small Colonial building—the York house, they call it.

Back and beyond the house, up a winding path with English ivy borders, is Roger's studio. The cedar-shingle structure, once an old barn, has two stories. The studio, with wide picture windows, looks over a kidney-shaped frog pool. As in any artist's studio, there are the easels, the paint-brush "bouquets," and bird paintings in various stages of completion. And there is Roger's ever-present couch. He thinks better lying down.

The lower floor has two large rooms, one lined with cabinets containing photographs, color slides, and research material. In the other room is a fireproof vault and drawer after drawer of Roger's collection of bird skins and stuffed birds—at least 1,800, including an 1879 specimen of the extinct passenger pigeon. There are boxes of unfiled material, though Barbara had through the years filed and labeled the many cabinets and arranged cameras, binoculars, and other equipment for Roger's convenience. "The big trouble," says Roger, "is to file away the material before you reach old age." Like many an older person, Roger thinks a great deal about his health and is "determined to stave off the grim reaper by any means—from dietetic foods to transcendental meditation, if necessary." He is always pushing, pushing to get "everything done" in his lifetime. He does take occasional breaks to jog, a mile in eight minutes or a walk for about three miles, and he does rigorous calisthenics, even before breakfast.

One of Roger's characteristics as a genius, although he is not an eccentric, is absentmindedness. He is notorious for it, usually blaming it on his preoccupation with birds. Barbara accepted it and said it was a fact of life that Roger had to be told everything twice.

"He is not scatterbrained at all, not what we think of as being scatterbrained," says M. Lorimer Moe, a lifelong friend and active developer of the Roger Tory Peterson Center for Environmental

Studies at the Jamestown Community College and also the Roger Tory Peterson Nature Interpretive Building at the Jamestown Audubon Society's Burgeson Wildlife Sanctuary. Moe says, "Roger simply has disdain for a lot of things others think are important."

Yet family and friends and business associates always seem to be shepherding him, making—and reminding him of—appointments, getting him off to trains and planes and meetings.

Absentminded or not, when there is a real emergency and there is no wife or secretary around to remind or prod him, Roger can rise to any occasion.

For example, in the summer of 1974 when Roger was on a trip to Greenland on the *Lindblad Explorer,* the ship, although designed to force its way through most ice fields, did in fact become icebound. Roger, as a renowned son from Chautauqua County, New York, had promised to give the wind-up lecture of the season at the Chautauqua Institution near Jamestown to mark the one hundredth anniversary of that fine old cultural institution. He had not only remembered his commitment without prompting, but was very determined to get there, ice or no ice.

As the *Explorer* approached Resolute, a community near the North Pole, ice blocked it completely. "It was a real cliff-hanger," Roger says. Fortunately, they were able to contact a Canadian Coast Guard icebreaker, the *Labrador,* which was nearby, and its master, Captain Paul Tooke, got Roger aboard.

Captain Tooke, it so happened, was an ardent bird watcher himself and he and Roger became deeply involved in long, night bull sessions about birds. It began to look as if he would not let Roger go to keep his speaking engagement. Furthermore, the ice was so thick that not even the *Labrador* was able to make the port at Resolute. The icebreaker, however, was equipped with a helicopter landing pad and Captain Tooke reluctantly arranged to have his fascinating guest flown by helicopter over to Resolute just in time to make the thrice-weekly airplane out of the area to Montreal and thence to Chautauqua.

It is typical of Roger that, in spite of his preoccupations, work, and many engagements, when he returned home, he immediately sent an autographed copy of his *A Field Guide to Wild Flowers* to Captain Tooke's young daughter, Shannon, in Bedford, Nova Scotia. He prizes her thank-you letter, which ended, "I also appreciate the fact that you personally signed it yourself for me."

Roger has many unusual qualities, some of which have been called "temperamental." But it is the temperament of a genius, according to Carl W. Buchheister, former president of the National Audubon Society, "and by the very nature of his genius, he finds any normal restriction on his actions very irksome. He wants to do what he wants to do when he wants to do it. If he wants to work right through the night, he will."

Roger thinks nothing of watching birds for twenty hours straight, then sleeping in a swamp for twenty-four hours. When the rare Ross's gull was found near Boston in March 1975, Roger went twenty-four hours without sleep, "high" on excitement. Food does not seem crucial to him, either, when he is involved with birds.

Guy Mountfort tells how he honored Roger once at the fashionable Savile Club in London. They had just finished *A Field Guide to the Birds of Britain and Europe*. Roger, always a compulsive talker on his favorite subject of birds, paid no attention to the waiter.

Mountfort finally broke in. "Roger, what would you like for your first course?"

Roger looked at the menu blankly and said, "Cherry pie."

As to clothes, Roger does not think it matters what people wear, including himself. At a recent National Audubon Society dinner he appeared looking distinguished in a black dinner jacket ("I forgot to bring my cummerbund," he confessed), but he is equally at ease in a bright red flannel shirt, lounging on a couch at the Sutton Place South, New York, apartment of Lars-Eric Lindblad. Lately he has become more aware of his "image." He likes turtleneck sweaters and, ever since Lars told him they were socially correct, he wears them on any occasion. He even wore one with his light blue suit when he married "Ginny" in 1976. He likes blue and it accentuates his blue eyes.

They say that Roger is indifferent to clothes, especially when he tosses them aside in piles in the corner, even on the *Explorer*.

This seems incongruous, for Roger shows meticulous care of his paint brushes, cameras, sharpened drawing pencils, and the thousands of filed exposures he has taken. He knows where everything is, and the little film containers have the names of the subjects, often scientific, as well as the places and dates where he did the photography.

He also has a memory bank for bird calls and songs, and his hearing is extraordinary as well. He usually identifies the bird correctly from the sound, even in foreign countries where he hasn't encountered that bird before. Despite his age, Roger's ears are as keen as they ever were. Richard Borden, the cinematographer who produces *Wonders of the Wild* documentaries, some of them including Roger, noticed his hearing acuity recently when they were birding near Concord, Massachusetts. Borden said, "I hear an oriole." Roger said, "Yes, and it is a young one."

Roger not only identifies birds by their calls, but he can imitate some of them, occasionally so realistically that a male bird has been reported to have flown after him in the woods thinking a rival was calling.

Roger has become far more than just an ardent birdwatcher. His achievements have been summed up by John A. Livingston, Canadian author and professor of Environmental Studies at York University: "The contemporary Peterson is artist, editor, writer, scientist, lecturer, compulsive traveler, compulsive photographer, film-maker, conservationist, naturalist. These 'field markers' are not arranged in any rank order, save for the first and last. The *real* Roger Tory Peterson, in my judgment, is an artist-naturalist. That is what the Jamestown lad set out to be, and that is what he is."

Part I

CHAPTER I

The Mischievous Boy of Bowen Street

HE was scrawny and wiry, a freckle-faced, hollow-cheeked kid, with unruly hair and an independent and rebellious spirit.

His love was nature. His hate was freckles. And discipline.

For his freckles he tried Stillman's Freckle Creme in regular strength, then in double and triple. But it did no good. The freckles stayed until he was a grown man.

Discipline was something else. To avoid it—any restriction or regimentation—he would go afield to be with his beloved nature and to be "as free as a bird."

"Birds have wings," he said. "They can fly where they want to when they want to."

This was Roger Tory Peterson, the boy, a very different sort of boy from the other kinds growing up in the hilly, factory-centered Jamestown, then a city of 45,000, in southwestern New York at the southern tip of Lake Chautauqua, twenty-five miles from Lake Erie.

Roger's friends were limited. One reason was that he was a loner. Few boys had any special interest in nature, certainly not his intense, absorbing passion for everything from birds to butterflies, from flowers to turtles. Furthermore, most of his classmates were older because Roger had gone to summer school two years, skipping ahead into high school when he was only twelve. The older boys thought he was, as Roger says, "some kind of kook." In the cruel way of youngsters but without real malice, some took to calling him "Professor Nuts Peterson" or "Bugs Peterson." One neighbor pal said, however, "we weren't really stinky." Mostly they were puzzled by him and amused at this "strangest boy in town," who sometimes arrived in school with such things as snakes, toads, or bird eggs in his pockets, sometimes smelling like a skunk after catching one in a butterfly net.

Probably the worst name he was called in high school was "Sleeping Jesus," not because of any religious bent, but because he frequently dozed off in class, his tousled head on his desk.

He was sleepy for good reason. He had a job delivering newspapers—*The Jamestown Morning Post*—and had to get up as early as three o'clock to serve his route. Of course this took him by his bird-feeding stations and he had to stop to put out some sunflower seeds. Sometimes he was late for classes, which brought down disciplinary measures from the principal. He used the newspaper money to buy his first camera, a Primo Number 9, a four-by-five plate model, to take nature pictures. In 1923, at age fifteen, he had photographed twenty-five species of birds. And he built a darkroom in the basement of the modest but roomy house at 16 Bowen Street, midway up a high hill overlooking the city, where he had been born August 28, 1908.

"We had corporal punishment of sorts in school then," Roger says. "One principal—a Miss Dixon—had her own means of discipline for the really bad boys. You just put your hands out and she would whack them with a ruler, a straight-edge ruler, until you cried. I had at least seven or eight such whackings in the course of one year, which was the record for our school. That was when I was back in the fifth grade."

One of the "bad things" Roger did was to refuse to walk out of the school "two by two like the animals in Noah's Ark." He would double back at the bell and go down the fire escape, behavior bad enough to get a ruler whacking. And once he poked the girl who sat in front of him with a pen point because, he says, "she annoyed me."

More serious out-of-school mischief was rolling garbage cans and auto tires down the streets, as steep as those in San Francisco. Roger was even accused of releasing the hand brakes of parked cars (as other boys had done) and starting grass fires.

Then there was the time he became involved in possible theft.

Not far from Roger's house there was a warehouse that belonged to a man from Erie, Pennsylvania. He came to Jamestown every weekend to inspect it. The warehouse was filled with all kinds of interesting things, including a small, old printing press. One of the boys in the neighborhood (not Roger) paid another boy five cents to break into the place and bring out one of those old penny-farthing bicycles with a high front wheel. Roger got into the place with the boys and they found some gilt printing powder near the press. They helped themselves.

When the warehouse owner came from Erie for his regular checkup, he found the bicycle missing as well as the gold powder.

He was a very clever fellow, who went around to all the houses in the neighborhood and looked at the doorknobs. On Roger's doorknob he found traces of gold powder. So Roger was incriminated. There was quite a bit of fuss about it, but nothing of importance happened.

Roger got into so many scrapes someone called him "the mischievous boy of Bowen Street." The father of one of his friends defended the boy. "There's nothing really *scoundrelly* about Roger," he said, but Roger admits that he "might easily have become the most notoriously bad boy in my home community had it not been for birds."

His father used a razor strap many times, for discipline was as much a problem at home as it was at school. This, of course, was in the days of "spare the rod and spoil the child."

Roger's father was upset, and rightly so, because the boy had no interest in pulling weeds and mowing the lawn. He said, "Why should we mow the lawn? Let the grass grow and song sparrows can nest in the shrubbery." This argument didn't impress his father. Roger's whole attitude was to let everything go back to nature.

Then, at the age of eleven, birds took over his life.

He was in the seventh grade when his teacher, Miss Blanche Hornbeck, started a Junior Audubon Club. Sponsored by the National Association of Audubon Societies, the Junior Club members bought, for ten cents, ten little leaflets about birds. Each one had four pages of text, with a colored picture by a reigning bird artist of the day—Bruce Horsfall, Allan Brooks, or the great Louis Agassiz Fuertes—and a page for the student to color. Members were given an identification button with the name Audubon on it to wear on their shirts. Roger's pin had a red-wing blackbird on it.

Blanche Hornbeck was rather slight, freckled (like Roger) with reddish hair, and about thirty-one years old. She remained in the Jamestown school system for only a year or so.

There was a neighbor boy, Carl Hammerstrom, also Swedish, who lived a few doors down and across Bowen Street. He, like Roger, fell under the spell of Miss Hornbeck's enthusiasm for birds. Roger found in Carl a friend with mutual interests. Roger recalls, with a memory amazing for one notorious for his absent-mindedness, that Carl and he took their first bird walk on April 8, 1920. It was to Swede Hill.

From their own steep hill, the boys could see their destination far across the town, with its furniture factories and railroad tracks below in the valley. Swede Hill was a green and rolling summit. Roger remembers that the day was "nice, with patchy sun."

Hammerstrom, now a retired physician, recalls the occasion of thirty-five years ago with warm nostalgia: "We started from the old quarry where my Swedish immigrant relatives had worked, digging out stones for foundations of Jamestown houses. It was our first serious birding. We had the Chester A. Reed pocket *Bird Guide* with us. We didn't have binoculars or cameras. The expense you know, difficult. Up and over the hills we wandered and we saw—birds!

"Finally we came on one apparently asleep on a tree. I gave it some name which was obviously wrong, but I sounded quite authoritative. Roger didn't agree exactly but said very little. And we walked over and actually petted the bird, which then flew off. It was what we called locally a 'heigh-ho,' which is a flicker, and that is what *Roger* thought it was. We checked it in Reed's."

And Roger says, "I touched it with my hand, my first flicker."

Miss Hornbeck had her class copy in watercolor some of the pictures in Elon A. Eaton's *Birds of New York*. Roger chose to do a bluejay painting by Louis Agassiz Fuertes. He was upset when some girl in the class got the credit for his painting. "I made a fuss," he says, "and they straightened things out."

Roger has always been partial to bluejays. "Bluejays have a lot of character," he says. "A bluejay is just *I AM*."

"One Saturday," Roger recalls, "a group of us went with Miss Hornbeck to the Hundred-Acre Lot, the school park, east of town. I remember only one bird, my first yellow throat. I also remember that two of the girls rolled their long black stockings down because it was so warm."

So intense was Roger's absorption in birds that he would go out to his feeding stations in the dead of winter. He wrote in *Bird Lore* many years later of his "ambitious" winter bird-feeding activity, together with Clarence Beal, "another kindred bird enthusiast."

"Every other day when the four-o'clock bell concluded our studies, we would don our skis and start for the woods at the edge of town with a knapsack full of grain. What few pennies we could scrape up were spent for sunflower seed, cracked corn, and suet. With us, winter bird feeding was a passion. At one time we had twenty different feeding stations in the woods near town. How I remember some of those trips, when the thermometer dropped to ten or fifteen degrees below zero! We would sometimes return with globules of ice on our eyelashes and little gray patches frozen on our cheeks."

Icicles dripped from their noses. Schoolmates tell of Roger's nose always running, not only from the cold but perhaps from an allergy of some kind.

At night the bones of his legs ached excrutiatingly from chilblains. His footwear was often inadequate. His feet were always wet. It was the same for most of the boys he knew. Most bedrooms in Jamestown had no heat, the only fire usually being in the kitchen range or an upright stove in the dining room or parlor. From the anthracite coal that was burned, black clouds of pollution hung over the city during the long winters. Icicles reached nearly to the ground and did not melt until spring. Jamestown averaged ninety-eight inches of snow a year, and in some years has had as much as four hundred fifty.

It wasn't easy, growing up in a place like Jamestown, not only because of the cold and the poverty, but because of the bitter discrimination against "furriners," especially the immigrant Swedes.

Roger was ridiculed not only for his almost eccentric interest in nature, but because he was a Swede. Inwardly the boys could not help but be impressed with his knowledge of things wild, even though they could not understand it. They could—and did—pick on him for his nationality.

Roger explains that the town was started by the landed English gentry who owned the many worsted woolen mills. Then came the Swedes, mostly untutored woodworkers. The English looked down on the Swedes.

A combination of poverty, religious repression, and the bright promise of America had driven thousands of Swedish families to the New World. The foothills of the Alleghenies were green with hardwood trees, just what the Swedes needed for making fine furniture. Eventually there were one hundred furniture factories in Jamestown, mostly run by Swedes. Many of the early English settlers moved on, still heaping insults upon the immigrant Swedes as they left.

"Here we were," said Dr. Hammerstrom, "sons of Swedes, first generation Americans, called 'Green Swedes' because we weren't supposed to be smart enough to peel bananas before eating them. There were signs saying 'No Dogs or Swedes Allowed,' and public places with posters—'Only English Spoken Here.' "

Even Roger's middle name, Tory, inherited from an uncle, *Tore* (Swedish pronunciation Toūr-eh), was changed by one of his uncle's school teachers to "Tory" on his school records—to give it a "respectable" English pronunciation.

One thing the discrimination did, according to Lorimer Moe, "was to intensify the immigrants' determination to succeed." And they did. Some of the finest furniture in the United States is still made in Jamestown by descendants of the Swedish pioneers, and many Jamestown Swedes went on to important careers as doctors, lawyers, and teachers.

This was the environment in which Roger grew up. It is possible that the ridicule and insults whetted his own almost fanatical desire to succeed, to prove himself, and to "show them."

Roger's father, Charles Gustav Peterson, had come, at age two, in 1873, from Varmland in the vicinity of Karlstadt, Sweden, with his parents, Nils Peter Peterson and Anna Sophia Folcker, whose family name was derived from a German forebear, one of two brothers, high-ranking army officers who fled Germany as political refugees to make a new life in Sweden.

Roger does not know why his grandfather came to this country. "When I would discuss our genealogy with my father," Roger recalls, "he would paraphrase Will Rogers to the effect that if you dig far enough even in the best of families, you will usually find one member who was hanged as a horse thief."

Grandfather Peterson died, apparently of a ruptured appendix. when Charles was only a small boy. His widow did the best she could to support her four children, doing laundry, baking bread, performing other menial tasks.

This was still the era of child labor, and the desperate Anna Sophia put Roger's father and a little sister in the mills before they were ten. People in those days carried their children to the mills even through the deep snows. The children worked for ten hours a day and were lashed with a cat-o'-nine tails if they slowed their efforts. Roger's father, who had only three years of schooling, took on as much of the responsibility of breadwinner as he could.

Tragically, Charles Peterson broke a leg skating. The leg was not properly set, and later, while swimming in the cold waters of Cassadaga Creek one March, he contracted what was then called rheumatism. Dr. Hammerstrom, who attended him in later years, says he had degenerative arthritis and that he was badly crippled, his right leg shortened. He was a surprisingly cheerful man, though there was never a day he did not feel pain.

Roger could never erase the picture of the deep and painful limp his father had. It handicapped him in earning a livelihood and sometimes led him to alcohol as a pain-killer. As a youngster, Roger sometimes resented, as children will, the fact that his father was not a "better provider." It was not until he grew older that Roger fully appreciated "the odds that this man struggled against."

Roger's only sister, Margaret, says the father drank only on paydays or holidays, which "messed them up" and "Roger and I hated him for it."

Not so his mother, who understood.

She was born Henrietta Bader, in Germany, in a little town near Breslau, now a part of Poland. She was pure Wendish stock. The Wends were a Slavic people who lived in a corner of Germany, keeping their own language. She was a beautiful woman with an olive complexion and long black hair that swept to her knees. Her eyes were dark brown, and the Italian tradesmen who came to the house often inquired if she was Italian.

Henrietta was brought to the United States when she was only four. Her father was an innkeeper abroad, as well as a contractor and builder of bridges. Roger believes he had business reverses and came to this country to make a second start. The family lived in Rochester. Henrietta, the youngest of four girls and one boy, was not expected to survive her babyhood. She never seemed to be in robust health. Yet she survived the longest, dying at ninety-seven in 1976. Some said she was the brightest of the family, and she had the advantage of some higher education. She attended a teachers' college and taught in the schools in Olean near Elmira, New York.

It was in Olean that Roger's father met and married Henrietta. He was then a personable traveling salesman for a men's clothing manufacturer, going to almost every state in the union. Some of his territory was covered by horse and buggy. Charlie Peterson was noted for his sense of humor, despite that painful hip, and he had a vast repertoire of jokes. He never went to church. He stated unequivocally that most churchgoers he knew were hypocrites.

Mrs. Peterson, on the other hand, was very active in the Holy Trinity Lutheran Church, then situated on West Fourth Street in downtown Jamestown. The couple had moved to the home of Charlie's father and mother after they were married. For many years, Mrs. Peterson was superintendent of the primary department of the Sunday school. Roger was confirmed in this church, but has never been quite sure what effect his mother's religion had on him. "There have been times," he says, "when I have felt that being a Lutheran and a Puritan with the fear of God in my bones may have given me guilt feelings that I have never been able to overcome. I have always felt a bit guilty about certain pleasures, and yet basically, I *am* a hedonist. I am quite certain, nonetheless, that my early days in the Lutheran Church have given me a more structured life than I would have known otherwise."

The first time Roger seriously questioned the Church was when the new minister came to visit his home. When his mother proudly presented him, she told the minister that Roger was interested in birds and natural history. The pastor frowned and said, "Well, that makes for unbelievers."

Not all of the Holy Trinity pastors in Jamestown shared this view. The Reverend E. E. Ryden recalled one Sunday morning that, when the general prayer had already been said, Roger arrived with muddy shoes and rumpled clothes. As he slid quietly into his mother's pew, the lad was heard to whisper apologetically, "I'm sorry I'm late, but the birds were singing so beautifully."

His mother nodded, and whispered back, "Yes, Roger, and God made the birds, too. Now bow your head and fold your hands."

Roger's sister Margaret (Mrs. Edwin Lager of Ventura, California), recalls that her earliest memory of Roger was in that Lutheran church. Roger was about five or six and she was a couple of years younger. The children were giving a historical playlet. Roger, starring as "Father of His Country," wore a wig and tricorn hat and a Colonial costume, complete with ruffled lace jabot and cuffs, which his mother had made from remnants. After his part ended, Roger did not come down promptly from the platform. He stood "looking dreamily out over the congregation at the stained-glass windows." The colors fascinated him, as colors always have. Margaret had to leave her seat and go bring Roger down.

His fascination with color extended even to making mud pies with his sister, with whom there was often considerable sibling rivalry.

"My mud pies," she says, "were just garden soil frosted with aster petals. But Roger found some actual potter's clay in an empty lot and shaped it into tiny graceful vases, which he painted in bright colors neatly, and baked them hard in Mother's oven."

Roger's father stopped working as a traveling salesman after his marriage and took a job in one of the metal furniture factories, the

Art Metal Company. Though Charles Peterson made as much as the other workers, he was usually hard up, and apparently was a soft touch when it came to lending money to a friend who needed it, possibly with the enticement of drinking. But he has been described as a hard-working, responsible wage earner and a fine cabinetmaker.

Henrietta was obviously a very good manager. As a young girl, her first job had been as a baby-sitter in a well-to-do household in Rochester. A trained nurse taught her expert baby care. She had learned to cook, too, in school, "sort of Pennsylvania Dutch with Swedish accents."

But she must have worked very hard. Living with them after Roger's grandfather died was his widow, who owned the house, "a difficult old lady indeed," who was ill a great deal of the time. The cousins lived upstairs in six rooms. Roger's sister said, "We had two rooms. We all shared the kitchen and bath. It is true we paid no rent, but Papa furnished the food, and did maintenance and gardening, while Mother cooked and cleaned, hand-washed and ironed. I remember tubs and washboards and a copper boiler and 'sad-irons' on the stove. Mother scrubbed the white maple kitchen floor twice a week, carried groceries wearily up the steep hill, did twenty-four-hour nursing when 'Mormor' or anyone else needed it, entertained and fed the old lady's callers, canned, picked wild berries, sewed, baked bread, taught Sunday school, saw that our pets were fed. And she *laughed*. Her discipline was easy. Everybody wanted her good opinion."

Roger's cousin Allan Jones says that he and six other cousins were born in the house and lived there from time to time. Allan raised vegetables and had more than ten dozen chickens and just as many pigeons and lots of rabbits. Roger had no interest in "farming" and refused to help Allan, which didn't help family relations any. The house must have been bursting—and with what confusion! No wonder Roger took to the woods and his birds.

Grandmother Peterson died in 1926; Roger remembers the date: "It was the day I saw my first cardinal."

Roger's father, who was twelve years older than his mother, died of a stroke when he was seventy-six. Out of necessity Mrs. Peterson worked at one time as a cleaning woman or housekeeper at the

Jamestown YMCA. Margaret says she made eighty-five beds a day and cleaned eighty-five rooms. Roger did what he could to help support her. Her subsequent marriage to a successful farmer, Lewis B. Saxton, brought her a well-earned period of comparative ease.

But what of the adolescent Roger and his relationship with his father? It was stormy indeed. In *Birds Over America*, Roger writes of his father's failure to understand his interest in birds, "so spontaneous I could not control it"; he tells of his excitement "just watching birds move, watching them fly."

His father would snort, "So you've been out after birds again! Haven't you seen them all before? And look at your clothes—nobody with any sense would stay out in the rain." Puzzled, he would shake his head. He simply could not understand Roger's stubborn interest in birds.

But underneath he did respect the boy's knowledge. Dr. Hammerstrom, who "knew Roger's father as only a physician can know a patient," says, "Charlie was always extraordinarily proud of Roger, even if he could not understand him."

It was probably this lack of understanding rather than lack of love that created the tension between father and son. But then it seemed that Roger was always in trouble. Roger was always being punished.

Once—in 1922—Roger used his father's $5.00 gold fountain pen to draw a sketch of a banded purple butterfly, which he sent to a contest sponsored by *The Buffalo Times*. The fountain pen was ruined and Roger was punished. But he won the contest and $2.00, and when the newspaper printed the sketch it said, "Roger Peterson, age thirteen, has sent us a very clever drawing."

The father was pleased. And he was pleased again when Roger came up with 99's in high school mechanical drawing class. This was something Charles Peterson could understand. But why couldn't Roger do better at shop—"manual training" as they called it then? He couldn't even make a bird house. Planing and hammering left him cold, whereas his father was a born builder.

And what about this business of chasing around after birds and butterflies, the quarrels with his sister, the fights with the kids? When the older kids ridiculed him for his nature "nuttiness," his mother would say, "Never mind, Roger, you'll show 'em."

But Roger's father worried. At one point, he went to the boy's high school mathematics teacher and spoke to him about the futility of a career based on bird study. Could the teacher dissuade Roger?

Although he promised that he would speak to Roger, he never did. He himself had more than a casual interest in birds and offered to lend Roger a bird guide he had purchased. Roger took it with excitement. But he was disappointed at the book's mistakes and other weaknesses. When he returned the book, he was glum, but did not comment, except to ask how many bird field guides the teacher thought could be sold in the United States. He replied that one person in a thousand might be interested, for a total at that time of possibly 130,000 altogether. Roger was not impressed.

It was Roger's biology teacher who really gave him bad grades, and with good reason. It seems that this teacher apparently wasn't up on her subject. "I would take issue with her from time to time," Roger recalls. "She didn't like that. She made the statement that the snowy egret was extinct and I had to correct her. What she said had been nearly true twenty years earlier but circumstances had changed and the snowy egret had made a comeback. I had no compunctions about bringing up such points in class. So my biology marks were not very good. I was a bit of a free spirit when it came to expressing my own views."

When Roger's mother heard about this problem she advised her son to be more tactful and to discuss differences of opinion with the teacher *after* class, not *in* class. This finally worked, and the teacher ultimately invited Roger to meetings of her "prestigious" Bird and Tree Club. His parents did not learn about it until Mrs. Peterson found a delicate little Madeira napkin in his pocket. It seemed that when the club met at the teacher's home, tea was served, and Roger absentmindedly put the napkin in his pocket. His mother laundered it and Roger returned it, with apologies. Later Roger did become a member of the Bird and Tree Club.

Roger did well in mechanical drawing, and he liked English. Surprisingly, perhaps, he became enthusiastic about "creative" poetry, and wrote a number of moving poems, some with nature themes. "The classes in English lit," Roger says, "were fun." It was during this high school period that his future career was set—writing and painting.

By this time many Irish immigrants, driven by the potato famine in Ireland, had followed the "Green Swede" furniture-makers to Jamestown. A number became saloonkeepers. After the Irish had become absorbed, "the Italians came and, of course, they were the low men on the totem pole for a while and called the usual nasty epithets." Roger says he grew up with Swedish-Italian gang fights. Rocks would fly. He got hit on the head and scarred more than once. "It was hell if you were alone and met a bunch of Italian boys."

When Prohibition came, all the Irish saloonkeepers became respectable cops and the Italians became bootleggers. "Instead of having fifty saloons in town, we had maybe five hundred speakeasies."

The Italians had a special parade on Columbus Day with the Knights of Columbus in their plumed costumes. That's when the boys used to get green apples and throw them at the cops.

The elder Peterson was not amused.

This did not, however, disturb him as much as Roger's obsession with birds. Who could make a living at birds? He simply could not understand. He called Roger a "damn fool" when he was angry, or possibly had had "one too many."

Curiously, Roger did not like his father's baldness. Charles Peterson had lost his hair when he was in his twenties. Roger had been afraid that he would lose his own hair when he got older. Although he had plenty of hair, he didn't want to take any chances and "took to rubbing Glover's Mange Cure" into his scalp.

While Roger was always being "picked on" by his father, Charlie Peterson could be warm and generous to others. "Maybe he was harsh with Roger," Dr. Hammerstrom admits, "but he was a good friend to me. He helped me dig for earthworms. And he had a wire net on a long rod we used for catching crayfish bait when we went bass fishing. Roger was off catching moths or butterflies or chasing birds or something."

Years later, when Roger's first wife, Mildred, visited the Peterson family, she found her father-in-law "a delightful man with a delicious sense of humor." She "fell quite in love with him," and remembers sitting on the floor and cracking jokes back and forth. "We were all laughing, having a wonderful time. Even Roger relaxed a bit, too," but, she added, "Roger's father just couldn't see Roger making a career in birding. He was as concerned for his son as any normal father."

At about this time, another influence came into Roger's life that was of vital importance to his future career. It was Ernest Thompson Seton's book *Two Little Savages*. This classic story, with the subtitle "Being the Adventures of Two Boys Who Lived as Indians, and What They Learned," became his bible, threadbare from reading. Roger's copy had an imitation birchbark cover.

The hero of *Two Little Savages*, twelve-year-old Yan, was also Swedish. He had difficulty in school and his classmates, like Roger's, were older boys. Yan's father had little interest in his son's birding. Roger sympathized with Yan and understood his life, for Yan wanted to run away and be free, as did Roger.

He also found inspiration in Seton's two hundred drawings in the book. Roger's talent for art was developing and the illustrations for quick identification of the river ducks and sea ducks in the book helped spark his yearning to know the characteristics in detail of every creature, especially birds.

In the introduction to his first field guide, *A Field Guide to the Birds*, Roger wrote:

> Those of us who have read Ernest Thompson Seton's semi-autobiographical story, "Two Little Savages," remember how the young hero, Yan, discovered some mounted ducks in a dusty showcase and how he painstakingly made sketches of their patterns.
>
> This lad had a book which showed him how to tell ducks when they were in hand, but since he only saw the live ducks at a distance, he was usually at a loss for their names. He noticed that all the ducks in the showcase were different—all had blotches or streaks that were their labels or identification tags. He decided that if he could put their labels or "uniforms" down on paper, he would know these same ducks as soon as he saw them at a distance on the water.
>
> Many of us, later on, when the sport of bird-study first revealed its pleasurable possibilities, tried to locate a book—

a guide—that would treat *all* birds in the manner that Yan had suggested for the ducks. We found many bird books, but although descriptions were complete and illustrations authoritative, the one thing we wished for—a "boiling down," or simplification, of things so that any bird could be readily and surely told *from all the others* at a glance or at a distance— that, except fragmentarily, we were unable to find.

Roger goes on to say that "we would select some point on each bird as being perhaps the diagnostic feature, though we could not be certain."

This, then, became the idea behind the Peterson field guides, the Peterson System of bird identification.

Seton's detail in bird identification fascinated him. Seton, for instance, in describing river ducks, noted that the males usually had shiny green and black on head and wings, and that the females were a streaky brown. He elaborated, "Red feet; male has pale greenish bill. Known in flight by white tail feathers and thin white bar on wing."

In the Peterson field guides there is a little arrow—or two or more—pointing to these distinguishing identification marks.

Roger has also used a feature of Seton's drawings to advantage— the distinctive silhouettes that have become a Peterson trademark and, as the bird painter John Henry Dick has said, "a new art form."

It was at about this time that Roger became a close friend of Clarence Beal's. Clarence, a couple of years younger than Roger, was the perfect companion with whom to study birds and camp in the woods in Seton-type tepees or lean-tos. They explored endlessly the lovely hills surrounding Jamestown.

Beal, now a successful landscape architect in Jamestown and a leader of the Jamestown Audubon Society, has written charmingly of his boyhood with Roger. "My first actual contact with Roger came in the winter of 1921–22, one cold February day when I had been filling my bird feeders with grain and suet; for some reason, perhaps a desire to establish his strength and superiority—Roger threw me down and washed my face in the snow. His mastery asserted, he never fought with me again."

Beal always knew when Roger was coming to his house because he would hear a birdlike whistle that went something like "whee, whee, yoo, hoo, whee, yoo whee." And there would be Roger, his cap on crooked and a knapsack over his shoulder.

The two boys, armed with the Reed bird guide and bird seed, would head for the woods. This could be Beckerink's Fields, Peterson's Pasture (no relation to Roger), "the old garbage field," Moon Brook, or the Hundred-Acre Lot.

"One morning, May 23, 1923, I helped Roger peddle his papers, starting sometimes at 2 A.M.," Beal recalled. "Then we headed up the outlet of Chautauqua Lake, listing all the birds we saw and heard. We boarded the JWNW [Jamestown, Westfield, and Northwestern Railroad] to Westfield on Lake Erie. We saw 123 that sunny spring day."

They talked about the books they were reading—*The Two Little Savages*, the Horatio Alger books, and Eaton's two-volume set, which was so weighty that Roger had to use his little red wagon and "push it up the hill" from the library a mile and a half from home. He went often to the library, roller skating sometimes. Even at that age he read *The Auk*—the American Ornithologists' Union publication—the *Wilson Bulletin*, as well as *Bird Lore*, which was to become *Audubon* magazine. There was also the *National Geographic Magazine*, for which he wrote years later, and *Handbook of Birds of Eastern North America* by Frank M. Chapman, curator of birds at the American Museum of Natural History.

They slept out. They caught crabs in the creeks and boiled them in big tin cans. They were Ernest Thompson Seton's two little woodsmen. They took many pictures, using Roger's Eastman Primo Number 9, which was excellent for birds and flowers.

The boys dreamed dreams. They also competed fiercely at identifying and listing birds, insects, and flowers. Competition has always spurred Roger on, according to Beal. He had a very stubborn determination to excel, which Beal understood.

Roger has asked his sister if she didn't want to be famous, and was surprised when she said no. Roger always knew he wanted fame, but he didn't realize how international it would be. Even in 1975, when he was chosen by the citizens of Jamestown "as the most famous person to have ever come from Jamestown," he was a bit "dazzled," said a local man. He had won by one vote over the actress Lucille Ball. Roger thought it was remarkable "that a naturalist could win such a contest."

Roger's birding had started with songbirds, like most bird watchers, but he later discovered the ducks. Perhaps the duck identification illustrations in Seton's *Two Little Savages* had influenced him. "I had no idea the water birds were so much fun," he said.

After making the rounds of his feeding trays on January evenings, he often heard the whistling of wings in the dark as goldeneyes flew over, headed for the Chadakoin River. "Later," he wrote in *Birds Over America,* "I found small groups of them swimming on this little wooded creek that drains Chautauqua Lake. By crawling on my belly through the loose snow that blanketed the frozen swamp, I could reach the up-turned trees on the creek bank undetected. My 4-power LeMaire field glasses, which I had bought in response to an advertisement in *Bird Lore,* plainly showed the round white face spots on the drakes that swam attentively around the gray females. In fascination I watched them throw back their heads and sound their strange nasal courting cries."

Roger was always interested in bird and animal behavior, including their mating habits. When the first airplane came to Jamestown—a truly historical event—he failed to see it. "I was watching two grasshoppers copulating," he says, "which shows my basic obsession was pretty strong."

When most people think of Roger, they think of birds. Few realize that butterflies and moths were equally important to him at one stage of his life. And he still belongs to the Xerces Society and attends its meetings.

Roger's mother, ever understanding, had made him a butterfly net and even went to the druggist with him to explain why her son needed cyanide to preserve his specimens, and she helped him hide it from the other children.

His father was less understanding when Roger brought home caterpillars and filled dozens of quart jars with them. He is reported to have thrown one out once when he was particularly fed up. "I had more than eight hundred caterpillars one year," Roger says, "chomping on the fresh leaves that I furnished every day or two. About a hundred and twenty-five pupated, but before the remainder could go into chrysalis the cold winds of October stripped the vines of their leaves and famine was upon my charges."

Roger combed the town from end to end for leaves of Dutchman's pipe, the favorite food plant of this particular butterfly, the green swallowtail, greeny black, with a row of orange spots under the wings four or more inches wide. One old lady chased him when he climbed her porch railing to pluck the last few limp leaves from her Dutchman's pipe trellis.

The caterpillars began to die. Some that attempted pupation ate each other as soon as their skin was shed. It was from some of the last survivors that Roger obtained midget specimens the following spring—butterflies scarcely more than two and a half inches across.

Another time Roger brought home cocoons and fastened them to his mother's lace curtains in the living room. All went well until winter came. Then, with the parlor coal stove glowing hot, the summerlike heat brought action. The cases softened and out came the insects to dry and spread their wings and turn into glorious lunas and Cecropia, Prometheas and Polyphemus. Soon they flew around the room by the dozens, "beautiful creatures in pastel shades of green, yellow, and red, laying strings of tiny sticky white eggs on the piano as well as on the curtains."

Roger's sister and his father were fit to be tied, but Mrs. Peterson was tolerant. And much to everybody's surprise, his father skillfully fashioned mitered boxes for Roger's collection. He also made yard-long steel cabinets to protect Roger's collection of insects. Roger ordered pins and labels from Ward's Natural Science establishment in Rochester and mounted the specimens meticulously.

Roger's night rambles in pursuit of moths were hampered by a Jamestown curfew law; all children had to be off the streets when the siren blew at 8:45. This really vexed Roger. The moths did not show up in any numbers until 9:15 at the earliest. He had discovered that the arc lights hanging high over each street intersection were a good hunting ground, especially the four lights bordering the cemetery on Lakeview Avenue. How to get there and not get arrested for breaking the curfew?

"There was a solution: I trotted down to the City Hall and explained my problem to the police chief. His action was decisive.

Turning to his secretary, he instructed her to type out a permit which read simply: 'This permits Roger Peterson to catch moths around streetlights until 11 P.M. Signed, F. Johnson, Chief of Police.' That piece of paper gave me a real status—a lot of status for a boy of twelve."

Roger has described butterflies in general as surely the most psychedelic of all insects "with their shimmering blue morphos, flashing like heliographs in tropical forests, and aristocratic swallowtails, patched and patterned with improbable combinations of black, yellow, red, and electric green, end products of millennia of evolutionary selection."

Elegant as butterflies are, Roger thinks the luna moth eclipses them in beauty and elegance. It "epitomizes everything that is fragile, elusive, and ephemeral."

Roger remembers very clearly the night he caught his first luna. He had been reading W. J. Holland's book on moths and was determined to catch one.

This was a night creature, of course, and Roger "borrowed" his father's kerosene lantern and set off toward Moon Brook, "appropriately silvered by a rising moon.

"Beyond the bridge, almost to the abandoned narrow-gauge railroad track, a luna, a real luna, flew across the road. Setting the lamp down, I tore into the woods after the pale ghostly form and with a lucky backhand sweep netted it. . . . Nothing I had ever seen before—bird or butterfly—could match the evocative, breathtaking beauty of this, my first luna."

Years later Roger dreamed about the incident. Everything in the dream was exactly the same as his original experience. With one exception. The one he caught in his net in his dream "turned out to be a delicate, nymphlike creature, quite naked."

Roger still recalls the dream and the emotions he had. Noting that since butterflies are basically a hobby of boys and not girls, he suggests that "perhaps it was some kind of adolescent dream of maidenhood, rather like Hudson's Rima in *Green Mansions*, not flesh and blood maidenhood, but an elusive gossamer and floss vision to be pursued and, hopefully, possessed."

It was about this time that there were reports of a specter being sighted in Lakeview Cemetery, floating over tombs, flitting between gravestones. But it could have been only Roger's long and filmy butterfly net. For some reason cemeteries are the best places of all to catch moths. Pretty spooky as it was to Roger, out there alone in the dark, he went many nights pursuing his hobby of the moment. The luna became almost a symbol of something "to be pursued and possessed."

The fact is he was not very much involved with girls at that time. When a classmate had rolled down her stocking on the school bird walk, he "noticed." And once later, in high school, he took a girl on a seventeen-mile bird walk. Seventeen miles! That was the end of *that* relationship! "My techniques were completely wrong as far as most young ladies of that day went," Roger says forlornly.

Nevertheless, Clarence Beal says that Roger "*was* interested in them." And another high school classmate, Marcia Harty, asked him many years later why he never went to parties. "He always seemed to be off chasing butterflies or birds," she said. His answer startled her: "Because I was never asked." She added, "I should have seen through Roger's shyness and invited him."

One need not think of Roger as a lonely or unhappy child. Like little Yan of *Two Little Savages*, he found compelling interest in all things wild and beautiful, but still found time to play or scrap with the boys in the neighborhood.

There was little organized sport in the Swedish community, a little baseball and football, but Roger did not participate. He was too slight in stature, though strong, especially in the legs from so many miles of walking and looking for birds.

Roger took up smoking at age nine, making cigarettes out of newspapers or a dried weed called curly dock, but he quit when his mother caught him puffing away behind the house.

Despite his almost abnormal interest in birds and butterflies, much of his boyhood was as normal as any Tom Sawyer and equally filled with longings to run away. Flying, like the birds, would have been the preferred way.

Botany also became a challenge to Roger in this period, and he developed a strong interest in flowers and plants and trees.

Clarence Beal used to go hunting with Roger for rare and special plants. Once when Roger was about fifteen, he and Clarence decided to have what they called a "Botanical Big Day," somewhat similar to a "Bird Big Day." Using Gray's *Manual of Botany* for a reference, the two came up with a total of 220 species of flowering plants. Roger pressed the flowers under the parlor carpet between pages of the newspaper. (This basic knowledge served Roger greatly in later years when he wrote and illustrated, with Margaret McKenny, *A Field Guide to Wildflowers*.)

There was a strong Boy Scout program in Jamestown and Roger was a member for a time, primarily so he might enjoy the privilege of using the Scouts' cabin south of town near the Frewsburg Swamp, "a good place for birds."

So the scruffy Roger "Nuts" Peterson grew, finishing high school at sixteen.

He received the highest marks in the class in art, history of art, and mechanical drawing. Under the photograph of a handsome boy with a proper haircut, the Jamestown High School Class of 1925 paid him respect at last in the class yearbook with this prophetic appraisal:

> *Woods! Birds! Flowers!*
> *Here are the makings of a great naturalist.*

CHAPTER II

The Beginning of an Artist

In the summer of 1925, two job possibilities appeared simultaneously.

Because of Roger's talents in mechanical drawing, he had a chance to become an engineering draftsman at the Dalstrom Manufacturing Company. To please his father, he did try it briefly, but he took his first week's pay and blew it all on camel's-hair paint brushes, which did *not* please his father. He quit.

The other prospect was an opportunity to do decorative painting of intricate Chinese subjects on the expensive lacquerwork cabinets made at the Union Furniture Company. The firm, now Union-National, Inc., was noted for its extremely fine products. It still produces this Chinese-decorated lacquerwork furniture.

For Roger, the job choice was easy—painting.

"Although the mechanical drawing job would have paid me more," he recalled, "I wanted to be an artist. The painting job paid only $8.oo a week at first, but I didn't care. I know it made my father unhappy because he regarded it as impractical when I could have done the more traditional and practical by taking the Dalstrom job and made more money. If I had continued my brief encounter there, I probably would have wound up being a drafts-man all the rest of my life. It was a real turning point."

Roger got the painting job partly with the help of his cousin, Allan Jones, who worked at the furniture factory. He took Roger and one of his paintings, of a kingbird, to Willem Dieperink Von Langereis, a Dutchman who was head of the decorating depart-ment of the furniture company. The colors were wonderful, said Jones, and the details—right down to the tiny pin feathers—just perfect.

"So I met this curious man," Roger says, "Willem Dieperink Von Langereis. Although he was from Grand Rapids, where furni-ture was mass-produced, Langereis put on a show of elegance, a façade of being a continental artist. He had a great long cigarette holder about out to here and made a great deal of his artistic tem-perament. He had a violent temper and the poor Swedes in the factory were just scared to death of him. But he liked me."

Langereis had been influenced by Aubrey Beardsley, the English illustrator and art editor of the magazine *The Yellow Book*, whose decorative pen and ink, black and white drawings and posters in the manner of Japanese art created an "exquisitely artificial style" before the turn of the century. This oriental quality turned up in Langereis' instructions for the lacquerwork furniture.

"He [Langereis] was getting some kind of a fantastic salary for those days—maybe $100 or so a week—while I," says Roger, "was getting eight bucks. This was back during the Prohibition era and there was demand for fine lacquer cabinets for bottles and glasses. We'd do the doors and sides. They sold at $1,200 or more, which was a lot of money in those days."

The Chinese technique of lacquering consisted of building up the lacquer layer by layer over a period of time—sometimes for as long as two years. The lacquer was a natural varnish made from sumac sap imported from Japan or China.

"But," recalled Roger, "we had a system by which we could put the lacquer on in about twenty minutes. We would simply take pumice and shellac and mix them to the right consistency and then trail it quickly off the *end* of a brush to fill an area. It dried im-mediately. In fact, it dried so quickly you had to be very dexterous to get it on without ruining everything. . . . Then, when the lacquer was all on and dried, you painted it with oils and gilt and in proper colors. So we would do a pagoda, a Chinaman, flowers or whatever."

Roger referred to the popular pieces of furniture as "booze cabinets," and said they usually had a black background for a base, but sometimes it was red. He never initialed any of his work, "but I could tell them now very easily. I have looked for them since, but I could never find one of my own.

"There were about six artists in the studio," he says, "one person doing the 'striping.' Very tricky, doing the striping—straight lines—gold—around the borders.

"I became very adept at doing this Chinese decoration *à la* Langereis. It took us several days to do a pair of doors."

It was Langereis who gave Roger his first encouragement about being an artist and insisted that he go to art school.

During the week, when Roger was doing his Chinese decorating work, his mind was never far from his interest in birds. He spent every spare moment in the woods watching them. He longed to know more about them scientifically, having read *The Auk*, and he saved up his money to go to one of the meetings of the A.O.U.

That fall gave him an opportunity. The meeting was in New York City at the American Museum of Natural History. Roger went, in November 1925, for a three-day session that was to be one of the most memorable occasions in his entire life—an event that was to set the pattern for his whole future. The formidable scientific society that sets the standards in ornithology brought ornithological "greats" from all over. Roger was to meet some of these men.

Not only that, but he was to see two of his own works at the exhibition!

Just past his seventeenth birthday in August, Roger had dared to submit two paintings to the art show. They were water colors. One was the kingbird painting, which had so impressed Langereis. The other painting was that of a hummingbird he had found frozen to death during spring migration.

He had managed to save $80. He took a train on the old Erie Railroad, which went as far as Jersey City and transferred its passengers to ferryboats for the trip across the Hudson River to Manhattan. The ferry ride in itself was exciting enough—his first. But more important, it gave him his first opportunity to see laughing gulls, one of the smaller members of the gull family and one that has a black head during the breeding season. Roger was delighted to see them and to know that they were finally recovering and becoming common again "after those damn bad years" during which they had been slaughtered for the millinery trade to decorate women's hats. It was a happy introduction to New York City.

Roger doesn't remember where he stayed. "Some old flea bag, probably, that didn't cost too much. I had just enough money to eat and buy my ticket home, but I didn't sleep in Central Park as some writer reported."

The museum itself was overwhelming. But the people he met were even more so. There was Ludlow Griscom, who was to become the dean of American bird watchers; Francis Lee Jaques, who was beginning his distinguished art career at the American Museum; Arthur A. Allen, founder of the Laboratory of Ornithology at Cornell University at Ithaca, New York; Dr. Frank Michler Chapman, curator of the Department of Ornithology at the American Museum of Natural History; and Edward Howe Forbush, the author whose career had so captivated Roger. Forbush was to show some of the plates for *The Birds of Massachusetts and Other New England States* painted by Louis Agassiz Fuertes. And Fuertes was there himself. Roger had good reason to be overwhelmed.

Fuertes was the bird artist about whom Roger knew most in those days. It was his bluejay he had copied from Eaton's *Birds of New York* in Miss Hornbeck's class. Fuertes was his ideal and now he had a chance to meet this man whose work he had studied so carefully.

Roger had gone to the museum the day before the meeting opened—to get oriented and to see where his own two paintings were to be placed. He said he "could hardly wait" to see them.

He went first to the main bird hall, where Francis Lee Jaques had recently started doing habitat groups—dioramas. Roger wrote in a foreword to the book *Francis Lee Jaques, Artist of the Wilderness World*, "I gawked for half an hour at the great, 2,700-

square-foot oval dome that formed the ceiling. Suspended from a painted sky on invisible wires were a variety of waterfowl and other birds, dominated by a wedge of geese."

Roger all but ignored the systematic displays in old-fashioned showcases that lined the walls. He could see only the Jaques display overhead. Finally he walked into an adjacent hall where he found an agreeable-looking man in his late thirties hanging an exhibit of bird paintings. These included a large oil of a great horned owl by Fuertes, several gouaches by Allan Brooks, a golden eagle by Archibald Thorburn—and Roger's own two creations.

Roger tried to make conversation with the man hanging the works and asked if Horsfall had done the aerial work in the other hall.

"Oh," was the offhand reply, "*I* did that."

The speaker was Jaques.

In time the two got to know each other very well and when Roger came finally to compare the works of Fuertes and Jaques, he said he had concluded that Fuertes, who had dominated bird art in this century's first three decades, "was primarily a portraitist and a brilliant one who has been the model and inspiration of many a young artist to this day. . . . But somehow, Fuertes could not put a bird into landscape convincingly. Three-dimensional activity—movement in space—was not his forte."

This, said Roger, was where Jaques excelled. His birds were in the landscape. This was one reason Dr. Chapman invited Jaques, a youth who had grown up on the Kansas prairies with gun and sketch pad, to prepare and paint the backgrounds for the new-style habitat exhibits.

For Roger the climax of the A.O.U. meeting was when he was introduced to Louis Agassiz Fuertes, who was touched by the youth's enthusiasm and talents. They went to the bird art exhibit on the second floor and looked at Roger's two watercolors.

"Just what the great man said about these drawings I do not remember," Roger wrote in the introduction to *Louis Agassiz Fuertes and the Singular Beauty of Birds*, "but I know he was kind. Later, as we walked down the broad steps to the first floor of the museum, he reached into his inner-coat pocket and withdrew a handful of red sable brushes. Picking out a flat one about a half an inch wide, he handed it to me, saying, 'Take this; you will find it good for laying in washes.' I thanked him and before we parted he added, 'And don't hesitate to send your drawings to me from time to time. Just address them to Louis Agassiz Fuertes, Ithaca, New York.' "

Roger did not, however, send any of his work to Fuertes for criticism. He wanted to wait until his paintings "were worth his time."

"And so, by delaying, I forfeited a priceless opportunity," Roger wrote, "for less than two years later Fuertes, only fifty-three, met his tragic death, hit by a train at a railroad crossing." His car was passing a hay wagon when the accident occurred near Ithaca.

"As for the paint brush, I never used it," wrote Roger. "I had discovered some white paint caked in the heel of the brush; the master himself had actually painted with that brush. Therefore, I put it aside as a treasured keepsake."

That day at the museum, says Roger, "I remember clearly the famous Fuertes large oil of the great horned owl on the ground against a background of dead leaves, a bold treatment that reminded me of a canvas by Liljefors, the Swede. 'This is the way I really like to paint,' Fuertes told me. 'I'm going to do more of it from now on.' "

Alas, he never did. He still had some of the plates for *The Birds of Massachusetts* to finish when he died. The last plates were completed by Allan Brooks.

Roger learned many things from Fuertes, one of which was the use of the three-dimensional play of light and shade, although he often favored unmodified flat color.

One disappointment for Roger was the failure, for some unknown reason, of Ernest Thompson Seton to make a scheduled appearance to speak at the convention. Roger had so wanted to meet the author of *Two Little Savages*.

Ludlow Griscom was there, of course, and made a great impression on Roger. And Roger must have made quite an impression on Griscom. On the day before the formal meeting, Roger was wandering over the museum, fascinated, when he chanced upon a dark-haired man busy in the bird department and introduced himself. The man was Ludlow Griscom. They chatted awhile and

Roger, who nurtured a reputation for being reticent, suddenly became bold enough to ask the great ornithologist if he would sign his application blank for A.O.U. membership.

"I just asked him," Roger says. "Brassy? Well, I guess it was, but you have to have more brass when you are young. Yes, I guess I did have a lot of brass."

Roger's sister, Margaret, tells of another incident where her brother's desire for nature information led him to an unorthodox, if not "brassy," episode in a museum. At seventeen, Roger wanted very much to see the Natural History Museum of Buffalo, New York, but he was working during the week and couldn't get there during exhibition hours. So he wrote a letter to the director and said he was going to be in Buffalo the following Sunday, and that he knew the museum would normally be closed, but would it be possible, because of his ornithological interest, for someone to let him in to see the bird exhibit Sunday morning?

The director was intrigued by the unusual request and wrote back that Roger would be welcome. The two agreed to wear a black-eyed Susan in their lapels to identify themselves at the train.

When the train pulled into the station, the museum director watched the crowd for his scientific visitor but the only passenger he could spot wearing a black-eyed Susan in his lapel was a teenager in knickers. When the director got over his surprise, he took the matter in stride, and after some serious birding talk invited the lad to his home for dinner. By the end of the meal he was even more impressed at Roger's expertise, took him to the museum, opened it, and escorted Roger around.

Within a year of Roger's historic trip to the A.O.U. meeting in New York, he was to exhibit again, this time when the Cooper Ornithological Club held its first American bird art exhibition at its first annual meeting in Los Angeles in April 1926. His entries were an oil of a great horned owl and a charcoal of a screech owl.

The entry in the catalogue stated:

> Roger Tory Peterson, a student working at present under the noted lacquer artist, Willem Dieperink von Langereis, is but 17 years of age and has barely launched upon his artistic career which has the promise of being a notable one. All his spare

time is devoted to sketching, painting and studying birds in nature. He used his camera as an ally in recording attitudes, postures and this early training will stand him in good stead when he comes to a mature mastery of his technique.

And indeed it did. But Roger's two owls were in good company even then, among the works of Allan Brooks, Bruce Horsfall, George M. Sutton, and Louis Agassiz Fuertes. Roger could not afford to go to Los Angeles, of course, but was proud to be included in such an important exhibit.

Langereis, too, was proud and encouraged Roger even more to study art. As a result, he set out to study in New York full time. He had saved enough money to strike out on his own.

It was not an easy decision for Roger to make—against his father's wishes and the tempting security of the decorating job at the Union Furniture Company. It was also unlikely that he could afford an ornithological education at Cornell University, though he had thought of the possibility and it appealed to him.

Roger was to tell an audience at the American Birding Association's first convention on June 16, 1973, at Kenmore, North Dakota, that "had I gone to Cornell, I probably would have become more traditional. I think my ornithology would have been better for the simple reason that some of my blind spots wouldn't exist. There are things I simply don't have because of this lack of biological training at an institution like Cornell. A lot of that I have picked up. I am what you might call a homemade ornithologist."

Going to New York proved a turning point in Roger's life. Elaborating on that fateful decision, Roger says there would never have been a Peterson System if he had not gone to art school. "My primary contribution—field recognition—could not have been made had I followed the traditional path as a biologist. Because of my art background I approached things visually rather than phylogenetically, hence the Peterson field guide system was born."

Roger went to New York to the Art Students League in 1927 and 1928, and to the National Academy of Design in 1929, 1930, and 1931.

CHAPTER III

Art School and Birding in New York City

AT the A.O.U. meeting in the fall of 1925, Roger not only had a chance to meet the key ornithologists of the day, but he also met for the first time three young men about his age who were to make names for themselves and who were to play an intimate role in Roger's own life.

They were Allan D. Cruickshank—born Allan Dudley Kingsley Courtney Atherton Cruickshank—who was to become a "modern Audubon with a camera" and who was to work for many years with Roger at the National Audubon Society; Joseph J. Hickey, who was to become Professor of Wildlife Ecology at the University of Wisconsin and an A.O.U. president, and Bernard Nathan, a boy from Brooklyn who was to interest scores of boys in Brooklyn in birding and was later a leader in the Boy Scout movement.

Roger saw Allan Cruickshank only briefly at that meeting in 1925. He was at the foot of a small step ladder on which Forbush was showing the original Fuertes paintings that were to be published in *Birds of Massachusetts and Other New England States*.

It was at a reception in the office of Dr. Chapman that Roger met Joe Hickey, who, at nineteen, was a year older than Allan. Both were students at New York University. Joe was president of his senior class one year; Allan, the following year.

Although Roger spent little time with either Hickey or Cruickshank at the A.O.U. meeting—they were in classes during the day—he did find companionship with Bernie Nathan. Both of them were impressed with the things they were seeing, and they were sharing their birding experiences. They went together on the field trips sponsored by the A.O.U. These were led by no less than the renowned Ludlow Griscom, the superexpert whom Roger was later, in his field guide, to describe as "the court of last resort" in matters of field identification.

On one of the field trips they went to Long Beach, Long Island, an entirely new birding environment for Roger. Long Beach was pure, wild beach then. "I got thirteen species of birds that day I had never seen before, including a Brünnich's murre." (The Brünnich's murre is a northern-breeding sea bird frequently confused in the United States with the razor-billed auk.) Roger was ecstatic. If he had been excited about birding and painting before, he was now so enthusiastic he could not wait to get back to Jamestown to earn enough money to begin a formal art career.

It wasn't until January 1927 that Roger's meager savings, so carefully hoarded from his pay envelopes at the furniture factory, made it possible for him to return to New York. Langereis had recommended the Art Students League of New York, located then as now in a handsome old three-story building at 215 West Fifty-seventh Street in the heart of Manhattan.

Reunion with Bernie Nathan was first on his program. He needed help in finding a place to live. They tried the YMCA in the Bay Ridge section of Brooklyn but there were no vacancies. Then Bernie suggested that Roger come and live with his family at 539 Fifty-first Street, Brooklyn. It was an apartment crowded with Bernie's mother and father, two brothers and a sister, but Roger was made welcome and was especially pleased to be in the warm and friendly home of his fellow birder. Bernie's father was in the wholesale grocery business, so there was always plenty of food.

At the Art Students League there were no entrance requirements nor were the students required to have had any previous training or to take an examination. Founded in 1875, the League has trained hundreds of successful painters.

Roger's first instructor was Kimon Nicolaides, whose book, *The Natural Way to Draw*, is regarded as a classic. Actually Roger, having excelled in draftsmanship in high school, had wanted to get into a class taught by Frederic Arthur Bridgeman, an accomplished draftsman and a master of anatomy who used a rather blocky technique when drawing. But there was no room for the youth. As it happened, Roger realized later that the Nicolaides approach to drawing was the one that influenced his painting throughout his life.

"He used," as Roger describes the teacher's technique, "a very light fluid line—a sort of feeling out of line, first lightly on the paper, then boiling, boiling, boiling, modifying and bearing on harder with bolder lines until the form asserted itself. It wasn't one of those block-out kind of drawings."

Roger's first day at the Art Students League was to be unforgettable:

"I, a small-town boy, stepped into the classroom for my first session with drawing paper and a model before me. Never having seen a woman in the nude before, except my sister, I think—I was a very sheltered ·and quite Puritanical Lutheran lad—I casually strolled over to a vacant easel and then, without looking up, sharpened my charcoal sticks and my pencils for about ten minutes before I lifted my eye to see what was up there on the stand in glorious living flesh. She was blond, bulky, and had good flesh tones.

"Of course," Roger added, "this soon was to become old stuff to me. Actually there was a period in art school when I could draw or paint a human figure much better than I could execute a bird subject."

Weekends, Roger and Bernie, always with a cigar weighing down one corner of his mouth, would go birding in such places as Brighton Beach, Dyker Heights, Prospect Park, and any other spot in Brooklyn where they thought a rare bird might turn up.

While birding and the study of art were Roger's two loves, he had the very real problem of supporting himself and keeping up art school payments. He took classes in the afternoon, so he could earn some money in the mornings. He got a job in a furniture loft on the West Side of Manhattan doing the one thing he knew best, refinishing and decorating furniture. Mostly the job called for painting roses and other flowers on cabinets and the headboards of beds.

This job lasted only two or three months because the boss, a Hungarian who was a good painter himself, said Roger's work was "too academy," which Roger assumed meant that his work was too stiff and studied.

However, after shopping around for a bit, Roger landed a job at the Deutsch Brothers, a furniture loft on 123rd Street in the Harlem area of upper Manhattan. One of his tasks there was refinishing furniture.

During this period Roger and Bernie attended the regular meetings of the prestigious Linnaean Society of New York in Manhattan on the second and fourth Tuesdays of every month at the American Museum of Natural History. Its members were both professional and amateur birders of all ages, and the boys were welcome guests, though Roger was not a member until later. The daily subway grind to and from his work became so burdensome for Roger that, when he returned to New York after his summer working vacation, he found a room closer to the furniture company, this time in a YMCA on 125th Street in Harlem. In those days, he found Harlem "quite fancy," but he found an Irish place where he could get lunch for thirty cents—beans and bread and coffee.

That year Roger's progress at the Art Students League was very rapid. A new instructor had been added to his list of outstanding teachers—the noted John Sloan. Sloan, at that time, was coming into vogue as a painter of the Ashcan school, so-called because it depicted the life of ordinary, everyday people.

Roger learned much from John Sloan. "To this day," he says, "I follow some of his precepts in my own painting. Sloan insisted that there was no such thing as shadow, so he eliminated cast shadows from his paintings and he advised his students to do likewise. I could never quite accept this. At that time Sloan was in his 'cross-hatch' period in which his drawings of figures were modeled and shaped with a crosshatch of numerous short lines.

"One day he came to class in a very jovial mood. He had had an exhibition in which practically all of his thirty-two paintings were sold."

In class one day, Sloan spoke of the National Academy of Design. He was strongly against the principles of the National Academy. Roger had never heard of it before. Sloan stated flatly that to be of the National Academy was "eternal damnation." Roger, being a neophyte, didn't know about these things, but thought he should investigate that school, and did. It was exactly what he wanted, so the next year he enrolled. He was an outstanding student.

"There was a revolution in art style at the time, and I, being young," explained Roger, "liked being in the stream of things, even though my instincts were in the direction of realistic, representational painting. So I was bothered by the fact that I was somewhat out of vogue and that painting went far to the left of Sloan."

The National Academy of Design, founded in 1825 by a group of professional artists, was modeled after the Royal Academy of Arts in London. Members are elected on the basis of recognized excellence. Audubon was once a member, as were painters such as Winslow Homer, Frederic Remington, Howard Pyle, and Norman Rockwell. Students, as well as members, are admitted because of their talent. They pay no tuition. To Roger, coming into real Depression years, this was well appreciated. Thanks to his natural talent, he was to remain there three years.

Roger knew that his main interest in art was birds and their environment, but he did not learn to paint birds at the National Academy. He did, however, learn realism, which was, he felt, what the Academy was all about.

First, students were put "on probation, working on plaster casts and busts," Roger explained. This was called "antique-processing." He found this interesting because of the emphasis on tradition, light, and shadow, and "where the edges come." Roger moved rapidly from the antique-processing probation class to more advanced classes.

Two of Roger's principal teachers were Raymond P. R. Neilson, portrait painter, and Sidney Dickinson, a foremost twentieth-century portrait painter whose paintings are represented in many national museums and who did notable portraits of John D. Rockefeller and all his sons.

The Academy in those days was up near the Cathedral of St. John the Divine at Amsterdam Avenue and 110th Street (now it is at 1083 Fifth Avenue). The building was long and barnlike, and had skylights. There were both male and female students, a young crowd. "Very good, most of them," Roger has said. They held their exhibitions downtown on Fifty-seventh Street at the Art Students League.

"A typical day at the Academy," Roger says, "would be to get there early to get a good seat so you could get a good view of the model and be able to work without bumping into your neighbor. The instructor would come around, give a touch here or there or provide some criticism of what I had done. I recall that one of my instructors, Neilson, went up to my drawing of a model and said I should soften her lips. He said, 'Make them look as if they should be kissed; don't make them so stiff.' At that time kissing girls was pretty far from my general routine."

During this time Roger continued to earn some money—not much—decorating furniture. He had switched his job to a refinishing loft studio on 132nd Street in Washington Heights run by Jan Do-Rio, a thirty-two-year-old man of Brazilian ancestry whose original name was Woisky. He had studied to be a monk, but it hadn't worked out. He played the violin and gave happy Saturday night parties that Roger sometimes attended "as a quiet-mannered guest." He was fascinated by the "international" atmosphere, the Portuguese language, the dress and behavior of the party people.

Much of the furniture Roger painted was for bedrooms, some with flowers, others with oriental designs, and, he said, "I'm sure most of the bedroom sets wound up in houses of ill repute, but I never investigated."

One of the beds, with a king-size frame decorated with French dancing figures and a heavy canopy and draperies, had not been claimed by the man who ordered it. Roger had moved meanwhile to be near his job. So the bed was carted up to Roger's new room at 182nd Street along with a bureau with Chinese figures—its styling clashing with the canopied big bed. But Roger was glad to have a comfortable and handy place to sleep.

Much of Do-Rio's furniture was "pretty horrible—not *elegant*" like the pieces he had decorated in Jamestown. Roger's employer, however, was pleased with Roger's work. He liked the boy, too, and his unassuming modesty, and invited him to come stay with him and his family in suburban Scarsdale. Do-Rio had a wife, Jean, and two sons, one adopted.

When the Academy had its big annual ball, a costume party, Do-Rio got Roger a date with a startlingly attractive girl from the Bronx named Andrea. She was not much impressed with the evening. Roger understood. "My dancing was terrible, you know." He was glad to drop the bored girl off at her home so he could go directly on a birding trip. "There I was in costume—and not a very imaginative one either, just an artist's smock and a beret, out in the marshes."

Of course, during those years at art schools, birding was constantly uppermost in Roger's mind.

Back when Roger was attending the Art Students League, he had taken off for South Carolina to see new shorebirds on his first June vacation period. He had read and been fascinated by *Birds of South Carolina* by Arthur T. Wayne, a great local authority on ornithology.

Roger wrote to him, and Wayne answered, "When you come down this way, be sure to look me up." So Roger painted eighty end tables with Chinese decorations—no rickshaws, but flowers and things—to earn $80. The fare was $69, enough to take a Clyde Line boat to Charleston third-class steerage.

Before Roger saw Wayne at his home in Mount Pleasant, South Carolina, however, he went out to Sullivan's Island across the bay to look for new birds. Edgar Allan Poe had been there when he wrote *The Gold Bug* and Roger remembered the description of the island—"little else than sea sand, and about three miles long . . . a wilderness of reeds and slime, a favorite resort of the marsh hen."

Sullivan's Island is next to the Isle of Palms, and Roger got a little boy to row him over for a quarter, "which was worth something in those days."

Roger had taken with him a small tent, which he set up on the beach. When night fell he went into the tent and started to sleep when he heard a sound, a strange sound. He decided it must be some kind of bird new to him. "Turned out to be a tree frog."

But the night was just beginning. He awoke to find a ghost crab nestling under his neck. Soon he found himself covered with ticks. Then came a tremendous thunder and lightning storm. Some goats came along and began chewing on the tent ropes. Next there came a heavy gust of wind and down went the tent on its thoroughly wide-awake boy. Finally dawn came and Roger packed his wet belongings and started an eleven-mile hike to Wayne's home. Roger was pretty disheveled, and "Wayne, who was an old man then, was a little mad because I was late," says Roger. "But it was hot, and the walk long." Before Wayne would converse with Roger, however, he walked over to the edge of his yard and pointed to a bird flying over the marsh.

"What kind of a bird is that?" he asked.

"It's a roseate tern," said Roger.

With that, Wayne invited him into the house and Roger stayed three days. "He was a perfectionist," Roger says, "and his study skins were the most perfect I have ever seen."

Wayne gave Roger a letter of introduction to Alexander Sprunt, Jr., at the Charleston Museum. Nothing could have pleased Roger more, and, as it happened, the meeting proved to be equally pleasing for Sprunt, who described the occasion in detail in his excellent book *Carolina Low Country Impressions*. Sprunt wrote how, in early June of 1927, a young man walked into his office at the Charleston Museum, and said he would like to know about a nearby locality where he could find some birds. He made a somewhat bedraggled appearance, his belongings in a sack slung over his shoulder.

Sprunt and his colleague Burnham Chamberlain were on the eve of starting a three-day trip to Cape Romain. They had chartered a boat to investigate the seabird colonies there. The young man asked if they could take him along.

"Interested bird students were few and far between in those days," wrote Sprunt. "Somehow there was something different about this tousled young man that pleaded his sincerity and interest. He finally remembered that he had not introduced himself. His name, he told us, was Roger Tory Peterson, and his home was in Jamestown, New York."

Three days were spent among the pelicans, skimmers, willets, and terns of the Bull's Bay area, all of which were new to Roger. Then one morning one of the skiffs was missing and so was Peterson. He did not return until sundown and had had nothing to eat all day. That evening, and all the time he was there, he lived in a sort of trance, sitting on the deck after dinner, staring with rapt expression across the water. He talked little.

The men were usually busy skinning birds, blowing eggs, and making notes for the museum. Roger was having the time of his life. He knew, wrote Sprunt, that he was living in a world where other men had some kind of place, that they supplied his necessities for continued existence, but it was with the birds that he was really living.

Sprunt finally got Roger back to Charleston and on the ship that took him north, with most of his thirteen dollars intact. "Seemingly still in a daze and with a characteristic gesture of brushing aside his forelock, he said as he departed, 'This has really been something, and I'll never forget it.' "

And Roger didn't. When his first *A Field Guide to the Birds* came out, he sent Sprunt a copy. In the inscription he said, "Our trip to Cape Romain was responsible for my introduction to at least thirty species in this handbook. That was some trip."

Sprunt wrote in his book that those who knew Roger in the early days could see how his zeal and hard work and determination foreshadowed his accomplishments, "for, rightly, he has achieved the status of the world's most famous artist-ornithologist."

On another memorable summer vacation from art school, Roger hitchhiked throughout New Jersey with two pals, one his *Two Little Savages* friend from Jamestown, Clarence Beal, the other, Edwin Stearns, a young minister's son from Caldwell, New Jersey.

"I was the original hippy," Roger has said, "but didn't know it."

"It was the Year of the Locust," wrote Clarence of the venture. "There were thousands of the insects 'waowing' and humming in the trees and bushes. They swarmed on every twig and their empty pupae cases hung from every tree trunk. The locusts were orange, not green as in the common cicada.

"First we went to Brigantine, north of Atlantic City. The town was glaring in the sun. On the white sands, terns, gulls, piping plovers, and bronzed people. And waving grasses in the salt marshes."

The Coast Guard gave the boys a ride out to Little Beach, where they planned to photograph the laughing gulls and black skimmers.

"Roger and Ed left me," according to Clarence, "in a photographic blind on the marsh, surrounded by gulls' nests. I had a rowboat with which to pick them up at the black skimmer colony later in the afternoon. Soon the gulls returned to their nests and I took their portraits from the hot shelter of the blind."

The tide rose (being from upstate New York, Beal was not familiar with the ocean tides), a storm developed, and Clarence set out in the little boat to find his pals. He became hopelessly lost and had to beach the boat. In the meantime, the Coast Guard had picked up Roger and Ed—rescued them literally. They all thought Clarence had been swept out to sea. So Roger sent a telegram to his parents and Clarence's in Jamestown that Clarence had been lost.

It was all very much like the Mark Twain story of Tom Sawyer and Huck Finn, with Aunt Polly thinking the boys were dead, when, at the funeral, they walked in.

A second telegram went off to Jamestown to tell Clarence's parents that he was safe. He had finally found his way back on foot to the Coast Guard station. The boys went on to Cape May.

Roger's summer vacation from art school in 1928 was spent at Camp Chewonki, at Wiscasset, Maine, where he was a nature counselor and where he was to return for the next five summers. But in the art school winters, on weekends and holidays, Roger found fulfillment of his birding passion in what was called the Bronx County Bird Club.

Roger has always been nostalgic at the mention of the Bronx County Bird Club. It certainly was different. It had no headquarters, no officers, no dues—only nine members, all teen-age

boys from New York City's borough of the Bronx with a remarkable driving interest in spotting as many different kinds of birds as
possible. Here is how Roger recalls the group:

"Nine sons of brick and concrete, in their late teens, were drawn
together from various parts of the sprawling Bronx—Hunts Point
Avenue, Woodcrest Avenue, and Van Cortlandt—by their common interest. How their youthful dreams took flight on the wings
of birds, among the vacant lots, dumps, and abandoned estates in
this northernmost of New York City's boroughs, is a saga in itself.
Typical of the melting pot that is New York, the parentage of
these nine lads represented almost as many nationalities—Swiss,
English, German, Polish, Russian, Irish, and Scottish. Later Swedish
was added when I arrived in the big city and was admitted to the
club as its first outside member."

It was a very tightly knit group that initially had strong reserva-
tions about letting in that outlander from Jamestown. After careful
examination and deliberation, however, the club gambled on
Roger.

One of the club's founders, Irving Kassoy, was to make owls a
lifelong study as a hobby while he went on to become a dealer in
precious stones in his professional life. He recalled:

"I did not feel anything toward him at first. We were curious
about him. He was very shy. I was actually disappointed in him.
He did not have the extrovert qualities that some of us had. But—
after the first one or two times we were out in the field with him, it
was all different."

But if members of the club were impressed by Roger's enthusiasm, knowledge, and keenness, Roger was equally impressed not
only by the club and its members but its ornithological contacts at
the American Museum of Natural History and the Linnaean Society.

Roger found the membership in the club "almost equivalent to a
course in ornithology at a university" because of the talent of its
members coupled with access to the professional and amateur ornithologists at the Linnaean Society and to Ludlow Griscom.

Griscom knew every bird. A great field man, Griscom had seen
every bird "in skins" and had shot some—as a boy. His accomplish-

PEREGRINE FALCON
Falco peregrinus

Published by permission of Mill Pond Press, Inc.,
Venice, Florida 33595

GREAT HORNED OWL
Bubo virginianus

Published by permission of Mill Pond Press, Inc.,
Venice, Florida 33595

BALD EAGLE
Haliaeetus leucocephalus

Published by permission of Mill Pond Press, Inc.,
Venice, Florida 33595

BARN OWL
Tyto alba

Published by permission of Mill Pond Press, Inc.,
Venice, Florida 33595

SNOWY OWL
Nyctea scandiaca

Published by permission of Mill Pond Press, Inc.,
Venice, Florida 33595

BOBWHITE
Colinus virginianus

Published by permission of Mill Pond Press, Inc.,
Venice, Florida 33595

RUFFED GROUSE
Bonasa umbellus

Published by permission of Mill Pond Press, Inc.,
Venice, Florida 33595

GOLDEN EAGLE
Aquila chrysaëtos

Published by permission of Mill Pond Press, Inc.,
Venice, Florida 33595

ments were called incredible. He is credited with bridging the gap between the shotgun ornithologist and the modern field biologist.

Griscom was a sort of a "loner," very positive in his statements. He parted his hair in the middle, had a very slight lisp, and the BCBC boys venerated him.

The original four members of the club, as Kassoy recalled them, "were John (Matty) Matthews, Dick Herbert, Joe Hickey, and I, and we were called the 'Hunts Point Dumpers' because birding was so good at the dump there. It was about a third of a mile square and there were salt-hay meadows. Occasionally we met John Kuerzi and his brother, Dick, of the West Bronx, and Phillip Kessler. John Kuerzi was a kind of a leader without anyone saying so. We got together in the finished attic of the Kuerzi home. There was a certain spirit that drove us."

Fred Ruff, who later joined the group, recalled that the little band "had little to guide us in our interests," adding, "We did have a few references though, the writings of Chapman, Griscom's *Birds in the Vicinity of New York City*, Reed's *Bird Guide*, the excellent plates by Louis Agassiz Fuertes, and Bent's government monograph. We, of course, didn't have the Peterson field guide, as its author was then floundering with us. We were fortunate in that we could generally have a sympathetic ear and an answer commensurate with the stupidity of our question or conclusion from such giants as Chapman, Chapin, L. N. Nichols, Charlie Urner, and Bill Vogt, to name a few. Through the rather meager material available to us, and the unyielding grilling we sometimes got at the museum, most of us, perhaps initially by osmosis, developed a sense of scientific accuracy—'there is no white but white and white is its name.' All of us have carried this concept regardless of the professions we pursued later."

When the club was getting started in the early 1920s, there was generally little public interest in the environment and only a few interested youngsters.

"As these kids grew older," Ruff said, "they expanded their range to the parks—Bronx, Central, Van Cortlandt, Pelham, and so on, learning more and experiencing more the 'soul food' which they never had on their concrete sidewalks or asphalt streets. By

43

happenstance, some of these kids ran across each other in their meanderings."

On one trip Ruff met Joe Hickey "and showed him a catbird, new to his list, and he showed me a towhee, new to my list. We found in Joe Hickey a born leader. In about 1922 we felt that a bunch of us should join together in a gang, club, or association. The mission of the group was to find and identify birds and report these to one another and to the Linnaean Society."

The boys held their first meeting in the parlor of Joe's parents' house near Hunts Point. Joe kept meticulous notes. Present were: Joseph J. Hickey, Irving Kassoy, Allan D. Cruickshank, Richard Herbert, Philip Kessler, John F. Matuszewski (later Matthews), John F. Kuerzi and his brother Richard, and Ruff. It was a gang with a mission which quickly organized itself into a club with the somewhat outgoing, all-encompassing title of Bronx County Bird Club.

After a five-minute business organization session, the next two hours were devoted to reports on birds and questioning each other about experiences.

The club had no girl members. "For some obscure reason birding, the obsessive sport," Roger has said, "is a more popular hobby among boys than girls at eleven or twelve. And if the boy becomes involved at that age, he is hooked for life."

Often the boys would go hunting for new specimens at the sprawling and beautiful New York Botanical Garden. One elderly gentleman strolling along the paths listened to their excited comments about birds and called to them. They thought he was going to blow the whistle on them, but instead he gave them an old pair of opera glasses. With only about two magnifying powers, they were not too effective, but to the boys who "hardly had two nickels to rub together in their pockets, the gift was a veritable bonanza."

To have a bird identification questioned hotly was a sign that you were "one of the guys," according to Allen M. Thomas, now president of the Saco Valley Audubon Society in Maine, who was not a BCBC member but birded with them as a guest. "If your rare bird report elicited no response, you were considered to be falsifying. I saw a man at the Linnaean Society 'cashiered' after he made so many 'way-out' reports. The word went quietly through the members that he was not to be believed. He was through."

It was not uncommon for the Bronx boys to eat supper at five, lie down from six to eleven, get up and pick up four or five fellows in the Bronx, and drive to Montauk Point, Long Island, or perhaps to Hawk Mountain, west of Allentown in Pennsylvania, arriving before dawn. Then they would bird all day long on six sandwiches, a large thermos of thick, hot soup and one of strong black coffee. They would be back on the road to arrive home about 1:30 or 2 A.M.

Roger said that for the BCBC boys, birding was "the fun of the chase," not the pursuit of science, or making a Christmas bird count census. "I like to think, though," he said, "that the boys in the Bronx set the standard and developed the technique by which many other groups now get the largest count in their regions. The Bronx boys were the first to check off a hundred species."

The friends Roger made during those years remained an influence in his life—Joe Hickey, author of the classic *A Guide to Bird Watching*, and Cruickshank, with whom Roger was to work at the National Audubon Camp, as well as at the National Audubon Society as lecturers and photographers. Allan did not remember seeing Roger until he met him through the BCBC. It was in 1930, he believed. "It was in the Van Cortlandt Park marsh at the northern border of New York City. I was wading knee-deep looking for rail nests when the cattails ahead parted and there knee-deep was the Big Swede."

Dick Herbert, another friend, became the greatest authority on the peregrine falcon—"the prince of predators"—before he died in the 1940s.

John Kieran, later sports writer for the New York *Herald Tribune* and "Information Please" radio expert, occasionally joined the boys on their bushwhacking through the swamps in search of Virginia sora, rails, and other marsh birds. He knew Roger well, since they both attended the meetings of the Linnaean Society. He was living in Riverdale at the time, and often heard the boys "a-whoopin' and a-hollerin'," clapping their hands loudly at the same time. Kieran wrote in *A Natural History of New York* in 1959 about these ventures: "The din was supposed to stir up—and frequently did—rails that might otherwise be left unseen amid the cattails and marsh grasses." Then, as sports reporter, he tells of the baseball game that "resulted in a real ornithological record for New York City."

It was between New York University and a rival collegiate team on Ohio Field, above the east bank of the Harlem River, on the afternoon of April 30, 1928. The red-headed Joe Hickey had Allan Cruickshank with him at the ball game. Suddenly they looked up and "saw a swallow-tailed kite (*Elanoides forticatus*) wheeling about in spectacular flights above the diamond and the competing baseball teams. So far as I know, this is the only record for that more southern and western bird within the city limits."

And where was Roger? In the marshes, looking for rails.

Roger tells of a time, years later, when Kieran called to ask if he knew anyone in the New York area who could imitate birds for his radio program. Kieran was to guess what birds were making the calls. Roger could imitate birds, and said he could.

So that evening, on "Information Please," he imitated a black-bellied plover, a screech owl, a loon, a chickadee, and a mourning dove, and one other bird—"I've forgotten what. Kieran got four out of the six. I think he missed the black-bellied plover. I remember he said of the loon, 'That's a pretty poor loon!'"

Recently Kieran said, "The Bronx County Bird Club was the most enthusiastic, active, and expert group of that age that ever existed—in my opinion."

A favorite place to "bird" was the Jones Beach Wildlife Refuge. Robert Moses, parks commissioner at that time, had decided to establish Jones Beach State Park, but came under pressure of conservationists saying he was ruining wild areas; so, he promised to make a "better bird sanctuary than anyone," and the Jones Beach Wildlife Refuge was the result. Roger says, "We used to have great get-togethers there with the old Bronx County Bird Club. We even had parties at the old shooting lodge and then go birding around the pond."

The BCBC never did disband officially. It was very cohesive until the boys started moving away from the New York City area in the years just after World War II. And there are no reunions. "The nearest thing to that would be when some of us would try to get together for the Christmas Bird Counts."

Roger says had it not been for the influence of the Bronx County Bird Club, "I would have devoted my life to painting. Birding would have been a hobby."

CHAPTER IV

Camp Counselor in Maine

THERE is, on the coast of Maine, near Wiscasset, a very proper and famous boys' camp called Camp Chewonki. It was here that Roger Tory Peterson spent five summers as a nature counselor. And it was here that he met the man who was to become a tremendous influence in his life—almost a father figure. His name was Clarence E. Allen. He had founded the camp in 1915, and was also director of the Rivers School in Brookline, Massachusetts, where Roger later taught. Roger dedicated his first *A Field Guide to the Birds* to Clarence Allen (jointly with William Vogt).

Clarence Allen wrote, thirty years later, in *The Florida Naturalist*, of the boy's scheduled coming to Chewonki. One day before the summer camp was to open, he received a telegram: "If you want your camp naturalist send me $39.40. I'm broke."

Allen did not know the sender, but Roger had been recommended by John Aldrich, a former counselor who had directed the camp's nature program for three years. Aldrich, who later became research staff specialist of the U.S. Fish and Wildlife Service, had met Roger at the Buffalo Museum.

Time was running out fast: the camp was to reopen, so Clarence Allen reluctantly sent the money. "How little did I know that I had made the best investment of my life."

Roger says he had previously bought the ticket to Wiscasset but lost it. "On the way, I stopped to see Joe Hickey, who was acting as a counselor—a lifeguard, I think—at an orphan boys' camp at Tivoli-on-the-Hudson. Somehow, in the course of stalking cerulean warblers near the camp, I lost my ticket to Maine and so had to send the telegram to Mr. Allen."

Roger hadn't realized the camp was about six miles from the train station, Monsweag, Maine, and he set out with two heavy suitcases—clothing for the summer and the ever-present old four-by-five Primo—on a terribly hot summer day. "I was a little on the skinny side," he says, "but I had extremely powerful legs and could walk the legs off anyone."

Clarence Allen's widow, Kay, recalls that Roger "really did not look like a well boy. He had been living in a hall bedroom somewhere in New York, decorating furniture, and breathing gas fumes. I guess it affected his health and he had lost some weight, too. Clarence said he was afraid the boy wasn't going to work out."

However, good Maine air and plenty of camp food soon put Roger "on his pins," Clarence wrote. "Roger convinced us with his zeal and interest and familiarity with birds and wildlife that he could make his contribution as a young counselor. He was able to impart enthusiasm and excitement to his young camp friends."

At Chewonki, "Roger led the boys up hill and over gullies, going up trees and up to your middle in swamps. That was man's work," wrote Allen. "They soon found out that every foot of the way revealed something new." They were explorers. Roger was a vigorous leader, and birdwatching became a sport demanding sharp eyes and staying powers no less rigorous than those demanded by football.

Typically, Roger would ask such questions as: Do you know how to spot the male monarch butterfly? Do you know goldfinches nest latest of all our summer birds because they wait for the milkweed silk to be used in their nests?

After weeks of this, Allen said, "it was no wonder that the voting at the season's end proclaimed 'nature' as the most popular activity. It had become just as respectable to win credits in nature as to win a tennis championship."

There were countless adventures. Roger fell thirty-eight feet from a pine tree while attempting to photograph an osprey's nest, but fortunately was unhurt. Roger has quipped, "I am never afraid of heights as long as I have my camera to hold on to."

Another time, Allen recalled, an unusual number of deer and moose came down from the north woods. Two panting boys rushed into camp one day and told Allen that there was a great moose at the Point. "I thought it was a hoax, but Roger apparently was impressed, for he grabbed his camera and rushed off to the Point, some three quarters of a mile away from the camp buildings." Characteristically, he approached within four feet of the moose and photographed the huge creature. Roger says the moose doubled back, surprising him—he hadn't meant to get so close—and he threw the camera in the brush and dived behind a tree while the moose rushed by.

Roger was fearless and indifferent to risks and danger when following a bird or animal, not always setting a good example perhaps for the boys in his charge, but stimulating them with the thrill of adventure. Many times, wrote the camp director, Roger would jump from a boat to the slippery ledges of the rocks and coastal islands offshore to band a colony of nesting seabirds or to look for a new bird for his list.

Allan Cruickshank came to the camp as a counselor one summer, and Clarence Beal joined the counselors one year as an assistant to Roger. "Chewonki was an ideal camp," said Beal, "and boasted a fifty-four-foot yawl with a full suit of sails and an old sea captain for skipper. Thus, we were able to visit many offshore islands to observe the seals, dolphins, whales, and the multitude of nesting seabirds: black-backed and herring gulls, Arctic terns, black guillemots, eider ducks, parrot-beaked puffins, and tube-nosed Wilson's petrels."

Beal recalls one canoe trip with Roger to visit a great blue heron colony on an oak-covered island in the Penobscot River. The photography was successful, he says, but "I will never forget the five-foot waves which nearly swamped our canoe!"

Nearly every one of the counselors was a champ of some sort. Many were from Harvard. Al Maley, who was to become Roger's closest friend later at Rivers School, remembers "we had the Harvard wrestling champ, the captain of the sculling crew, the fencing champ of New England, the northeastern tennis champ—from Princeton. . . ." Roger says, "I was not champion of anything."

Al Maley recalls that "four years out of five the camp boys voted Roger as the counselor who did most for the camp."

One of the things Roger did that was fun was to take the boys "sugaring" for moths at night. Of course it took special dispensation to stay out beyond the normal hours.

They would make a mixture of vinegar and sugar—very heavy with sugar; to have done it properly would have required stale beer and rotten bananas. Using a paint brush, they painted the mixture on tree trunks on a hot still night and then later went around with a lantern, butterfly net, and cyanide jar. "The special moths we found at the sugar," Roger says, "were the big Catocalas, which have beautiful underwings. When resting on a tree trunk the upper wings look like bark—but when spread, the very beautiful rose-colored or orange or yellow underwings are visible. Of course, the problem was to catch them without damaging them. A butterfly always flies upward when it leaves a flower. So after clapping the net over it you hold the netting up and the butterfly flies into the cul-de-sac. On the other hand, a moth drops, so you place the net below when they're feeding at the bark. A very different technique—moths drop, butterflies fly up.

"Our night of adventure was the great thing because you could sometimes give a variation, play a trick, pretend there were ghosts, if you were leading them through some little country cemetery."

There had been an old chicken coop on the farm that they made into a museum. Roger would take in wild flowers, put them in jars, and label them.

There was a wonderful frog pond, where they caught turtles and frogs. "I hope they never sprayed it," Roger says. "It has taken people many years to appreciate environmental values. We were not as aware then as we are now about these things."

Roger liked a girl there, Nancy Thornburg, who often sketched with him. Also there was an attractive school nurse whom Roger escorted shyly through the woods to a lovely point called Blueberry Hill, about the highest point in camp, recalled Clarence Allen's son, John, a junior counselor. "There was a moon," said John, "and they sat on a bench, admiring the view, when all of a sudden he heard a bird whistle or toot down in the woods, so without further ado he wandered off into the woods, leaving this young lady sitting there. Time passed. No Roger. Finally she made her way back to camp. To say she was irate is putting it mildly. I don't think she spoke to Roger again."

Kay Allen tells of Roger, in the first year he was at Camp Chewonki, sitting on the back porch of the little farmhouse at the camp, whistling a whippoorwill call. "Roger did it so well he brought in the whippoorwills from all over the woods. We had them the whole night long. And everybody was so mad at Roger. No rest for anybody, the whippoorwills calling each other."

Clarence Allen "watched Roger like a father watching his own son," John Allen once wrote years later in a letter to Edwin Way Teale, the noted nature writer. "The distance that Roger had come from those early days, when many of us despaired of getting him to complete his work or to be on time for anything, to his present industrious habits is, of course, a delight to me and to all his friends."

It was at Camp Chewonki that Roger lost the treasured paint brush Fuertes had given him and had taken with him to camp. It slipped from a shelf and fell in a crack in the floor. Roger thought about it a lot during the winter. "It was too valuable to lose. So the next summer I had the floor ripped up and there was the handle of the paint brush, but mice had chewed off all the bristles."

Clarence Allen took Roger to the Rivers School the end of the summer in 1931. As Allen once said, "It took but a few days to strike the tents when camp closed and put the equipment away for the long Maine winter. But what to do with the young man without a job, nearly broke, with nowhere to go? 'How about coming to Boston and helping me with the science department at Rivers Country Day School?' I asked Roger. We offered bed and board, a quiet place to work and some pay."

Roger accepted quickly. For the next three years he was at Rivers School, learning to be a Boston "gentleman."

CHAPTER V

A *"Gentleman's School"*

THE Rivers School was a private day school, a prep school for sons of "gentlemen" in the Boston suburb of Brookline, across the Charles River from Harvard. It was started as an open-air school in 1915 at Coolidge Corner, at the suggestion of a group of prominent physicians who taught that fresh air promoted health.

Mr. Robert Rivers, the headmaster, believed in keeping all the windows of the school wide open. The boys in the classroom sat with their mittens on all winter long. They had a kind of bag—no zippers then—which they sat in, and each had an electric foot warmer they called a "kiosk" to heat his feet. The kiosks were electrically controlled from plugs under the floor.

Kay Allen says with a smile that the reason so many doctors in Boston couldn't write prescriptions you could read was because they had learned to write with their mittens on at Rivers. The fresh air was supposed to have made the boys ruddy and strong, and they did not mind the cold, even the frozen pens and fingers. But the teachers couldn't take it. Many resigned.

Mr. Rivers used to walk around the school bundled up in his raccoon coat and look up at the French windows. If he saw one closed, he'd go in and push it out wide and criticize the teacher.

When Mr. Rivers retired because of ill health in 1929, Clarence

Allen, coming from the Country Day School, a nonrefrigerated academy in Newton, Massachusetts, installed wood-burning stoves. The rooms became suffocating.

Because he had not been trained as a schoolteacher through normal college channels, Roger could not teach subjects for credit. He did teach natural history, which Clarence Allen believed was very important to every boy's education. Roger also taught drawing and painting.

Separate cottagelike buildings stood around a yard, each housing a class of some twenty boys. The administration building had been the main farmhouse, and beside it there was another house that was used for kitchen and dining room.

Roger was given a small upstairs room in the administration building, cubbyhole size, about six by eight feet, with one window and two small lights. It was in this room that he made most of the drawings and laboriously worked out the text that was to be his first field guide to the birds.

Since Rivers was a day school, with about 180 pupils, it was deserted at night. Clarence Allen often let Roger use his office, which gave him more room to spread out his papers.

Once a burrowing owl shared Roger's room. He fed it hamburgers and an occasional mouse. The Franklin Park Zoo of Boston did not wish to keep it. "They thought it would be a bit tricky to keep a burrowing owl," says Roger, "so John B. May, at that time state ornithologist of Massachusetts, gave it to me." The burrowing owl bobs and bounces about when agitated, according to Roger's own field guide, and this one was not a very healthy owl to start with. But Roger fed and cared for it until the Franklin Park Zoo was willing to take it, "where it belonged in the first place."

Roger has said that Al Maley had more influence on him at Rivers School than anyone else except Clarence Allen. Maley lived on the second floor over the dining room, but since the day school served no evening meal, Roger and Al often ate in the Greek restaurant in Brookline village. Al, while interested in birds and nature, was, in fact, the school's ancient history teacher. "In this monastic life," Maley says, "Roger and I were close friends, but he never tried to teach me about birds, nor I to hold forth on ancient history to him."

In spite of their close friendship, for a long time Al didn't know that Roger worked at night on his *Field Guide to the Birds*. He did know that it was necessary to go to Roger's room in the morning to wake him up or he would never have made a morning class. The room was "a mess—easels, paints, birds' skins. Roger probably never made his bed or hung up his clothes. He was always in such a dream. He didn't see the mess.

"After some months," Al Maley says, "Roger showed me the silhouette drawings on ten-by-sixteen-inch Whatman board, and I knew that it would be a great help in identification. I didn't know that it would revolutionize the art. The infinite capacity for taking pains was all there, and I marveled at the accuracy of both the black and white and water-colored pictures. And I knew that Roger had better damn well be right, since there is no one ready to draw critical blood more than a fellow naturalist."

The classes ranged from first to twelfth grade, and it was a challenge to keep the younger ones both learning and entertained. Roger didn't discipline the boys too heavily. The truth was, he says, he really didn't know how. Having been a rather impish boy himself in Jamestown, he understood their restlessness. And, he said, "I never had the proper teacher's training. It always bothered me that I was not quite aware of the techniques of discipline."

Roger had boys in his classes almost as old as he was. There was one very difficult one. "This fellow," says Roger, "was determined to go to the old Howard Burlesque Theatre in Boston. How was I, his teacher, supposed to keep him on the straight and narrow when he would drag me off to the old Howard?" Just how reluctant Roger was to go see a burlesque is debatable, but he says he still feels guilty about it. "This was nothing any proper schoolteacher should have done."

In class the only way to keep discipline was to keep the boys "so damned interested that they would forget to cut up." Of course Roger knew birds from A to Z, but he had to teach astronomy and geology too.

The text Roger used in his natural history classes was an attractively illustrated book called *Trees, Stars and Birds* by an Ohio schoolteacher, Dr. Loren Mosley. "The only thing that bothered me somewhat was the stars part," he says. "I had no background in astronomy so I merely kept one day ahead of the boys." And in a school of this sort where classes didn't go from grade to grade, he sometimes had boys left over from other classes the year before. "They soon got onto my vulnerable points."

But it is doubtful that he had any vulnerable points when it came to birds. "He was a Pied Piper with the boys," wrote Clarence Allen. Mrs. Allen says, "He had the boys with their mouths hanging open, wanting to touch him, clinging around him, hating to see him go out of the classroom. Only twenty or twenty-one, he was a terrific young teacher."

Roger was always teaching with live things, live birds. "He would bring a bird in, set it down on the desk, and talk about it to the boys," says Kay, "and the bird wouldn't mind!"

Once, from one of his field trips to Wellfleet on Cape Cod, he brought back a bittern. "I was walking over the marsh," Roger says, "with my friend Dave Garrison, who was to be my successor at Rivers School, and there was a bittern that had eaten so many small fish it couldn't fly. So I jumped on it, and the fish rained out, you know, and the bittern took one look at me, saw my eyes, threw his head back, and I got a beak through my cheek." (The scar doesn't show—"a little thing"—but Roger has always been conscious of the Peterson profile.)

So Roger took the bittern back to school. "We had some long glass cases in the attic, and I put the heron behind the glass and started to do a drawing right there. He would try to sock me, but the glass would stop him." After finishing the sketch Roger released him.

Then another time (Roger never forgets a bird), he had some trouble with a sick cormorant that had a wounded eye. The students were up on the beach near Ipswich, Massachusetts. They took the bird back to the school. Not one of the boys had noticed that it was not just an ordinary double-crested cormorant. It was the European great cormorant. The next morning Roger played a joke on Clarence Allen. He put the large bird on the back of the headmaster's chair. When he came in the next morning here was this great black thing sitting there, staring through its one good eye.

This cormorant would not eat any of the coarse fish at four

cents a pound, but it would eat smelts at forty cents a pound. Its bad eye obviously wasn't going to recover. Roger took it down to the Boston Museum of Science and "they just drooled," he said. They needed a specimen of the European great cormorant for their collection. And inasmuch as it wasn't going to survive, they very kindly put it to sleep and "it became a specimen."

In the attic of the main building Roger found a lot of mounted birds, among them an Eskimo curlew, now very close to extinction, and a heath hen, now completely extinct. Several of the specimens were more than a hundred years old. Ducks and shorebirds were well represented in the collection.

At Rivers he appropriated one of the empty rooms at the school and made it into a museum. There were glass cases and the birds were assembled there for the boys to study. It was truly a great collection, and a rare opportunity for Roger. All he had to do was pick out a bird skin he wanted, take it to his room, and draw his picture.

In another building there was a room with many windows. Roger turned this into a studio and taught the students how to paint, how to handle oil colors, how to mix paints and apply them to drawing board or canvas.

It was here that Elliot Richardson, later to be Ambassador to Britain and U.S. Secretary of Commerce, among other government posts, got his first taste of natural history and painting. Richardson was Roger's best student. He won both the art prize and the natural history prize.

Richardson is the most famous of the boys Roger influenced at Rivers. And certainly Richardson influenced him. Much of his proper Bostonian quality rubbed off on Roger. Not only was Elliot in his classes at Rivers, but Roger used to go to the Richardsons' lovely home to tutor Elliot and his brother George.

Their mother died when Elliot was two and their father was paralyzed from a stroke. The boys were brought up by a devoted housekeeper, a Miss Brown. On Easter vacations and such, Roger sometimes went with them to Cape Cod—not exactly baby-sitting, but teaching and "companioning" the brothers.

"I used to take them birding," Roger remembers. They lived on the Cape right next to the Outermost House, about which the naturalist Henry Beston wrote his classic story of a year he spent on the Great Beach of Cape Cod.

Dr. Wyman Richardson, one of Elliot's uncles, had also been an amateur naturalist and the boy's interest was developed by family and environment. The uncle wrote *The House at Nauset Marsh* and it was here on the Cape that Roger stayed with Elliot and George.

Most of the men in Elliot's family had been great surgeons and physicians. But one uncle was a lawyer and Elliot decided to follow in his footsteps. He studied law at Harvard and was a cartoonist on the *Harvard Lampoon*. His favorite humor book was *Punch*.

In 1974, when Roger received the Golden Key Award, an honor conferred each year by the American Association of School Administrators and other educational organizations on a teacher who has helped shape the career of one of the nation's prominent citizens, Richardson presented the key at the annual convention. He said Roger had taught him more than painting. "What I think he taught me more than anything was the importance of observation. When you went out on a field trip with Peterson, you took in every movement and sound; you saw things; you took an interest in what was around you. And this can apply to other things in life—the cultivation of an ability to make the most of a situation you're in."

The Golden Key Award came forty years after Rivers School and Roger had seen him only once in the intervening years.

The following fall, 1974, when Richardson was speaking at a Connecticut Bar Association annual dinner in Hartford, Roger was there to receive the organization's award for Connecticut Citizen of the Year. Neither had known the other was going to be present.

By the time Roger had spent three years at Rivers, others had influenced and "refined" him. "Everybody around me had good Boston accents," says Roger. "My Jamestown accent was more midwestern than it is now, and they would correct me on pronunciation. And the kids always called me 'sir.' Every time they addressed me, it was 'sir.' For a young person to be given the full treatment—it was very nice, indeed, extremely! Calling me 'sir' was a straight procedure. This was bred—bred in the bones."

Clarence Allen did much for Roger's social education, as did Kay. She had lived with a brother and a sister whom Roger had dated on occasion.

Roger, says Mrs. Allen (now a handsome widow in Camden, Maine), used to come to their apartment quite often. "He was a footloose young man on campus, still what you might say 'a raw boy' just out of the country. And he would sometimes do *horrible* social things. My brother would swing on him and say 'Roger, you can't say things like that, you *can't. This* is the way you do it.' Then there was the awful night—we were going to some faculty party or something. Roger came in a tuxedo. And below the sleeves —I guess they were a little short for him—was his long-sleeved winter underwear hanging down! We made him take off his coat. He had come from birding and just kept his heavy underwear on. My brother fixed him up."

Another time, when they were going to a party, Kay's sister noticed smoke coming out of Roger's pocket! Roger, who was just beginning to smoke, didn't know what to do with the cork tip from his cigarette, so he put it in his pocket.

Again came that familiar fond phrase that so many people use when telling Roger's stories: "That's Roger! You have to look after him."

Roger's interest in girls bloomed during those Rivers School days. One girl he dated was Nancy Thornburg, his friend at camp.

"I enjoyed Nancy's company very much while I was in Boston," says Roger. "I could level with her in a completely natural, unself-conscious way, which was a rare relationship in my youthful days. However, even though she was only about two years older, she regarded me more as a kid brother than a romantic companion. She had an apartment on Beacon Hill and we often went to evening sketching classes and life classes in Boston. That was in the days when Bohemian life in the thirties touched Boston. Nancy was more interested in Al Maley, my best friend at Rivers." But Al was unresponsive. He was more interested in one of the young teachers of the lower school, Kappy (Katherine) Sanders.

Roger was always happy to be called in from time to time to the classes Miss Barrett and Miss Sanders were teaching to show his knowledge of birds for the enlightenment of their students—and show off his own knowledge, no doubt, for the lovely young teachers.

Another one of them baked a lot of cookies for Roger to eat when he set off once to visit his parents in Jamestown. "However," he says, "being so completely bird oriented with a kind of tunnel vision at the time, my peripheral vision failed to perceive the signals, a deficiency that seemed to correct itself in later years."

Along with Roger's increasing social graces and interest in girls came an increased development in his sense of humor. And a delightful sense of fun.

"My most memorable experience with Roger," Kay Allen says, "was one night when the faculty at Rivers decided to have a pung ride. [A pung is a kind of openwork sleigh, flat with runners in front and back, not covered over.] Somebody got the pung and the two horses and the drivers and the hay and stuff. Oh, we had a tremendous snow. It was night, moonlight, and we were having a great time. No drinking or anything. We had the teachers and the young assistants. There was Al Maley and all."

And Roger turned into a clown. He purposely kept falling off, with everybody screaming. Then, says Kay, "he would run behind with all his might and land—the whole length—on top of everybody. Nobody could stop him from doing it. He was just unmanageable—all that energy and spirit—this *flying* through the air. Oh, he had a great, light wonderful side to him when he was young at Rivers, just very frivolous. It could be almost on the rough side, like jumping on the pung on top of everybody."

On the very serious side in those Boston days was the august Nuttall Club. To belong to the Nuttall Club was an honor. When Roger was first proposed for membership he was not approved. It was not because he was not a gentleman or a member of an old Boston family or a Harvard student. It was because when his name came up one of the members said, "He was too cocky about his records." Roger said they thought "I was too sure of myself, too brash, so confident about the rare birds I'd seen, that this member questioned whether I was reliable."

Roger learned of his first and only blackballing in a curious way. He had the mumps. The physician who came to treat him was a member of the Nuttall Club and confided to Roger the reason why Roger had not been accepted. He liked Roger and advised him, "When your name comes up again for membership, as it will, I would suggest that you play a more modest role."

Roger was made a bona fide member of the Nuttall Club a year later. In the meantime he found birding companionship with a group of boys from Cambridge—the Harvard Bird Club. Roger said he was even then "privileged to attend the Nuttall Club meetings as a guest."

The Nuttall Club meetings were usually held at one or another of the old homes on Brattle Street in Cambridge. They were a very small group, usually between twelve and twenty men attending. (No women then.) Aside from a formal paper each meeting, "we had a few minutes of field notes recounting things that various members had seen" records Roger.

"One game that we played occasionally," Roger says, "was an identification test. A tray of difficult identification problems would be brought into the room. Usually about twenty-two bird species were represented, numbered one to twenty-two. Each of us would write down our identifications on a slip of paper and hand it in. I recall that Ludlow Griscom and I tied with a perfect score one night. We, of course, knew the tricks of one-upmanship that would be likely to be played. If there was a bird that looked like a rather nondescript Lincoln sparrow, we would immediately put down 'immature swamp sparrow' because we knew that in that plumage swamp sparrows are sometimes mistaken for Lincoln sparrows by the tyro. Even though there were usually at least three or four tricky specimens of this sort, we were aware that we were being tricked, and did not fall into the trap."

One of the men Roger met at the Nuttall Club was Francis H. Allen. It was a fortunate acquaintance, for it was Francis H. Allen who, at Houghton Mifflin Company, Boston, accepted Roger's first book, *A Field Guide to the Birds*.

CHAPTER VI

The Birth of
A Field Guide to the Birds

THE origins of Roger Tory Peterson's *A Field Guide to the Birds* were not simple. And it is rather remarkable that the book, with its Peterson System of bird identification, was ever published. Roger was only twenty-five, unknown, unsophisticated.

Of course, the idea of the book came from those early days in Jamestown when, as he describes in the introduction, the influence of Ernest Thompson Seton's *Two Little Savages* sparked the dream of a "real" field guide to the birds, plus the years of birding with Ludlow Griscom. But there was to be a whole series of amazing circumstances and coincidences that culminated in the Houghton Mifflin Company's purchase of a "gold mine"—the Peterson Field Guide Series, which has grown to twenty-one titles.

Francis H. Allen, Houghton Mifflin editor and chairman of the board of the Massachusetts Audubon Society, had, of course, met him at the Nuttall Club. And Roger had, as a matter of fact, sent Allen an earlier book proposal on an entirely different subject, which Allen had rejected. So Roger was not exactly a stranger to the editor when he took the field guide manuscript in.

Houghton Mifflin, though "very much impressed with the

book," according to Paul Brooks, who became Roger's editor, was "fairly cautious and the contract was conservative for the new find." It had a lot of drawings and four-color plates, which were quite expensive to reproduce in those days. The publisher did not even pay royalties on the first one thousand copies, but Roger was so thrilled he didn't care.

Richard H. Pough, then with the National Audubon Society, says that he ran into Francis Allen at an A.O.U. meeting at the American Museum and Allen told him about the Peterson manuscript. "What do you think of the work that Roger's done?" he asked Pough. "Do you think that we shall sell very many copies?"

Pough, who had seen the material, said he thought it was great. When Allen added that his firm would publish it if Pough would guarantee it wouldn't lose any money, Pough said he was so sure that he would have put up the money out of his own pocket. (Pough later published his own bird guides for the National Audubon Society, over a million of which have sold and brought much income to him and the Audubon Society.) Roger's manuscript also had the blessing of John B. May, then State Ornithologist of Massachusetts.

One report says that the acceptance of the manuscript was immediate and a telegram went to Roger the day following Allen's receipt of the manuscript. Even if this is not so, Francis Allen and Paul Brooks were confident about the book. According to Paul:

"On that morning in 1933, Francis Allen didn't need the binoculars he always kept on his office desk to realize at once that he was looking at a brand-new species of guidebook. 'Peterson's book,' he wrote in his editorial report, 'is conceived on entirely new lines. The principal feature of the book is diagrammatic drawings to show the appearance of the bird in the field. The figures on each plate are so arranged as to bring together the species that are most similar and most likely to be confused, and the diagnostic marks of the species are pointed out by arrows. It is a book that would appeal not only to beginners but to the more advanced ornithologists and I think will prove practically indispensable to students of birds in the field.' "

Brooks' enthusiasm for the book was more youthful. In his memo he said, "I think I am in a fairly good position to look at his book from the point of a beginner. It seems to me an excellent job." And he felt they could count on a "moderately good, steady sale."

The field guide sold two thousand copies—all they had published—the first week, "and they had to scramble around to get it reprinted to meet the sudden demand." Now, about two million copies have been sold; one hundred thousand a year.

Paul Brooks always felt the book would sell well, even though it was published during the depths of the Depression, but some were skeptical. One said it was just a "tool" guide; another, that it was a sort of "cookbook."

One evening, after Houghton Mifflin had taken the book, Paul Brooks was dining at the home of Judge Robert Walcott—then president of Massachusetts Audubon—and Paul mentioned the book with great enthusiasm. Walcott said, "Oh, Paul, how much is it going to sell for?" Brooks said, "$2.75." Judge Walcott answered, "Oh, nonsense, you can't sell a bird book for that. Look at those fifty-cent guides."

A year later Brooks was again at the Walcott home for dinner. Walcott had forgotten their conversation of the year before, and he said, "Paul, do you know about this new bird book everybody's got in his pocket?"

Roger was very excited about his book. He used to walk around Harvard Square, "where I went very often on a Sunday morning to join up with the group from the Harvard Bird Club to go birding, and in the bookstore, the Harvard Co-op, there was half a window full of my books—just a whole big display of them! You know, when it's your first book, and you're not sure at all how it's going to go, and you see this window full of them . . ."

Creatively, *A Field Guide to the Birds* owes its beginning to the late William Vogt, author of *The Road to Survival*, population expert, and an early friend of Roger's. It was to Vogt, along with Clarence Allen, that Roger dedicated the first field guide.

Roger had met Vogt at the American Museum in the late 1920s, when both of them occasionally turned up at meetings of the Linnaean Society. Vogt, not long out of Bard College, was a drama critic and nature columnist for five Westchester papers.

"I first met him," Roger recalls, "in the washroom at the museum. I was trying to wash the oil paint from my hands, having come from work—I was decorating furniture at that time and attending art school. I was trying to get the crud off my hands and he asked me about the stain and what I did for a living. I told him, and we got to know each other. I would take him on field trips on a Sunday. We birded with the Bronx County Bird Club, which, because they couldn't get rid of us, finally let us into their club as the first non-Bronx members."

Vogt, shorter than Roger, was badly crippled with polio, which he had contracted as a teen-ager in a summer camp. Occasionally when he was in the field with Roger he would stumble and fall, but always preferred to pick himself up.

"He showed me the flowers," said Roger, "and I showed him the birds."

On one of these occasions, Vogt asked Roger, "Why don't you put your ideas down on paper?"

Vogt later wrote in *The New York Times* of that day when he and Roger discussed a possible book. They were birding on the Hudson, counting ducks, in December 1930.

"The river," wrote Vogt, "was Whistlerian gray, and the light mists softening the outlines of the east and west banks gave us something of the sensation of hanging in space. The few hundred canvasbacks floating off the end of Croton Point, their reflections clear in the calm river, were part of the sense of the void. We were taking part in the 1930 census of birds, and it was the canvasbacks we had come to see. A barely perceptible (to me) note fell from a flock of small birds overhead, and my companion said with unchallengeable assurance, 'Siskins.'

"Roger possessed a prodigious keenness of sight and hearing, and on this particular December morning I was again impressed by his expertness. I was a mere bumbler by comparison. 'Roger,' I said to him, 'you know more about identifying the birds of this region than almost anyone else, and you can paint. Why don't you pass on your knowledge to other people in a book?'

"I was more excited about the possibility than he, but we discussed it through the mile-long walk back to the car, along the inshore marshes." They walked through the cattails, developing the plan for the book. The illustrations would be kept simple, like those Seton had done in *Two Little Savages*. It would concentrate on identification; song descriptions would be attempted only when they would help with identification.

"Who'll buy the book if I write it?" said Roger. "Nobody knows me."

"I finally guaranteed the book's sale," wrote Vogt, "with no justification whatever, that if he would do the book I would get it published."

Later, while Roger was working on the book, Bill Vogt suggested that he write several magazine articles. "I did one for *Nature Magazine*," Roger said, "called 'Half a Mile Away,' on identifying gulls, illustrated it with drawings, and pointed out the field marks. Bill introduced me to Richard Westwood, the editor. It was during Prohibition days and we went to a speakeasy in New York City. One of those places where there was a little window on the door where one was scrutinized before he could enter. This, of course, was not my world at that point, being a law-abiding Lutheran from the country, and I felt very wicked and guilty and apprehensive. But the deal was arranged."

This was followed by three stories in *Field & Stream*. Roger was paid $155 for all three, which included the drawings. One was on sea ducks, one on marsh ducks, one on bay ducks. "These articles were rather historic in a way," says Roger, "because I was telling sportsmen how to identify their ducks. Often the typical duck hunter does not know what he is shooting. The editor of *Field & Stream* felt they should be educated. I myself have never been a duck hunter."

An amusing sidelight concerning those three articles occurred some years later. Roger was in Sweden and had met the Prince of Lichtenstein, "a large, corpulent man who was a great sportsman and hunter." He said, "Oh, you are Roger Peterson. I have the articles that you did for *Field & Stream* with the drawings of the ducks. I put them up where I could study them—in the bathroom. Aquatic, you know."

Vogt, true to his promise to Roger about selling the field guide, took it to five publishers. Roger can remember only three. Little, Brown was one of them, but they were planning on doing a Thornton Burgess bird guide and they thought Roger's would be competitive. (The Burgess book for some reason was never accepted.) Putnam also rejected the book, as they already had a series of nature guides.

Bill told Roger he was writing Houghton, Mifflin to see if they would be interested. But Roger arrived before the letter, accompanied by Al Maley, who drove him to Boston in his sputtering Essex.

Thanks to that earlier meeting with Francis Allen at the Nuttall Club, he had been allowed to enter the sacred portals of Boston's most prestigious publisher.

Reviews of the field guide from professional ornithologists were mostly favorable. Chapman, of the American Museum, said that "twenty years ago the book could not have been written," the implication being, according to Roger, that otherwise he would have written such a book himself. "At that time, bird identification was largely made over the sights of a shotgun." Ludlow Griscom had come along and showed the "old boys" how to do it with proper observation. Now Roger had given them a guide to carry in the field, with the little arrows to show the individual markings. In the second edition, with well over a thousand diagrams of individual birds, in fewer than fifty of them was it necessary to use more than two arrows. Four arrows on a bird occur exactly twice.

The only review that depressed the sensitive Roger came from a man he idolized, John Kieran. According to Roger, Kieran had written his review largely from the publisher's blurb on the inside jacket, which said, "This book will at once take its place as an indispensable companion for Eastern bird students," implying it could take the place of binoculars, or so Roger interpreted the statement. Kieran had preferred the word "helpful" rather than "indispensable."

Kieran said recently, "My admiration for Roger's work and my delight in our almost lifelong friendship remains. Roger has been a hard worker, immensely talented, and deserves every bit of the success he has attained." Kieran goes on, "Roger is the recognized world leader in bird portraiture."

The book has become a valuable collector's item. Alongside Audubon's elephant folio at the Rare Bird Books section of the 1975 Animals in Art exhibit at the Royal Ontario Museum there was a first printing of Roger Tory Peterson's *A Field Guide to the Birds*, and with it a first jacket. Actually there were three editions exhibited: 1934, 1935, and 1947.

The overall theme, arranged by David M. Lank, reads "Four Centuries of Animals in Books" and "The Most Successful and Influential Bird Books of All Time."

The placard under Roger's books in the glass case read, "Without doubt, the greatest stimulus for popularizations of wild life has been Peterson's phenomenally successful 'Field Guide Series.' The bird books—in their various language editions—have been adapted to national or regional avifauna, and the format has been used in literally dozens of other works, ranging from animal, tracks, astronomy, shells, to nestlings. Peterson's great art and profound knowledge have assured his place in the first rank of the artists of natural history."

How much is a Peterson first printing worth? At least one, complete with dust jacket, sold for $1,200. And how can one tell if it is an authentic first printing? "Well," Roger advises, "check the plates of the whistling swan's neck, and the one of the egrets. The engraver didn't clean up the whites entirely and left some gray screen in the necks of both birds."

It was not until 1961 that Roger did a complete revision of the original book, with thirty-six color plates instead of four.

But this was long after John H. Baker, who later became president of the National Association of Audubon Societies, had seen the original plates of the field guide at an A.O.U. meeting at the American Museum in 1933 and asked Roger to leave Rivers School and come to the Societies. On November 1, 1934, John Baker became its executive director, and it was on that same day that Roger went back to New York to become a member of the staff and, subsequently, educational director, and, later, an Audubon lecturer and writer.

Part II

CHAPTER VII

Roger Joins
the Audubon Society

At the National Association of Audubon Societies, Roger's first job was to produce a new and different cover for *Bird Lore*, which later was to become *Audubon Magazine*, now simply *Audubon*.

Although Roger was not a calligrapher, he did change the lettering. The first cover was a black and white drawing of a rough-legged hawk as viewed from above as it flew over the wintry landscape. They were limited to two colors, black and one other. After this rough-leg appeared, Roger received a letter from Arthur Cleveland Bent. Bent said the hawk painting was one of the finest bird paintings he had ever seen. This pleased Roger very much.

When he tried to surpass himself on the second cover with a composition showing five shovelers jumping from the marsh, it was a disaster, though Roger said the concept was valid.

Bird Lore had been acquired by John Baker in 1934 from Dr. Chapman of the American Museum, who had owned and edited it. It usually appeared in a rather pale green cover with old-fashioned lettering and some thought it looked more like a religious tract than a modern magazine. Baker's instinct was to have an Audubon Societies' publication that was appealing and modern.

THE WORLD OF ROGER TORY PETERSON

It is necessary, because of the intertwining of Roger's life and career with the Audubon organization, to know who John Baker was and what he did to help bring it up from a membership of only 3,500 to a membership of more than 350,000 today.

John Baker had been a Wall Street broker, and had been chairman of the board of the National Association of Audubon Societies, when he succeeded Dr. T. Gilbert Pearson.

Baker has been described as a Boston Brahman, "an impressive, rather formidable man, darkish of complexion and with a shiny pate and a short bristle mustache." His mother ran a private school for boys in Boston, and his father was George Pierce Baker, the great teacher and producer of drama at Yale. John Baker's hobby had always been birds; he had a deep ornithological knowledge. He was anything but a politician. He rubbed many Audubon members the wrong way and was actually disliked strongly by many people who did not react well to his direct, often pragmatic ways. He frightened members of his staff also, and was never adept at smoothing people's feathers. Roger says Baker would not compromise when the welfare of birds or other animals was at stake, and for this stubbornness he made a number of enemies. So it was not only his sometimes glowering personality that turned many people against him.

On the other hand, Baker had great integrity and "perhaps," says Roger, "accomplished more in his years at the helm of the Society than any other administrator." Among the fundamental projects he started were the Audubon research program, the teaching camps, teaching centers, plus the lecture programs through the country, as well as acquiring *Bird Lore*.

Baker made William Vogt editor of *Bird Lore* and assigned Roger to him. Roger painted most of the covers.

Roger's contributions to *Bird Lore* were articles on methodology for the use of teachers who planned to interest their pupils in birds. Roger had always regarded himself as a teacher wherever he went—at Rivers School, at various camps, wherever a child or grown person showed an interest in birds or nature.

John Baker, that first year, recognized this talent. One of the first things he did was to send Roger around to the various school systems in the Northeast where they were using the Junior

Audubon Club leaflets, and also to a half dozen or so children's museums in existence, to evaluate the impact of the leaflets and the Audubon educational work.

The leaflets, up until that time, had been written by William Dutcher, Audubon's first president, and Dr. Pearson. Pearson was "an excellent field man," Roger concedes, "but the leaflets were written almost as though they expected their fellow ornithologists to pass judgment on them, rather than the school children for whom they were intended."

Roger changed all that. He also believed that there should be some distinction between texts for the younger children and the older ones. He planned two sets of texts, one for those nine and under, and one for those ten and over.

With his talent for writing and painting, as well as for teaching, and with the help of publicity generously given by a national teaching publication called *Our Weekly Reader,* membership in the Junior Audubon Clubs again reached 400,000 or more, the peak of their popularity. Each leaflet, selling for ten cents, and each with a colorplate, told of an individual species.

Nothing like this had ever been done before. Carl Buchheister, retired president of the National Audubon Society, says that these leaflets were more important in educating people about birds than Roger's field guides. Not only the children in school, but the parents at home, absorbed the knowledge in those Junior Audubon Club leaflets. Carl said that Roger shares with his reader, regardless of age, "that naïveté, that feeling of wonder, of excitement about nature that he had as a child, that he had as a boy himself—and never lost."

The leaflets reached nine million children during the years Roger wrote them, says Buchheister. They were common in the back hills of South Carolina and in New York City and in Wyoming. For the first time in their lives, youngsters read something about the natural world—about an owl, a hawk, what they do, what they eat. Roger re-created in his writing all the things he felt about birds. It was Roger Tory Peterson who got young people started. He had the ability to share his knowledge and the desire to do it.

It wasn't until Roger went into the Army in the early 1940s that the pattern of the Junior Audubon Clubs changed. One reason was that the United States Government no longer permitted the public schools to collect money from children for any purpose. Roger always felt that it was unfortunate that the leaflets on individual species had to be discontinued. Ecology, the new approach the Audubon Societies began to stress, was fine, but, he said, "people do not start with an ecological concept. They acquire it through using some specific springboards such as birds, plants, or whatever in nature. To expect children to become 'instant ecologists' is presumptuous." At about this time, Carl Buchheister was teaching Latin at the Lawrence School, a private institution at Hewlett, Long Island. One of his students was Mildred Washington, who was to marry Roger Tory Peterson, Carl playing an innocent role in bringing them together several years later.

Because of his interest in nature, Buchheister organized a group of the youngsters—ages eleven to fourteen—into evening classes in wildlife. It was a sort of club and fifty or more boys and girls signed up. They had a little building where they met on Friday evenings, had a big fire in the fireplace, and cooked hamburgers and hot dogs. Adults were not allowed, so the young people were not self-conscious or inhibited in any way. A couple of them would make little talks about some bird or about something in nature that interested them. The others would ask questions, referring to Buchheister only as a "presidential advisor." Sometimes they had an outside guest.

Roger was one of them.

Somebody told Buchheister about a young man who had just come to the National Audubon to write about nature for children. Carl didn't know Peterson from Adam. He was not even a member of an Audubon Society at that time, but he did get in touch with Roger. It was in the winter of 1935—Roger had been at Audubon only since November 1934. "Lo and behold," Carl says, "the man who came to my class, coming out in the Long Island train from New York, was Roger Peterson. He was tall, very thin, had a very sharp, pointed aquiline nose. He acted very shyly and modestly but was not at all fearful. He wore a sort of business suit which needed pressing badly. He was not a Brooks Brothers fashion plate, but he was not in a Daniel Boone camping-out outfit either.

"And how he held the attention of those children! Completely natural, unpedagogic, just acting as if he were a boy with his own interest in nature, talking to fellow boys and girls. A marvelous, completely enthusiastic interest, no trick of oratory, no trick of presentation, just coming out as natural as a boy in a meadow who had found a screech owl in a tree hole and was talking to his friends. At lectures he projected that he was feeling it all—how a bird lives, what kind of head it has, what kind of feet. What happened was that every single kid sitting on the floor had his mouth open, because here was somebody who was feeling it all. He could tell little stories and examples of his own adventures. It was as if the youngsters were out there in the woods together."

Carl had not introduced Roger as the author of the *Field Guide* or artist and writer of *Bird Lore*. He was not yet known as "the great bird man." In fact, Carl did not know anything about him then himself, but said he learned more about the screech owl at that lecture than he had ever known.

Meanwhile, Roger was living in Greenwich Village, getting his first taste of Bohemian life in the Prohibition era. He had a small apartment at Milligan Place, just a block or two from the women's jail on Eighth Street and Sixth Avenue. "I recall," he says, "on New Year's Eve I could hear the hubbub in the jail as the inmates rattled their tin cups across the barred windows at the stroke of midnight."

Robert Porter Allen, director of sanctuaries at Audubon, and Roger's neighbor and intimate friend, lived at Patchin Place, in the apartments made from old stables, just around the corner from Roger, and it was natural that the two Audubon naturalists would travel back and forth from the Audubon offices together. In fact, Roger was not only attending the sparkling Saturday night parties at the Allens but eating most of his meals there. Bob's brother John, who was an art director for *Fortune* magazine, lived with the Bob Allens. It was Johnny who brought into the household the artists and actors and musicians who turned the apartment into hilarious bedlam. Johnny had cancer, but never complained.

Bob's wife, Evelyn, was a musician as well as a marvelous cook, a caretaker for Johnny Allen, and a sort of mother confessor to Roger. He used to lean on her in many ways. At twenty-seven he needed to know more about people than birds. He would get the buoyant, attractive woman, a few years older than himself, to listen and advise and share his confidences.

Johnny had an apartment at Patchin Place connected with his brother's. "You went out through a front hall into our apartment," says Evelyn, describing the Village layout. "We had a kitchen under our apartment. You went down a circular stairway into the kitchen. And Johnny and Bob and I hired a woman to cook for us. Jenny. Because Johnny was making $90 a week with *Fortune*—in those days it was *something*—and Bob was making $45 with Audubon, we could afford it." They fed everybody who dropped in.

They had a little backyard, and Bobby, their baby, played under the eyes of the girls in the women's jail. "These poor girls would sit up there in the cells and watch the baby, and they used to sing and yell to him." They also yelled down to the Allens' attractive guests in the backyard, "Come up and see us sometime."

Johnny's adjoining apartment was made into the living room, where they had a grand piano, and a bar was set up between the living room and his bedroom. This bar became the favorite of many of the young artists—like Roger—and included many people who were at *Time* and *Fortune*.

Into Roger's life came such people as James Agee, the reviewer and essayist. Roger dated his sister Emma. There was Van Heflin, then an unknown actor; Charles Lemar, the costume designer; Charles Tenno Jacobs, one of the first staff photographers of *Life*; Victor Hammond, the art expert; Joseph Kastner, copy editor of *Life*, and his wife, Barbara. Kastner was later to work with Roger's paintings and articles for the magazine. Along with a number of musicians and orchestra leader friends of Evelyn's, there was Vincente Minnelli, the famous stage-set designer and movie director. "Of course," says Evelyn, "we had all those funny people from Linnaean and Audubon. Bird people."

Johnny drank heavily there on Patchin Place, perhaps "because he felt so awful," says Evelyn Allen.

Roger drank very little. For the most part, he sat just watching and listening. And talking with Evelyn and confiding. For some reason, they all called Evelyn "Cull," and Roger would say, "Cull, let's talk about life."

"I knew Roger like this," says Evelyn, folding her arms and

hugging herself. "We had great love for each other. I think it was very obvious to him that Bob and I had a very physical, satisfying relationship, and I think this was something Roger wanted for himself. I don't think he had this and it's too bad he didn't have enough of it in his young life, for I think Roger would be physically and sexually very strong."

Perhaps it was his Lutheran upbringing that kept him from "sleeping around," as was happening all about them in Greenwich Village, Prohibition surroundings. It was not as obviously permissive as some sexual behavior was to become, but was a pretty morally lax Bohemian period. (Roger was to say later that he had sex only with his wives.)

The Allens knew nothing of his background. He never seemed to hear from his parents, nor did they come to see him. Roger joined Joe Kastner and Bob and Johnny for lunch now and then at one of the speakeasies near the Chrysler Building, where they worked. Roger was quite shy and quiet—until somebody got on to the subject of birds, when he was eloquently garrulous. At Patchin Place, Roger could be violent too—more emotional perhaps than violent—about things that concerned him, such as bird identification or conservation, waving his arms—he was "extremely vehement," according to Evelyn.

Birds, however, were not the subject of general discussion as much as life, art, politics, and whether or not Johnny should go out and buy pork chops or lamb, or whether some guests on WPA really hadn't supplied their share of booze. Bob and Evelyn, lively people, were often arguing and even throwing things, and Evelyn, pregnant again, didn't always want to prepare meals when the cook wasn't there. "Evelyn was a spirited, buxom girl, terribly worried about Johnny," says Kastner, and he adds, in front of his wife, Barbara, who was also there during the Patchin Place days, "Evelyn had the softest lips I've ever kissed." Roger says that Joe said, "It was like being kissed by a butterfly."

Evelyn and Bob Allen, increasingly worried about Johnny, thought he would be better out of New York, and they moved to Freeport, Long Island, where Johnny could sail his little dinghy and paint and study birds. They took Roger with them. They thought it would be healthier for him, too, in the country. Roger was still scrawny and thin, and he missed the birds. They took Allan Cruickshank with them too! Allan was also at the National Audubon Societies by then. He got a room down the street from the Allens in Freeport, but ate his meals with them. So, on work days, it fell to Evelyn Allen to get the three members of the Audubon staff—her husband, Roger, and Allan Cruickshank—off to the train for New York.

Roger had a room and bath off a balcony, and Evelyn made him hang up his clothes and reminded him to take showers—Roger had reverted to some extent to his pre-River School "proper" teaching days—and to get him up in the morning was a real chore. "I was rather 'kookie' myself in those days and it was a house full of 'idiots,'" she says, "practicing my Bach all day, caring for the babies and cooking for the boys."

Allan—"Cruicky" they called him—was always a practical joker. Roger simply could not keep up with him. They were the closest friends and the bitterest of rivals, always competing on bird counts, in photography, even in girls. Cruicky was handsome, tall, bright, and clownish. He was an expert at bird calling and loved to deceive Roger whenever he could. The two, pitting their talents against each other, profited from the competition.

The story of one of his most absurd pranks on Roger occurred when they were all at Freeport. Cruickshank's widow, Helen, tells it this way:

"One morning, when Allan went over to their house at the crack of dawn before Robert and Roger went off to New York, Roger was so excited, Evelyn could not persuade him to eat. He had found a 'rare' magpie, a dead magpie. Roger wasn't sure whether it was a European magpie that had come westward, or a black-billed magpie that had come eastward. He wanted to take it to Dr. Chapman at the American Museum for identification. He had it all wrapped up in a shoe box and it was on the breakfast table. Roger could eat nothing in his excitement.

"In the process, one of the children—little Bobby or Alice—upset the milk. Evelyn got a dishcloth and mopped it up. Roger went upstairs for his coat or something, and Allan, just as a joke—he didn't know it was going too far—opened the kitchen table drawer and put the magpie in it. And he put the dishrag into the shoe box.

About that time there was a terrific confusion. Bob yelled for everybody to get going, the children were upset, more crises, the bus was coming, Evelyn shouting and roaring at everybody to hurry. Roger rushed out with his package. Allan was a bit concerned, but not too much, evidently; he was enjoying his prank.

"As soon as they got to New York, Roger went straight to Dr. Chapman's office at the museum. Dr. Chapman was impressed with what Roger had to say, and he called in Dr. Robert Cushman Murphy. 'And now,' said Dr. Chapman, 'it's time to show us the magpie.'

"The box was opened and—the dishrag!"

Roger's astonishment was no less than that of the head of the museum, and Murphy, always rather austere, didn't think it was a bit funny. Chapman understood and asked Roger to come back the next day. It was an experience he never forgot and probably one for which he never *quite* forgave Allan.

The Allens moved from Freeport soon after Johnny died. They moved into a little place in Amityville. It was near South Bay and the birding was good. Roger and Allan, back in New York, shared the weekends as often as they could.

That summer John Baker conceived the idea of a camp in Maine for teachers of nature subjects, and Roger was sent off to inspect the site in the summer of 1935.

CHAPTER VIII

Romance at the Audubon Camp

In Muscongus Bay, Maine, Hog Island was the site chosen by John Baker for the first Audubon Camp for Adult Leaders. Roger had made his survey to see if the birds and other wildlife and plants made the island as desirable as Baker thought it was for his purpose. He wanted a place where those interested in nature and nature education—principally counselors, teachers, Scout leaders—could go and learn about nature firsthand. "We must find a way to equip a teacher better to teach," said John Baker. But others who wanted to learn about birds and animals and the out-of-doors could come too.

"Hog Island was a paradise," Roger wrote, "a garden of Eden." He had had a glimpse of it a year or so before when he was a counselor at Camp Chewonki and had sailed past it. "I remember seeing a white-tailed deer among the ferns."

The island is about sixty miles north of Portland. The shopping areas were Newcastle and Damariscotta. Roger knew the outer islands too—Eastern Egg Rock, Western Egg Rock, Little Rock, and Old Hump Ledge, with their cormorants and gulls.

Baker had first heard of Hog Island when Millicent Todd Bingham, who owned the island, came to him with snapshots, among them some of young herons in the nests of their treetop rookery and a seal balancing on a rocky ledge. Baker, according to an article in *Audubon*, was politely interested, and then Mrs. Bingham said she would like to protect in perpetuity the island with its virgin spruce forests and wildlife.

"Just what I want," Baker said.

Most of the island's three hundred acres had been purchased by Millicent's family in the early 1900s. It had been protected from shooting and other depredations for over twenty-five years. Her father, a professor at Amherst College, and her mother had loved summers on the island. When her mother, a widow, died in 1932, Millicent's determination to fulfill her mother's wishes to keep the island from spoilage led her to the Audubon Societies. An arrangement was made to lease the island for one dollar a year.

At the northern end were some buildings—"just what I want," Baker repeated. They were acquired through the generosity of a Dr. James M. Todd.

Mrs. Bingham was as happy as John Baker. "When I walked through the woods and listened to the thrushes, the cry of the osprey circling overhead, or the boom of the great horned owl at night," she wrote, "I could never feel that I owned such a place. It seemed rather the property of all who cherish it likewise in years to come."

Roger had taken many pictures to show Baker. He struggled with an antique 35-mm motion-picture camera Baker had lent him—"Do what you can with it," he had said.

Charles Fenno Jacobs, one of the pioneer photographers of *Life*, whom Roger had met during his Greenwich Village days through Joe Kastner, went with Roger to take still photographs. That was in June 1935.

"We made our headquarters in the old ship chandlery on the property," says Roger, "and fed high off the hog on lobsters that we bought at the lobster pound at nearby Medomak. But at the end of a week, we were scarcely speaking to each other because of the unmerciful kidding I got about the size of my four-by-five Graflex camera, a revolving camera so huge that Charlie insisted I could use it for a darkroom to develop my pictures in." It was clumsy and hard to move around. Charlie said "it was a superstructure."

Roger really got irritated. "I picked up a lobster and threw it at him."

One does not think of the gentle-voiced Roger Tory Peterson of ornithological and lecture-hall fame throwing lobsters in a temper. But Roger admits to "having a sort of a temper." And throwing things when he is angry. Once he threw a bottle of castor oil at his father when he tried to doctor Roger. Someone tells of his throwing a picture he had painted, perhaps because he was not happy with it. And once a vase. Roger has said of himself, "I do have quite a temper, being of Scandinavian background. I would probably be quite capable of going berserk, not fearing for my own life if pushed far enough. It is rarely that I lose my temper but when I do, it upsets me very much. I do not like it. When I am very angry I can be very articulate and can cut a person to ribbons with a few words." Not "swear words," according to Roger, who says "most people using such epithets do so because of their lack of imagination in using the language. It's an easy way out." Roger claims, "When I swear, which is very rarely, it *really* means something."

He may have sworn at Charlie Jacobs that day on Hog Island, but they were soon photographing together again.

"We photographed a heron colony," Roger says, "a very fine nest, about twenty feet high in the tree. Granite below. Spruce trees around it. I had a blind on a small islet on the rocks, but the spruce tree obscured the nest. I decided I could bend the spruce tree out of the way so I could focus on the nest. I shinnied up the tree, tried to bend it. But you can't bend a spruce like you can a birch sapling. I leaned back. The spruce snapped like a matchstick. I came down on my back on the rocks. I had a horrible back for several weeks. I had nearly broken it."

Later the film, "poor as it was," was put together to be used for publicity to attract people to the camp the following season.

Carl Buchheister, who had left the Massachusetts Audubon Society, where he had been director, and who knew the Hog Island area well, was hired by John Baker to head the camp. So on June 10, 1936, Carl and Roger, who was to be the leading bird instructor, were there and waiting for the first arrivals.

John Baker had told Buchheister that it was important to have a moving picture of the arrival of the first campers. Carl agreed.

"Mr. Baker," he said, "I know that can be done. We'll get Roger to take all the pictures. He's the only one who can do it." Roger had the camera and the film. The night before the historic day, Carl warned Roger that at five o'clock in the morning they would be going down to the railroad station. Roger was to set up the camera so that pictures could be taken of Carl greeting the people as they got off the train.

Roger hated getting up in the morning as much as the old camera. They did get to the station. It was a good, clear morning. As the train came around the bend the whistle was blowing. Roger had his tripod and camera set up. He waved and told Carl where to stand. Roger was the happiest of men as he snapped the camera.

Later in the morning he came to see Carl with a *"look on his face*, like an absolutely sick great blue heron. He had that long nose and a dreadful downcast long look." Carl asked, "What in hell is the matter with *you*, Roger?"

"I—I didn't have any film in the camera."

It was Roger, too, who had arrived at the camp without a key to his trunk. So about every four or five days, Roger would go to Harriet Buchheister, who ran the camp with Carl and mothered Roger as women always have. "Who's going to town?"

"What for?" said Mrs. Buchheister, guessing.

"I want them to get me some shorts." Every time anybody went to town Roger asked him to buy him a pair of shorts. He piled the soiled ones up in the corner of his cabin. He was rooming with Allan Cruickshank, who was always neat and told Mr. Buchheister, "You asked me to room with him, but I can't stand it. So I fixed him! I got a pole with a nail on it and a great big can and I lifted every one of those things and put them in the can. I put the lid on it."

Away it went with the refuse collector.

Carl was fond of both Roger and his competitor, Allan, and saw them through many practical jokes during the Audubon years. There were, however, other incidents that first year that were not funny:

Roger had been asked by William Vogt for some illustrations for a very important monograph by Margaret Morse Nice, a Columbus, Ohio, ornithologist. She had made a very exhaustive, definitive, scientific life history of the song sparrow, and the Linnaean Society was publishing it. Roger, Vogt, and Buchheister, of course, were all members of the Linnaean Society, and it was logical that Vogt should ask Roger to do the illustrations. Roger should have done them before he went to camp. But Roger, who defers and defers and defers, didn't do it.

After about a week at camp, Carl Buchheister received a letter from Vogt: "Roger Peterson hasn't sent those drawings for Margaret Nice's monograph on the song sparrow. I need them badly. The deadline is approaching rapidly. Please tell him to get those drawings *done*."

Carl said to himself, "I'm not the boss of Roger Peterson outside of camp. This is not my commitment. It is something that has to do with the New York office." But he did show Roger the letter.

Roger said, "They're always after me to get things done. *I'll* get them done."

Another letter came from Vogt. "Get the guy to get those drawings done."

Again Carl went to Roger, who said, "Well, you know, he's always doing this to me. *I'll* get them done."

On the fourth or fifth day later, a telegram came. "And," said Carl, "you know the trouble we had getting telegrams out there from the mainland. But a boat came over with the telegram. It read something like this: 'Deadline tomorrow. Must have sparrow drawings. Get them in the mail. And then tie a twenty-five-pound rock around Peterson's neck and throw him in Muscongus Bay. [Signed] Bill Vogt.'" Carl showed the telegram to Roger, who was greatly annoyed.

But that night he went to his room and kept the light burning the entire night long. At 6:30, when the staff came in for breakfast and to get their day's assignments, Roger came in and threw a big envelope on Carl's desk. "Well, there they are."

"I opened the envelope," said Carl, "and there were absolutely incomparable drawings of song sparrows. A whole bunch of them! Young ones. Old ones. Eggs. A whole lot of stuff. I asked Roger if he had been up all night, and he said, 'Yes.'

"That," said Carl, "was the genius of Roger Tory Peterson. He was born a genius to do what he wanted when he wanted to. By that very nature of his genius he found any normal restrictions on his actions irksome. A genius wants to work when he wants to work."

At the Audubon Camp there were some restrictions that even Roger, the genius, could not dispute. One was curfew. Campers had to be in their rooms at 9 P.M., even Roger, although Roger behaved as if he were above it all.

One day Roger suggested that he take the students owling. Carl was concerned about the timing of a night walk. Roger explained that since it was June they would have to wait until at least ten o'clock, when it got dark. Roger was adamant about the importance of owling and Carl was worried about the campers being out after curfew. At first Carl would not permit the walk, but finally he gave in. He noticed that all the students who went on this trip with Roger were young ones, mostly women. "Roger was a good-looking guy—he could be immensely attractive and nobody could be as bright and articulate as he. But the point is Roger never listened to anything you said. I had said, 'I'll make one exception. I want you back here within an hour.' He got out there. He forgot about me."

Baker always went up to the camp every two weeks to see how things were going, "looking into everything. Listening." He made everybody nervous, according to Carl. "He'd come into my office at night after the students were put to bed and pull the blinds down. He and I would sit there and talk shop. About the Society. About birds. Baker was a damn good ornithologist."

"Having any trouble with people minding the rules?" Baker would say, and Buchheister would answer, "Don't worry about that, Mr. President. I've got that under control, Mr. Baker."

"Fine. Very good."

One night about twelve o'clock Carl took Baker up to his cabin. "We didn't have bathrooms. There was a little wash house up the hill. We didn't have electric lights. I had a flashlight. We hadn't walked more than fifty feet. And my God, I heard a rustling and a jumping and footsteps and then all of a sudden I heard somebody whine and cry. Dark, you know."

Baker said, "What's that?"

"I don't know. Not a raccoon. So we went up where the noise

was. The staff had been making a ditch, plumbing or something—
and in this ditch was this girl! A young blonde. She had run and
fallen in the ditch. She was holding on to her ankle and groaning
like a son of a gun. Somebody else was running away."

Carl asked her, "What caused you to be out at this time of
night? You are supposed to be in your dormitories at nine o'clock!"

"She said she was taking a little walk. An owl walk."

Whether that was the reason Roger was not assigned to the
camp the following year he says he does not know. Or whether his
marriage that winter had anything to do with it. But at this
juncture Allan Cruickshank took over and taught the bird courses
and was known as "the Dean of Women." He was there twenty-
two years.

When Allan died in 1974, one of the islands in Muscongus
Bay—Eastern Egg Rock—which the campers visited often to see
the nesting cormorants and gulls, was bought for an Allan D.
Cruickshank Wildlife Sanctuary. It was dedicated in 1976 to the
memory of the ornithologist, wildlife photographer, author, and
long-time National Audubon Society staff member. The seven-
acre island, eight miles from the Audubon Workshop on Hog
Island, is now the site of a project to restore the Atlantic puffin to
some of its former range.

In spite of all the "Roger stories" and escapades, Roger did a
remarkable job as bird teacher. And he started the first bird census
there. That first summer 223 men and women from as far west as
California and as far south as Florida attended one or more sessions.
There were five sessions, two weeks each. Many came for a chance
to be led in the field by the already well-known Roger Tory Peterson. They came from all walks of life—from a New York fireman
who liked to feed pigeons from the firehouse roof to a dean of the
graduate school of education at Harvard University. And many
couples.

One of the students who came was Mildred Washington, who
was just twenty-one years old. She came to Hog Island because of
her genuine interest in nature, and because she knew Carl
Buchheister, who had taught her about nature at the Lawrence
School several years before. She had never met Roger. Nor, when
she did, was it love at first sight—for either of them.

Roger said of himself, "Being one of the very few young eligible males in a sylvan camp dominated by females was like being a cock ruffed grouse on a drumming log. It was inevitable that I was to be selected by one of the young ladies who came as a student. It was Mildred Warner Washington."

But other observers of the romance remembered that handsome, exuberant, outgoing Allan Cruickshank had already caught her eye. Allan, apparently, was not aggressive enough. Perhaps the competition, ever present with Allan and Roger, whether it was in bird identification or photography, extended to girls. Some at the camp said that Allan appealed to her more, and claimed that Mildred admitted that if she couldn't get Allan, she would show him that she could get Roger. True or not, it was a tempting choice— two handsome bright young men in a setting of rarefied air, magnificent beaches, rich woods, and nature ablooming all about them. Mildred lost some of her interest in birds and concentrated on humans. Her mother, Mrs. Whiting Washington, was not too far away in North Edgecomb, Maine. Mrs. Washington liked Roger and Roger felt at home with her. She was a real birder, and an expert at carving wood replicas of birds. She was pleased to see the romance develop.

A pretty brunette with a very attractive figure, Mildred was active and emotionally vibrant, inexhaustible on birding trips. She had heavy eyebrows and long lashes and curly hair. She was all girl.

Also, she was in the Social Register. And she was a descendant of the George Washington family, which may have impressed Roger.

On September 24, 1936, an item appeared in *The New York Times'* society columns, a special from North Edgecomb, Maine:

> Mrs. Whiting Washington of Trail's End, this place, has announced the engagement of her daughter, Miss Mildred Warner Washington, to Roger Tory Peterson, son of Mr. and Mrs. Charles G. Peterson of Jamestown, New York.
>
> Miss Washington is the daughter of the late Bowden Washington and a descendant of John Washington, an uncle of George Washington. She attended the Mary C. Wheeler School in Providence.

Mr. Peterson is the educational director of Audubon Societies and is well known for his bird paintings. He studied with Willem Langereis and also at the Art Students League and the National Academy of Design in New York City.

The wedding will take place in December in Wiscasset, Maine, near here.

And so it did, on December 19, 1936, at St. Philip's Church. "Our wedding," says Roger, "was a very social one. I was in top hat and tails." Roger found himself listed in the New York Social Register. (He had been in *Who's Who* when he was twenty-six as a result of his field guide.)

Roger writes of Mildred's genealogy, "It was quite extraordinary. She was a great-great-great-great-great-great-granddaughter of George Washington's uncle. She was also descended from two Vice Presidents, as well as Robert Fulton, DeWitt Clinton, and some of the old Dutch governors, and could trace her lineage back to King John of England, as well as about eight or nine of the barons who forced him to sign the Magna Carta; also the kings of France and Spain, etc. A most extraordinary lineage, quite in contrast to my own, whose parents were immigrants from northern Europe."

Miss Elizabeth Tillinghast was the bride's only attendant. Clarence Beal was best man. Ushers were Carl Buchheister, Richard Pough of the Audubon Societies, and David Lloyd Garrison.

Mildred was a very strong-willed and spirited girl, and she and Roger, although strongly attracted to each other physically, had emotional incompatibilities from the time they met. In fact there was some arguing at the wedding that made some members of the wedding party nervous for the future of the marriage. One guest wondered if they would—or should—go through with it.

Roger and Mildred spent their honeymoon at the Château Frontenac in Quebec. "It was hardly the place to do any birding," said Roger, "being the Christmas season. The only bird I recall seeing, and only one, was an Iceland gull on the open water of the St. Lawrence River near the city docks of Quebec."

The couple did not have much money when they were married,

though Roger was back at Audubon as educational director. They set up housekeeping in an apartment at 22 East Eighty-ninth Street, and Roger says Guy Emerson, a former president of Audubon, lent him a few hundred dollars to help furnish the apartment, but Mildred denies it.

By the time Roger was married he had acquired his first car, a second-hand Buick. Richard Pough and Peggy Brooks, of the Audubon offices, gave him driving lessons.

"Peggy and Dick Pough did a good job of teaching me to drive," Roger believes, though others, counting up the accidents Roger has had on the highway, may wonder. It had been predicted even then that Roger, because of his single-mindedness, would probably get himself killed if some rare bird flew across the road. "I was always conscious of this, and refused to be diverted," Roger says. However, on his first trip to Florida with Mildred, he did go to sleep at the wheel, he admits, and ran off the road. No harm done.

Roger was rapturously in love those early days of marriage. They say, some of them who were at Audubon then, that "Roger was hardly able to keep his mind on his work."

It is amazing what an enormous amount of work he did—painting, writing, and revising the *Field Guide*, as well as working for the Audubon Societies, which John Baker was building into a strong and effective organization for nature education and conservation.

CHAPTER IX

Mildred and the
Ivory-Billed Woodpecker

DURING those busy years at the Audubon Society and his fascination with Mildred, Roger was asked by Baker to do more and more lecturing. At first it wasn't easy for Roger. He had been a self-conscious young man, but soon developed a talent for storytelling. Audiences found many of his anecdotes charming and amusing. One of the stories he told always brought appreciative laughter. It was about his first lecture.

John Baker had sent him to the Brooklyn Academy of Music to speak to an audience of children. Allan Cruickshank was with him, fortunately, for Roger was terrified when he found there would be more than 1,500 youngsters present.

"I'm in trouble, Allan," he said. "You've got to help me out."

So he persuaded Allan to sit in the balcony. Roger started his talk with a ghost story involving a screech owl. He could imitate a screech owl most realistically—a heart-stirring, spooky sound. The children were sitting on the edges of their seats when all of a sudden, from the distance, came an answering screeching screech owl. Allan, in the last row in the balcony, had played his part well. The lecture was a great success.

But that wasn't all, Roger continues the tale. "I had touched up my slides with a little paint to make them more effective, but the heat of the projector melted the paint, which ran down the heads of the warblers and robins." From where he stood on the platform, he could not see what was happening. The children were screaming with laughter. When Roger found out, he laughed, too, sharing the hilarity of the situation.

This was long before the Audubon Screen Tours—so successful even today under a different name: the Wildlife Lecture Program. Roger often got hooked into talks that were real headaches. One was for an audience of only eight, he recounts. "In our apartment that evening Mildred and I were having dinner with the Jaques, dear friends. Halfway through dinner, I realized that I was supposed to be downtown in half an hour, giving this talk. So I hurried down. There were only nine people. One woman, a rather abrasive type, said, 'Well, I hope you are entertaining. We had another nature speaker, Cleveland Grant, last week and he wasn't.' I blew up. 'I'm sorry, but I am not nearly as good as Cleve Grant and I don't intend to be entertaining.' She stalked out. I had an audience of eight."

Another time John Baker sent him up to Worcester, Massachusetts, where they had a kind of bird day each year for the schools. A captive audience. "In those days I had only old-fashioned colored lantern slides. The auditorium had one of those projectors where the light slowly built up while the picture slowly got brighter and brighter every time a new slide came on." The only way Roger could let the operator know when he wanted to change a slide was to put a handkerchief on the end of a billiard cue and drop it across the screen. "It was a miserable lecture," said Roger. "I had a cold. And the management complained to John Baker that I wasn't wearing a dress suit."

On that same jaunt, Roger was to give eleven lectures in four days, "almost turning mental flip-flops." In Rhode Island he spoke at the Rhode Island School of Design on bird drawing and on the paintings of Audubon; at a garden club; the Rhode Island Audubon Society; a private boy's school in Newport, and to a bunch of small black children about nine years old—all with completely different approaches to his lectures.

Finally John Baker realized that there had to be more organization, more thrust to the lecture program. "We were just learning, feeling our way, at the Society," Roger says. "By trial and error we became professionals."

So Baker started a well-organized lecture program throughout the country, employing top lecturers, preferably showing films instead of still pictures. By going from town to town on one-night stands, the operation became economically feasible. These, initiated during the war years, were called the Audubon Screen Tours.

Roger was pulled into this program after his stint in the army. But not being a motion-picture photographer at the time, he had to use excess footage that other photographers couldn't use. It was full of splices. In one lecture the film broke eleven times. Using "seconds" and discards did not please him, so he invested in his own equipment and took his own movies. This became very expensive.

Roger felt that the screen tours built Audubon membership. "Instead of having forty members in a club, they would soon have four or five hundred or maybe a thousand. The screen tours gave the members an active thing to do. Also, they were entertained. But that was not our purpose. It was a sugar-coated treatment of natural history. People also got educated as to what conservation was, what ecology was, what the environment was."

Roger's "educating" procedure was to go into a city and have dinner with the officers or sponsors before his lecture, sometimes speaking about some local conservation problem to which he had alerted himself. For instance, Roger would ask, "What effect would the town's plan have on the local mockingbirds and cardinals?" In Bermuda there was a problem of saving a marsh. Roger mentioned it both at a dinner and from the platform and moved the people to take action and save the area.

There were bound to be lectures that were disasters. One time the mechanically controlled screen started to roll up. "The picture got narrower and narrower and narrower and finally disappeared," laughed Roger. And the problem of travel was great. Giving a lecture every night could be rough. At first Roger took trains. Later he drove. "A more pleasant way of doing things," says Roger, "of course." When Roger was married to Barbara, his second wife, she not only drove but supervised the projection.

The daily distance was sometimes more than three hundred miles, which was very hard, and as time went on, the Societies reduced it to two hundred miles between cities, but even that could be rough. Most of the lecturers became real troupers, able to act fresh at a banquet before the evening lecture. "I found that I rolled fine for three weeks, but after that I was a bore," admitted Roger. The Society did the booking for lecturers and took care of the itinerary, which helped.

Today the Audubon Wildlife Lecture Program covers about two hundred different cities in the United States and Canada, and also in the Caribbean, the Virgin Islands, and Puerto Rico.

During the early days at Audubon, Roger had taken part in a morning bird program on WOR, giving bird news right after the regular world news broadcast. He would report happenings on rare birds seen here and there, what migration was on, etc. It was only once a week. "Fortunately," says Roger. He so hated to get up in the morning.

This was before he had a wife to get him up, so he used the old trick that John Barrymore is said to have originated. He sent himself a Western Union message. An actual messenger was supposed to come to the door. "That worked pretty well," Roger says. Then there came a time when the message, "Get up," didn't get him up for the program. And another time when he couldn't make it he suggested that Douglas Orbison, then also on the Audubon staff, go to deliver the broadcast. But Douglas couldn't find the station.

"So that was the end of *that* bird program."

When *Bird Lore* changed to the *Audubon* magazine, Roger became even more active in writing for it. Of course he designed covers, too, but his column, "A Bird's Eye View," ran for years. Many of these articles had to do with his travels.

He also "overhauled" the Boy Scout merit-badge study booklet on birds, "just a matter of cleansing," "sanitizing," the merit-badge requirements. How, for instance, could a boy be required to see forty birds if he lived in an area such as Hawaii where there weren't that many different kinds? The Girl Scouts and the Camp Fire Girls came for advice, too, and he represented the Audubon Society at meetings and especially at the big Boy Scout jamborees.

There's a story about Roger when he was working in the educational department of the National Audubon Society, keeping his irregular hours as usual.

John H. Baker, then the new president of the Society, in his rigid, demanding, businesslike way, had hired a female efficiency expert. When she went into Roger's office, she often found him sitting around with his feet up, staring out the window for long periods of time. Finally the efficiency expert couldn't stand it any longer.

"Would you mind telling me *what* you are doing?"

Roger replied, "I am *contemplating*. And if you can tell me whether I am doing it efficiently, you are better than I think you are."

A Field Guide to the Birds was selling widely during this period. It had given a boost to the whole Audubon movement, stirring a great new wave of interest in the natural world, on which the Audubon movement revitalized itself. Many years later Roger was given the Audubon Medal, largely in recognition of this contribution.

He made other contributions to the Audubon Society. One was the gift of an oil painting of whooping cranes. A limited, signed, and numbered edition of 750 prints, twenty-four inches by thirty inches, was offered to new life members enrolling in the National Audubon Society for a fee of $1,000. (This print, now sold out, brought in $750,000 in life memberships over the years.) The original painting was presented by the Society to Baker when he retired.

In the late 1930s there was an uprising that resulted in an exodus of some of the fine, staunch members of the staff. One of them was Bill Vogt, himself a fomenter of this unfortunate "palace revolution." Vogt wanted John Baker thrown out, largely because of his arrogance, but the board, having given Baker the job in the first place, backed him. Baker was able to get Robert Cushman Murphy to arrange for a research grant from the Guggenheim Foundation to send Vogt to the Chincha Islands in Peru to study the guano production by the seabirds.

Roger was untouched by the change in the staff and continued to write for *Audubon* under Peggy Brooks, who became editor.

Peggy was a delight to the office and did the work of three. She was constantly spilling over into laughter. No wonder Joe Hickey spent so many happy hours in the Society offices. He married Miss Brooks.

And where was Mildred during these growing-pain days of the Society in the late 1930s and early 1940s? According to Mildred:

Her marriage with Roger was having growing pains, too.

Mildred wanted children.

Roger did not want children.

Mildred loved music.

Mildred loved people.

Roger loved Mildred.

Roger loved Roger.

Theirs was a passionate, emotional marriage, no doubt of that. Birds brought them together, and Mildred, says Roger, "was very keen on birds, having acquired this interest from her mother. She was as tough as nails when we were on field trips; she would always accompany me."

Said Mildred, "Basically, we had little in common except birds." She gave up the idea of having children. "Roger did not love children. He wanted no young fry." Says Roger, "I did want children, but not until our marriage was emotionally stable."

Their apartment on the corner of Madison and Eighty-ninth Street was a comfortable one. A long front hall branched off to what Roger called his studio. It had north light, but Mildred thought it was on the dismal side, and it had a "horrible lamp."

When Roger came home after a day at the Audubon office, he painted or wrote.

Mildred had her musical friends and belonged to a singing group, the William Byrd Chorus, named after the composer of madrigals. On Friday nights they all met and sang madrigals and solemn music, and then launched into songs like the Yale "Whiffenpoof" song. And they sometimes went down to a restaurant, the old German American, and sang some more. They drank beer—"big bunches of beer," said Mildred, and they passed the steins around the table. It was fun.

Mildred also spent a lot of time with a brother of whom she was very fond.

Roger was writing and painting and lecturing.

Mildred went into volunteer work, and not just a momentary thing. It was a five-day-week job at St. Luke's hospital, a service program for underprivileged people. Mildred loved people. She loved children. There was a Spanish family under her wing, "with adorable children." Little Teresa, especially, who was four.

Mildred took her off to Maine on a vacation trip to see her mother. This got Mildred into trouble with the hospital administrators, who said she wasn't supposed to do that sort of thing. Roger, "though not loving children," was furious at the institution. Mildred said he called the woman at the hospital who had criticized Mildred about taking Teresa and called her "a damn bitch" and "slammed down the phone when he talked with her."

"Roger had a COLOSSAL temper," Mildred said. He has admitted it, but few people believe it. Even Mildred couldn't believe it until they had their spats. Sometimes they were more than that. "Nobody had ever blown up at a Washington," she said. Mildred was horrified when this happened, or when Roger threw things. Roger admits they "simply would have darn near killed each other" if they hadn't separated.

"It was that simple," Mildred said, remembering without emotion, shrugging, "but all of us have a bit of the devil in us."

Mildred was a strong-minded person. She took after her mother, and a grandmother who had seven sons, and had to be strong-minded.

In spite of the tempestuousness, however, Mildred and Roger had many happy birding days together: there was the time they saw the ivory-billed woodpecker.

Mildred had always wanted to see an ivory-billed woodpecker. When, as a child, she had been ill with tonsilitis, she was forced to stay in bed. Her mother brought Mildred "her Forbush" (*Birds of Massachusetts*) and other bird books. Mildred said she sat there poring over these, utterly fascinated. "The ivory-billed woodpecker was the one bird I was determined to see. I just *had* to see it. I don't know why. It wasn't only because it was rare and nearly extinct—I wasn't aware of that sort of thing then. I can't remember just what went on in my mind. But it was something very important. I really don't know why. Someday I would have to see that bird."

The ivory-bill has caught the imagination of many people, not only Mildred's, and not just because it is so rare. The ivory-billed woodpecker is twenty inches long, with a wing spread up to thirty-three inches. The male has a flaming red crest; the female, a black crest. But they both have dramatic white stripes down each side of the neck to the shoulders, blending into the whole rear edge of the wing, which is also white.

"Unreal birds—downright archaic," says Roger.

"The ivory-bill feeds mostly on trees that have been dead two or three years," writes Roger. "It takes about that long for decay to set in and the first insects to attack the wood—the fat whitish grubs of borers that tunnel just beneath the tight bark. In another year or so, these subsurface borers disappear. Decay strikes deeper into the heartwood, but the ivory-bill is no longer interested. The tree now becomes fodder for the pileated [woodpecker], which continues to rip open the tunneled wood until the tree, blasted and crumbling, falls to earth."

The opportunity came for Mildred to see the ivory-bill—a first sighting for Roger too—on a vacation in 1942. They took a whole month to "just sort of meander and wander around the country, without having to do anything on a book—just meander and wander, watching birds," Mildred says, "and perhaps get some pictures for *Birds Over America*, which Roger had planned to write."

They still had the first car Roger had ever owned—a second-hand black coupe. The couple decided to go through the Alleghenies to the Mississippi and follow the river from Louisiana to Minneapolis to visit her old home on Lake Minnetonka. Her deceased father, a radio engineer, had set up the first radio station when she was about eight years old.

"It was just a fun trip that summer. We'd been out doing work on the *Western Field Guide* (the wife it's dedicated to is *me*)." This trip was a vacation, said the very feminine Mildred. The "eternal dilettante," she called herself. Roger took many good photographs, too, some of which appeared in his books. "This time we would just go where we pleased, when we pleased. Oddly enough, we did not often squabble on bird trips."

On their meandering, they went to the famous Singer Tract in Louisiana, where, it was said, lived a rare ivory-billed woodpecker.

The Singer Tract was an 81,000-acre wilderness in Madison Parish in Northern Louisiana. Four fifths of it was in low-lying sweet gum, oak, ash, elm, and pine. It was one of the last tracts of virgin forest with logging rights. Singer, of the Singer sewing-machine family, had sold it to a lumbering company in the late 1930s. Brutal commercial cutting was destroying it ruthlessly. Not until 1941, when about 40 percent of the tract had been cut over, did the Audubon organization become involved. John Baker appealed to President Roosevelt to preserve it as the home of the ivory-billed woodpecker, and lumbering was halted, despite the fact that timber was needed in the war effort. Later, controlled logging was resumed.

Mildred, Roger, and an old friend, Bayard Christy of Pittsburgh, were there in the Louisiana swamp on a little path, just standing there, when they saw the ivory-bill. Mildred's dream come true. They had nearly missed it by a hair. Then they saw another. Two females. Mildred told of the impressive event this way:

"After two days of searching, Roger said, 'Come on. We've spent enough time here. Let's go.'

"And I said, 'I've wanted all my life to see an ivory-bill.' "

It wasn't as important, according to Mildred, for Roger to see an ivory-billed woodpecker as it was for her. "Maybe a psychiatrist could say why," she said.

"Roger kept saying we were wasting time. 'It's just silly.' He was tired, and it was hot. But I was stubborn.

"We had been prowling around, listening, Roger saying we were just wasting time and we were fighting about it. I got furious. 'I've wanted to see this bird all my life and I won't go until I see this ivory-bill. You can take the car and go on if you want to, but I won't leave until I see the woodpecker.' Roger said I was being a silly ass.

"And just as we were arguing, Roger said, 'Shush.' We both stiffened. And right over there—less than fifty feet away—two of them. Ivory-billed woodpeckers! We just stood there."

The fact that they were females was a faint shade of disappointment to Mildred. But the argument had ended. "I don't remember what we said later. I may have said, 'I told you so.' We'd been 'spitting' at each other and squabbling, like two fools."

It was all forgotten as the two ivory-billed woodpeckers flew away, their white stripes shining in the sun. Seeing the birds was one of the most ecstatic moments of Mildred's life. Roger was thrilled, too, but to Mildred it was a childhood dream realized.

Mildred had always been up to her ears in birds, became a member of the A.O.U.—"just an associate," she said, "but so was Franklin Roosevelt." (She belonged to the Maine Audubon Society and birded with its members.)

It is her hope that the ivory-bill will someday be seen again. The last ivory-bill was seen in the Singer Tract in December 1946. A female.

Even to this day Roger receives sight reports of ivory-bills, but they are never confirmed by competent observers. There still may be ivory-bills in Cuba, but no ornithologist has been able to check this recently.

In *Birds Over America*, Roger described in glowing terms how, with Christy, they sighted the ivory-bills. Christy, who had just turned seventy when he joined Roger and Mildred in Louisiana, had wished most to see the ivory-bill before he died. (What is the appeal of that "unreal bird"?) The book, which Roger started to write after his stint in the army, was published in 1948, six years after he broke up with Mildred. She said, "I was edited out, removed from the text, in toto."

When Roger, years later, described the marriage with Mildred, he intercrossed his fingers—"we were like this"—and pulled them apart. His first real passion. His first divorce.

In 1942, after one of their mutual "colossal" tantrums, Mildred moved out. They had tried to pull things together, Mildred going to psychiatrists, and Roger cooperating by seeing one too. But there was no use. Roger's area was just too limited for Mildred. She missed life. Birds weren't everything. "I was just an eternal dilettante," she said again.

A new Audubon secretary, Barbara Coulter, brought some papers to the Peterson apartment from the Audubon office one day —"along with a couple of pastrami sandwiches," Mildred remembered vividly. She thought that Barbara had an eye on Roger, and when Roger worked late at the office, Mildred noted that he was the last to leave. It didn't take a psychologist to explain that one reason for Mildred's emotional upheaval was her faltering marriage.

During this period a trace of epilepsy sometimes turned up in Mildred under stress, never in public, but the very thought of which terrified Roger. Mildred's doctor, Gothard Booth, whom she saw four times a week for four years, assured the couple that the problem could be corrected by psychotherapy.

But the failing marriage added to Mildred's nervous condition. Mildred is said to have had a drink or two too many at Audubon conventions, and if she had a problem on occasion, friends say, "it came long after they were married"—and "with good reason."

Mildred went back to her volunteer work, to her music, and eventually married an electrical engineer, Edward Busse, from whom she was later divorced.

They had three children—Steven, a son, a daughter, Mrs. Charles Terry, and another son, Mildred's "remarkably wonderful" son, who was killed in a bicycle accident not far from their home in Freeport, Maine, shattering her life.

Mildred had named her "wonderful" son Peter.

Roger wrote in a copy of his first *A Field Guide to the Birds* this inscription to Mildred: "To a girl with a real sane appreciation of birds." She giggled when she showed it to friends at Freeport, Maine, in 1975.

Mildred lived in a weathered, shingled house, built on the foundation of an eighteenth-century house that had burned down many years before. There, in a room full of antiques and walls of books, Mildred welcomed her guests graciously among the fading upholstered furniture. The ashtrays were full of cigarette stubs, and on the table was an original copy of *A Field Guide to the Birds*, worn from use.

Any emotion, any pain, had gone out of the distant relationship with Roger. "I went into a pretty bad tailspin for a while," she said, "but recovered in due course and managed to discover that the world was still there."

Mildred, who enjoyed boating, often sailed alone among the islands in the salty bays near her home in Maine. One midsummer day in July 1977 her boat was found capsized; it was empty. Later her body was recovered. Although she was a good swimmer, she had drowned.

CHAPTER X

War Years

ROGER was enormously shaken over the divorce from Mildred. "There were certain things about that first marriage that were right. And yet it couldn't be." Furthermore, Roger hated the idea of living alone. He has said this on many occasions: "I am horrified at the thought of living alone."

He married Barbara Coulter, curator of the Audubon photo library, on July 29, 1943, a short time after the divorce.

It seemed the thing to do. "I had never given Barbara any indication that I thought she was pretty nice, but I thought, 'I don't want to live alone.'"

Barbara was one of two women that he knew who Roger thought at the time were, well, possibilities. "I just set out on a deliberate campaign at that point," he admits. "And Barbara would be . . . I tried her first, and that was it. I took her out and all that. She was aware, of course, that things had split up with Mildred. They say when you marry again you get a carbon copy of the first. You *don't*. Barbara was quite different from Mildred."

Roger had been very much aware of Barbara for some time. She had been Robert Allen's secretary first, sitting in the office next to Roger. Bob had a perfectly wonderful sense of humor. He kept the office filled with laughter and gaiety. Barbara had an especially lovely voice. Roger, listening next door, could hear the happy go-ings-on, the ripples of laughter. "Being so near," he says, "I had a good chance to observe a person." And being a "loner," he some-times joined them.

Evelyn Allen has always said that Roger needed guidance and help. And Barbara was a good manager, more than just a typist-secretary. "Bob thought she was highly efficient, a 'lalapalooza.' . . . Barbara," she adds, "was just thrilled to death with Roger."

Barbara herself has said, "I was madly in love with him when I married him." Barbara realized, also, in Roger, his potential for being a "great man." Even today she calls him "the great man," though many times she has called him "my child."

It was Barbara, one friend said, "who brought out all the things in Roger that make him great." Recognizing his genius, she longed to get her hands on him "and make him go." Skillfully and artfully, and with real affection, Barbara was able to "manipulate" him in the right directions.

There is no question that Roger also saw the advantages in marrying Barbara in furthering his career. It worked both ways, of course, as one of Roger's early school friends has said: "Barbara was one who saw the advantages in marrying Roger—and made the most of it." After all, he was very attractive and "eligible."

Who was this girl who, for thirty-two years of her marriage, subordinated her entire life and interests to Roger?

Not breathtakingly beautiful, and perhaps not as pretty as Mil-dred, Barbara was attractive, slender, brown-haired, with a good figure, and with that particularly melodious, happy voice. She was an only child, a descendant—on her mother's side—of pioneers who made the trek to western New York State from Massachu-setts. On her father's side, Barbara has been told, a member of the family had been a Revolutionary, deserting from the Hessian troops in Virginia to join the Colonial forces.

Barbara's parents went to Seattle, where Barbara was born, and later to Atlanta, Georgia, where her father was southern district manager of the Bucyrus Erie Steamshovel Company. He traveled a lot. Barbara spent her childhood in Atlanta and acquired a strong southern accent. In the hot summers, she and her mother went to Spencerport, near Rochester, New York, to her grandfather's farm, and Barbara rode her first horse—a sixteen-hands-high carriage horse—at the age of ten, and worked with the draft teams. Those were enormously happy days. Riding became a lifelong love. Later Barbara taught riding in girls' camps in the Rockies.

When her family went back to Seattle, Barbara was sent to a speech school because of the "suthen" accent and came out with an "all-purpose" accent.

The family was always interested in natural history. Barbara was brought up on the Reed *Bird Guide*. "It was always on the window sill of the family breakfast room. We checked every bird going through mother's garden. We didn't know of the Peterson 'bible' in those days."

Barbara is Scots-Welsh, a Protestant. She studied music and opera in Seattle and always loved it there. She does not like cats—they eat birds: "Cats belong in a barn."

She came to New York to study for two years at Columbia University. Mark Van Doren was her professor of literary history and drama. She went to Katherine Gibbs Secretarial School. She held a few jobs as secretary-receptionist and then went to the National Audubon Society. She first worked with Robert Allen on his monograph on the roseate spoonbill. This finished, she took over the photo and film department, which "needed an overhaul as much as anything," she says. "The person who had been in charge had been ill. Everything was 'scrambled eggs.' Mail wasn't being answered, local Audubon people weren't getting the films they ordered." Efficient Barbara pulled everything together.

There was a retiring room for females at the Audubon offices, with a full-length couch in it, a cupboard, and a hot plate. Here Roger often retired to think. (He thinks and sometimes dictates best when lying down, as Barbara says, as if on a "psychiatrist's couch.") Although Roger claims he never appropriated the lounge except at night, Barbara said the girls had a difficult time getting in there because Roger was using it as his "working place."

Roger says Barbara has been secretary to three top ornithologists—Robert Allen, William Vogt, and, ever aware of his standing, Roger Tory Peterson.

When Barbara and Roger became engaged, Roger gave her an original painting of a cedar wax wing for an engagement present.

"It is the only bird with a yellow band on the end of its tail," he said as he gave it to her.

And she married Roger.

John Baker did not approve of husband and wife working for the same organization, so Barbara had to leave. Meanwhile, Bill Vogt, having been freed from his guano studies in Peru, was with the Pan American Union in Washington, D.C. Vogt had known Barbara's efficiency well at Audubon and he asked her to join him at Pan American Union.

World War II had changed the scene for Roger too. Roger wanted to serve his country—and he had always wanted to travel. "I did not want to get killed and 'mopped up' before I saw more of the world," he admitted. He was thirty-four years old.

"It looked as though any man my age would certainly be in the services by now," he explains, "and I wondered whether I still had a choice as to the direction an army career might take.

"Irving Kassoy, one of the young men in the Bronx County Bird Club, and I, after reading Robert Lockley's book on shearwaters, had an idea. We would like to get into the Signal Corps, which, in World War I, had used pigeons as message carriers. Carrier pigeons were not yet obsolete, but Kassoy and I thought we had a better idea.

"If the Pacific was to be an extensive theater of war, why not use seabirds as message carriers? We hoped we would be sent to some interesting tropical islands to investigate the use of shearwaters, petrels, and other oceanic birds to carry messages from ships to islands, etc. We carefully researched our material and drew up a plan that we sent to the Signal Corps. The answer from the Army was a polite 'No.' "

Soon after the Army rejected the bird message-carrier proposal, Roger was drafted.

"At the induction center I listed myself as an artist. I should have called myself a biologist, but my academic training had been basically as an artist, and there was always camouflage." He landed in the U.S. Army Corps of Engineers. They placed Roger in the publication center at Fort Belvoir, not far from Washington, D.C., where he was "stuck" preparing training and instruction manuals.

But it made it possible for Barbara to be with him. Housing was hard to find in the war years, especially near Washington. They rented a third-floor apartment in a friend's house in Alexandria, Virginia—a living room, a bedroom, bath, and kitchen.

Barbara worked for Vogt at Pan American and typed his *Road to Survival*. She also typed Roger's *Birds Over America* in her spare time. She worked for Vogt until she was pregnant with Roger's first son, Tory.

It was inevitable that Roger's war years—1943–1945—would be in some way involved with birds. And it was inevitable that Roger would contribute to the U.S. Army Corps of Engineers in his own unique way, with distinctly Roger Tory Peterson know-how.

Among his valuable contributions were the following:

First, plane identification—the aircraft-spotting technique—was based on Roger's bird identification method—the Peterson System.

Second, Roger was able to illustrate and prepare instruction manuals for the Army based on his experience at the National Audubon Society with the educational material for the Junior Audubon Clubs. And, of course, the *Field Guide* text was an asset, too, for it showed his ability for concise editorial presentation. Some of the manuals Roger helped prepare dealt with defusing land mines, road building, and assembling Bailey bridges. "On one occasion," he says, "we had to work extra hours under pressure preparing the instruction manual that would be used in assembling the bridge to cross the Rhine in the great Rhine offensive. It was assumed that other bridges would have been blown up by the retreating enemy and that the advancing army would have to build its own temporary bridges. As someone quipped, 'One slip of the ruling pen and an army might be lost.' We got a special citation for that job."

Third, Roger's knowledge of colors and art led to work with the Army's camouflage program.

Fourth, Roger entered into DDT research for the Air Corps, which had gone into it in depth even before the U.S. Fish and Wildlife Service became active in chemical spraying.

"The men I trained with were being sent off, one by one," says Roger. "I was held as 'indispensable,' because at that time only combat officers were needed. And yet I was a bit too young to be given a direct commission. So there I was, with a group of other often unhappy artists illustrating instruction manuals.

"Nearly every one of the men in the company, about twenty or so, were top-rate illustrators, designers, calligraphers, or painters. At the time they went into the Army, each of them must have commanded incomes of $25,000 a year on the average. I was perhaps the least affluent, though already well known because of the *Field Guides*. When our small group crossed the parade ground to our barracks, there was a prewar annual income of half a million dollars."

Frustrated, and at sword's point with each other as only artists could be, no two agreed with any other two about anything. Their views about art were at the root of it. As for technique, the group could be divided into two basic categories—"the noodlers," those who made their drawings so meticulous that they could be examined under a magnifying glass, and the "hot licks boys," those who painted broadly and finished off their work with a few bold sweeps of the brush. None of them had more than the rank of staff sergeant.

The acceptance of Roger's aircraft-spotting techniques came about in an unusual, serendipitous way. Joe Kastner, who had known Roger so well back in the Greenwich Village days, had been asked by *Life* magazine to work out some way whereby the average citizen could spot enemy planes. There was concern in the United States that enemy aircraft might appear over our shores to drop bombs. Airplane spotters were on the alert, particularly on the roofs of some of the large seacoast cities. There was urgent need to be able to identify enemy planes quickly. So *Life* conceived the idea of putting a section in the magazine—a section showing citizens what to look for.

Joe Kastner talked with Roger, gave the artist-researchers at *Life* the *Field Guide to the Birds*, and told them to come up with something similar that could be applied to aircraft. The feature was called "The Plane-spotters Handbook," and it told how both enemy or friendly planes could be recognized by several basic things, just like birds: silhouette, pattern, and dihedral (wing angle).

Whereupon, impressed with this excellently done feature, the

Roger with his mother,
Henrietta Bader Peterson,
1909.

Roger's father,
Charles Peterson,
1907.

Roger, in a church play, 1915.

Roger Tory Peterson's birthplace, 16 Bowen Street, Jamestown, New York.

Roger as a boy on Bowen Street.
Clarence Beal, Jamestown, New York.

High school graduation, 1925. His yearbook picture was captioned: "Woods! Birds! Flowers! Here are the makings of a great naturalist."
Globe Studio, Jamestown, New York

First job: painting Chinese decorations on
lacquered furniture at age 17.

The 43rd Annual Meeting of the American Ornithologists' Union, November 1925. Roger is at top, third from right. Others are Howard Cleaves, far left, Courtenay Brandreth, third from left, John T. Emlen, now president of AOU, above Brandreth's head, E. H. Forbush, bearded man above woman's hat, Louis A. Fuertes and Alexander Wetmore, to right of Forbush.

American Museum of Natural History

(Above) Roger with Jan and Jean Do-Rio. While going to art school in New York, Roger worked for Jan, painting decorations on furniture.

(Left) Roger with Richard Herbert examining peregrine eggs on Palisades.

Allan Cruickshank

Mildred Washington Peterson, Roger's first wife.

John Hopkinson Baker, National Audubon Society president, 1934–1959. *Conway Studio Corp.*

Roger positioning his "paper dolls" before
painting a picture.
Edwin Way Teale

1943: Roger goes to war.

(Inset) Barbara Coulter Peterson, Roger's second wife.

Barbara with one of her Morgans, Old Lyme.

James Fisher, who traveled 30,000 miles in the U.S. with Roger in 1953 and coauthored *Wild America*.

Roger with Ludlow Griscom, pioneer birder, 1955.

Left to right: Carl-Frederick Lundevall, Swedish translator of *A Field Guide to the Birds of Britain and Europe;* Guy Mountfort, Roger, and P. A. D. Hollom, coauthors, in Sweden.

Roger and colleagues at the Palacio, Coto Donana, Spain, 1956. Bottom, left to right: Rosemary Jamieson, Lady Alanbrooke, Lord Alanbrooke, Guy Mountfort, Eric Hosking. Top, left to right: George Shannon, John Parrinder, James Ferguson-Lee, RTP, Jerry Jamieson, James Fisher.

Roger receives an honorary degree.

Roger lecturing to king penguins at South Georgia Island, 1976.

Arthur Godfrey, RTP, and Charles Lindbergh at Stone Harbor to dedicate a bird sanctuary.
New York Times

Carl Buchheister, former president of National Audubon Society, and wife, Harriet, examine a puffin picture of Roger's.

Three outstanding bird painters: Don Eckelberry, Arthur Singer, and Roger Tory Peterson.

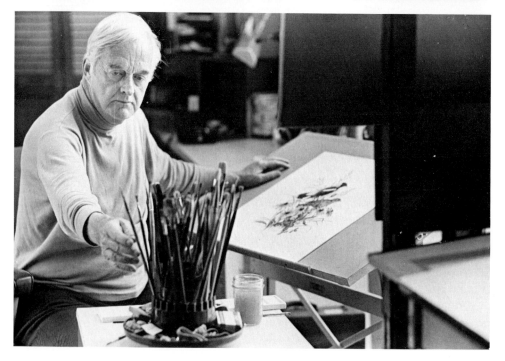

Roger painting in his studio. *Paul Hosefros/New York Times*

Roger with mockingbird, in Patagonia, 1975.

Relaxing on the *Lindblad Explorer*, 1971.

Roger and Virginia Westervelt on their wedding day, May 1976.

Armed Services planned their own instruction manuals along the *Life* identification lines. "Its genesis," says Roger, "went right back to the bird guides. The *Infantry Journal* lifted straight from the field guides one time, with credit, the basic elements of field recognition!"

The Army learned another thing or two from Roger at Fort Belvoir about birds. Not one to be afraid of brass, Roger went all the way up to the commanding officer to save the nest of a horned lark he had found on the parade ground.

"I can't remember whether it was eggs or small young, but when I found it there was about to be a parade which was to pass right over it.

"Under ordinary circumstances, I'd go through sergeants and up to the captain. But these particular sergeants had absolutely no sympathy with something like a lark's nest on the parade ground. I did happen to know a captain or two and even a colonel. I was known as the bird man and this colonel had contacted me and said, 'My daughter, my eleven-year-old daughter, is very keen on birds. Would you take her out on a bird walk?' I did, and I showed her her first redstart."

So, it wasn't surprising that the line of the parade was rerouted. "Which is something to do when you're only a private," Roger said, grinning.

On February 12, 1944, Roger wrote Clarence and Evangeline Beal, "I am still with the publications section at Belvoir, but am living off the post in Alexandria. We still have the pleasure of doing the 'infiltration course,' where we crawl on our bellies for a hundred yards through barbed-wire entanglements under a hail of machine guns fired just over our heads. For dramatic effect and to tone up our nervous systems they set off fourteen charges of nitroglycerin in our midst." Then Roger gets back to his basic interest—birds. "Birding is quite good near Washington. Got a one-party list of fifty-one species on a Christmas census around camp. Nothing unusual, but it was interesting to have a total of eighteen bald eagles and six black vultures."

Roger was painting, always painting, during this period too. "I have just finished three more bird prints—bluebird, snowy egret, and roseate tern," he wrote Beal, and thanked him for a Kodachrome of water lilies—"It's a honey, and I hope to use it soon in some way in one of my prints, perhaps in the one of the wood ducks."

At the tiny Alexandria apartment Roger's painting was being done in the bathroom. There the walls were white and gave the right light for night work. Roger was at Belvoir during the day and had only nights to work.

During the last months of Roger's army tenure in 1945, it was requested by the Air Force that Roger be transferred to Orlando, Florida, to do some special work on DDT research. "This new wonder chemical," Roger reports, "was to be used in the Pacific to rid certain islands of mosquitoes, etc., and it was questioned by several of the biologically oriented officers then in the Air Force whether the use of these chemicals might not make a biological desert of some of the Pacific islands.

"The two biologists in particular were Alexander Klots, who was later to do the butterfly field guide for my Houghton Mifflin series, and Earl Herald, the fish man, who later would become head of the Steinhardt Aquarium at Golden Gate Park in San Francisco, and whom I was to choose to do the *Field Guide to the Fishes of the Pacific Coast* for my series, still to be published.

"Certain sample plots of five acres, mostly on state land not far from Orlando, were to be sprayed with various strengths of DDT and then compared with unsprayed control plots. I was to census the bird populations before and after. Herald was to check the amphibians, fish, etc., while Klots took note of the insect populations.

"I made repeated trips throughout the three-month period to check these plots. It was a bit late in the season because nesting was over for the most part, and thus I spent the dog days in the flat-woods of Florida and had a most interesting time, usually with a command car at my disposal, and a WAC to drive it. My last three months in the war were literally one continuous birding trip.

"We found that a small enough dose of DDT could kill the mosquitoes and still even spare the bees, and that the larger doses were not necessary. In fact, five pounds per acre could be directly lethal to birds.

"However, at the time, we had no idea about the residual effects and that birds that were in long food chains, such as pelicans, peregrines, etc., would be so adversely affected. Our work was a beginning of some of the research which Rachel Carson so intelligently interpreted later."

In Washington, Rachel Carson and Roger became good friends. They were both directors of the local Audubon Society and she had learned the birds from Roger's field guide.

While on one of the Air Force excursions to an area near St. John's River, Roger says, "I ordered my driver to pull the car to the side of the road, one wheel off and one wheel on, while taking a picture. Standing there near the open door photographing the St. John's marshes, a rickety car came barreling down the road. It plowed into the rear of my car and the open door struck me down. I was picked up, dazed, by a passing army officer. My nose was broken and I had cuts around my eyes and cheekbones which showed the exact shape of the focusing hood into which I was viewing at the time I was struck."

Barbara was not with Roger during his Florida days. She was busy being pregnant and preparing a new home at Glen Echo, Maryland, on the C&O Canal.

Roger's stint in the Army ended in 1945 but Glen Echo remained the Peterson home for ten years. Nettie May Burgess, of the Washington Audubon Society, owned the house and rented it to the Petersons.

The house had been the slave quarters for the farmhouse next door. A charming and quaint, modest little house just above the tow path that goes along the Potomac north of the city of Washington, it was a good house for a naturalist. "We are right on the edge of the woods," Roger wrote Clarence Beal, "and I can see pileated woodpeckers from my window; barred owls hoot at night; both scarlet and summer tanagers live in the huge oaks over the roof; Louisiana water-thrushes, Kentuckys, etc., nest in the back of the house, and even bald eagles fly over—saw two yesterday. Also osprey."

One of the unique features of the house was an indoor garden about three feet deep and twelve feet long, just inside a long picture window. "There was a small drainage hole to the outside patio through which excess moisture might drain out when the garden was watered," Roger wrote. "The local chipmunks found this hole, enlarged it, and made their own passageway into the garden. In due time a five-foot black snake, searching out the chipmunks, also found himself inside our living-room garden. When the doors were open in our upstairs bedroom at night, as they usually were, flying squirrels would sometimes enter and more than once we found a flying squirrel spending the day in the fold of the heavy draperies. Woodpeckers of half a dozen sorts patronized our suet and feeding trays."

At Glen Echo naturalists from all over the world came to see Roger—the *Field Guide* was a worldwide hit—and many American celebrities and old friends came to see them. Barbara was also busy raising young Tory and then Lee, their second son.

When Tory was about four he did something that Kay Allen said Roger could never forget.

"Roger always did his painting at night. He was a night person. The children could not disturb him. They were forbidden to go into his studio. Roger had a new painting practically finished. And Tory went up and smeared it all over with paint!" (Did he just want to be a painter, too, or did he do it for rebellion?) "The boy—he was so *tiny*," said Kay in her emphatic way. "And Roger was *so mad*. You can't imagine Roger getting mad. But I tell you— you should have seen him! Roger works so carefully, so precisely; he put hours and hours on that painting. I think he could never forgive that boy for destroying it. How Tory got into the studio, I don't know." (Whether it was at that crucial moment is a question, but Tory lost much of his interest in birds. He became an investment banker.)

The Clarence Allens saw the Petersons at Glen Echo often. Kay tells a wonderful, typical Roger story: "One night we were at a party in Washington, Roger and Barbara and all. And Roger announced suddenly, 'I'm leaving now. I'm going down to the Washington Monument. There is a full moon and it's the height of migration—October.' Hundreds of birds in fall plumage would fly straight into the lights of the monument. There were two or three other couples there, so they all went too. We went, of course. We picked up many dead birds. Roger would identify them right off. He took a lot of them home—skins for his painting."

Roger had been trying to get the National Park Service to turn off the lights during the fall migration. They finally did. He was also influential in getting the Empire State Building to turn off its top lights during migration.

One day when the Petersons were living in Glen Echo, an FBI agent rang the doorbell. He was connected with the House Un-American Activities Committee investigating the celebrated Alger Hiss–Whittaker Chambers spy case.

He wanted to know if Roger had ever received a letter from Alger Hiss. They were trying to trace the typewriter on which the Pumpkin Papers were supposed to have been written. "As you know," Roger explained, "it was a poor miserable prothonotary warbler on the Canal that was responsible for Nixon. He made his name because of the Hiss–Chambers trial."

Nixon, then a California congressman at the famous investigation, was trying to establish an association between Hiss and Chambers. Hiss had denied their friendship. In a closed session, Nixon asked Chambers if Hiss had any hobbies that Chambers might remember.

Yes, said Chambers. Hiss was a bird watcher.

Nixon asked if he ever mentioned any special birds.

Yes, a prothonotary warbler. He said he had seen one around Glen Echo near the C & O Canal outside Washington.

Later, when Alger Hiss was ushered into another secret hearing, Nixon questioned Hiss about his interest in ornithology. At that point, another committee investigator, Representative John McDowell of Pennsylvania, asked quietly, "Did you ever see a prothonotary warbler?"

Yes, "a beautiful yellow head, a gorgeous bird. I saw one down by the C & O Canal."

Nixon was well aware of what this intimate knowledge implied. It was a crucial moment in the Hiss hearings.

Roger, known as the authority on birds, would have been a logical person to consult about whether there could be a prothonotary warbler living near Glen Echo. "And I had seen one," says Roger. But the FBI agent asked only if Roger had ever received a letter from Hiss. "I have not," Roger told him, nor had he ever met Hiss or Chambers. Parenthetically, the young agent said he was a bird watcher too. So Roger got him to be program chairman of the Audubon Society of the District of Columbia.

Hiss said recently, "I still think the prothonotary warbler was my most exciting 'first.' "

In 1953, Barbara and Roger decided it was time to put down roots, and not rent in Glen Echo anymore, so they set out to find a new home. The Petersons looked all up and down the coast for just the right place to live.

Roger had given a "crying voice of doom" speech in California on pollution and pesticides, and, like many others at that time, was concerned about the atom bomb. He was searching for a place away from Washington and New York, logical spots for the bomb to be dropped. He even visited Hildegarde and Victor Weybright, publishers of Roger's paperbacks, just outside Baltimore, to consider that "safe" area.

Barbara and Roger finally settled at Old Lyme, Connecticut. (That was before the nuclear submarine base was located at nearby Groton.)

At last Roger had a more efficient studio in which to do his work. It had been a two-story barn with a stable below housing two Arabian horses. Roger took out the stalls and made it into a film-editing room, adding a fireproof vault for his collections and irreplaceable paintings.

Back of the studio is an old graveyard that goes back to pre-Revolutionary times. It is reputed that a former occupant of the property hanged himself from a rafter in the barn. The other one did away with himself in the house. They were both artists.

"I recall," says Roger, "that when Barbara and I first moved into the house formerly owned by an elderly woman with her two eccentric sons—ghosts still seemed to be around. The first two or three nights that we slept in the house, we could hear creaks on the stairways, groans, and crackling of the walls."

Barbara says she was not too anxious to buy the house. She thought they should rent and live in it for a year before they decided on a permanent abode, but Roger was adamant. Rebuilt and redecorated, it became the lovely "home among the cedars," which Barbara and Roger mentioned so often in their New Year's letters, which they sent in place of Christmas cards.

One of the stories Roger sometimes tells about himself during those first years at Old Lyme was about the time he went to an optometrist in a nearby town. The optometrist was new to the community, too, and had not heard of Roger. He checked his eyes and glasses, noted his quite gray thatch of hair, and observed:

"Your eyes seem fine, but, you know, as we get older it is a good idea to exercise them more."

Then he added, "Why don't you take up bird watching for a hobby?"

Roger just nodded agreeably and modestly kept silent, not telling the doctor that virtually his entire life had been spent bird watching.

Another story Roger tells of those early days in Connecticut was about his son Lee, aged nine, and a copperhead. Apparently there was a den of the dangerous snakes on the ledges up above the house. One day, when Lee was sitting on the steps outside the house fixing his butterfly cage, Barbara came to the door and discovered a copperhead sunning itself about five feet away from him. She rushed into the house crying, "Roger, do something!"

Roger did something. He went into his study, loaded some film into his Leica camera, and rushed out to take a picture of the snake, which had disappeared into the ivy.

Barbara would not speak to him the rest of the day.

Birds and butterflies are not the only kinds of wildlife plentiful on the Connecticut property, and in the years Roger has lived there he has seen things come and go and sometimes come again. The plants, too, vary from year to year. Mushrooms, for instance, along the path from the house to his studio, may be absent for a long time, then produce profusely. "I have not documented my observations," says Roger. "I simply make a mental note of the variations and changes as I walk the path."

And he hears every sound. "I hear a robin talking," Roger will say when there's none in sight and nobody else can hear a chirp. His hearing acuity is amazing.

He first became aware of this when he was in high school and was in a movie theater with a girl, he says. "I could recognize any number of bird calls above the movie action. Finally I just closed my eyes and had a good time counting the different species I could hear. I found it much more interesting than the movie." And per-haps his companion.

Years later Harvard scientists tested Roger's ears and reported that he had the most acute sense of hearing in their experience of testing. Roger thinks it may be largely a matter of training. "I've been listening to birds since I was eleven."

CHAPTER XI

Free-Lancing:
Field Guides and Other Writing

ROGER had been writing for some time before the Petersons moved to Connecticut. "When we started writing," Barbara says, "toward the end of the war, we thought maybe we could do it for three months, maybe six months." John Baker wanted Roger to go back to the National Audubon Society full time, but Roger was anxious to prove himself as a book writer. He wanted to write, he said, more "interpretive things." The first *Field Guide*, *Bird Lore*, and the Junior Audubon leaflets and other functional articles in the Society's publications were interpretive to some extent, but served to whet his desire to educate and teach nature to a wider audience, to be "an opinion-maker." But to make a living at it was another thing.

"I thought I'd like to free-lance," says Roger, "but if my income dropped lower than, say, $5,000, I'd have to get back to a full Audubon routine."

His income never dropped to that level and he did not return to the Society's staff. From then on it was full-time writing and painting.

His first important book, other than the *Field Guide*, was *Birds*

Over America, published by Dodd, Mead in 1948. Arthur A. Allen, professor of ornithology at Cornell, said, "This will stand as the best record of bird watching in the mid-century." It is semi-auto-biographical and into it Roger poured all his feelings about birds and told of his experiences starting from those childhood days at Jamestown. Roger's own photographs—105 of them—illustrate the book. It is dedicated to Barbara and the foreword says, "Most of all, I am indebted to my wife, Barbara, who, as counsel and amanuensis, has made my task a smoother one."

Roger was rather surprised at the way money began coming in. Sometime during this period, when the Clarence Allens were also in Washington, Roger went to Clarence and said, "What do you do with money when it comes in so fast? I don't know what to do with it."

Clarence said, "Do you have a lawyer?"

"No."

"Then get a broker, a good broker."

Roger is an excellent writer. He writes, he says, "visually, with the same power of observation that I use when painting." There is poetry in Roger's writing. The first luna moth he described: "pale green with a furry white body, fernlike antennae and graceful twisted two-inch tails." Snow geese: "skeins of snow geese weaving patterns in the sky." And kingfishers, as he described them in the early Junior Audubon leaflets: "Like vegetables, young kingfishers grow toward the light. For nearly two weeks the naked red-skinned babies lie miserably on the cradle of fish bones waiting for their eyes to open." To read those booklets he wrote for young people is to visualize the beauty of birds and nature in a way unexcelled. Poetry had been one of Roger's favorite subjects in high school in Jamestown, and it shows.

What also shows is his training—and natural tendency—to organize his writing, much as he does his painting. The use of graph paper from his mechanical drawing classes, the architectural development of an idea, a concept—these characteristics show through in his written words. For a man so notoriously disorganized in living habits, with a memory that Barbara has said requires "being told everything twice," his work is a model of *plan*.

Roger, being a nontypist, writes in longhand on long yellow

legal pads. Though he says he could type it with two fingers.

Through the years Barbara found his handwriting easy to read. "I've very seldom had trouble, but I was with him so long. . . ." Roger interrupted to say, "Well, it depends on whether I want to write well or not. If I'm hasty, it's hard to read. But I can write legibly."

In recent years Roger dictates more, keeps a recording machine by the living-room couch, where he reclines and lets the words flow. He has another in the office, and one in the studio up the hill. "Very often I do it here in the living room, just to change the locale."

Roger writes with a felt-tip pen, "though I think if I were writing to make it look good, I would use a proper pen. I cannot use a ball-point. You have to hold it upright. And as a result when you are getting older your joints don't have the flexibility. With a felt-tip, you have the free flowing. You can almost draw in the air. Felt-tips are perfect for autographing books." As for signing his prints (up to six hundred in a day), he uses a pencil.

Roger is as concise an editor as he is a writer. He says he does "work out a kind of a structure" when he writes, but "I might modify tremendously in the course of writing it. And I might readjust. I think we all do that. But I tend to write fairly close to length."

This was necessarily true in the field guides with their "headline" space, but Roger was equally well organized in the many articles he wrote for magazines—among them the *National Geographic, International Wildlife,* and, of course, *Audubon.*

The work he did for *Life* magazine was more in the line of "picture stories," and these began in 1938, when he was at Audubon, continued while he was in the Army, and lasted until 1948. "I produced twelve picture stories for *Life* with a total of fifty-six pages," Roger says, "more pages of paintings than any other artist up to that time."

Roger's contact, of course, at *Life* was Joseph Kastner. Joe came to Roger one day and suggested that he do a color story for *Life.* He said that the *National Geographic* had, through its articles on natural history, discovered that there was a very large responsive public just waiting for this kind of nature story. Joe said that *Life* could help build a national interest in birds much as Roger's field guides seemed to be doing. The field guides had set off sparks.

Roger produced a six-page article. It dealt with bird migration, which was early that spring. It was published on May 23, 1938. There was a lively page of colorful warblers, a page of herons and other marsh birds, and two pages of colorful songbirds handled rather schematically, like the field guide. "*Life,*" says Roger, "received more favorable letters from readers than they had for any previous color story, except in their art section."

It was this issue that was chosen to be buried later in the Time Capsule at the New York World's Fair, to be dug up one thousand years later for historians to examine our way of life. In this issue, Roger recalls, there appeared that famous photograph of Hitler and Mussolini reviewing a vast Fascist demonstration in Rome. "There was also another full-page photograph of Franco being enthroned and a full page of Franklin Roosevelt. The historian who studies this issue in 2938 will learn not only about a world and its leaders edging toward World War II, but will also learn that the spring migration of birds was a week early in the year of 1938. Wars and their leaders come and go, but the birds will probably be performing their yearly ritual more or less on schedule."

After this first story appeared, Henry Luce, who owned *Life,* came into Kastner's office and told him that the story should have started with one huge bird for a lead-in—a full-page vireo, or a full-page warbler, for example. The comment that Luce dropped so casually reflected in every one of the succeeding color stories that Roger painted for *Life.* The stories always started with one full-page smasher and then a series of small storytelling spots.

After each story was painted, Roger usually furnished the factual material from which the captions were written by Kastner, and Roger went over them to see if they were correct.

One time Roger found eight errors that had crept in through the office routine. The article was on gulls and other seabirds. Two of the errors were "real boners," says Roger, "the other six simply slightly unsanitary statements, easily cleaned up. We corrected all this, and then turned the new draft over to one of the office girls, a young lady who was, at that time, very much in love. Her head was in the clouds. Absentmindedly she turned in the *uncorrected* carbon and all the eight errors appeared in the magazine. Naturally my friends blamed me for the booboos."

Another story had to do with birds of prey. This involved a rather large black and white drawing of two vultures picking at the carcass of a skunk that had been killed by the roadside. Roger portrayed one of the vultures plucking gingerly at an intestine that was partly withdrawn from the skunk's belly, trying to make this as artistic as possible without being offensive. "This drew a comment from Dan Longwell, chairman of the board of editors, who complained that I made my vultures *too* dainty. 'They should really get right in there when picking at guts,' he said."

One important article Roger painted was one of bald eagles. The opening page depicted a bald eagle plunging after a cottontail rabbit. "Apparently the art editor didn't like my rabbit"—Roger smiles—"and without telling me about it, instructed one of his staff artists to 'doctor it up.' The result was a real cute, Walt Disney bunny of the Molly Cottontail type. I was enraged. My rabbit might not have been the best rabbit, but at least it was *my* rabbit."

At that time Roger, still naïve in some ways, did not know that an artist should ask for the return of his originals, and that the fee was for reproduction rights only. "In fact," says Roger, "the fees were not at all what they should have been, and when in the Army, I learned from my friend Glen Fleischmann, that the *Saturday Evening Post* paid him something like $1,000 for a double spread, I passed the word along to Kastner. He agreed that *Life* should certainly not pay less than the *Post*."

Many of Roger's original paintings were actually lifted by various *Life* staff members and pirated away. "I was told," says Roger, "that one senior editor went off with the blue jays—blue jays mobbing a screech owl—and when I finally was able to retrieve some of my originals some years later, more than half of them were missing."

Roger feels that his paintings in *Life* often had a far greater impact than he realized at the time. "As an example, I might cite the famous Argentine bird artist Axel Armachastegui, whose paintings now go for $10,000 to $15,000 and up. When we were introduced by Aylmar Tryon during a luncheon in London, Axel told me that my *Life* paintings had triggered him. He marveled at them but could not determine how they were done. I used Windsor Newton watercolors, which were not available at that time in Buenos Aires. Armachastegui finally arrived at a technique using Chinese inks and crow-quill pens, a very meticulous technique for which later he was to become famous."

During the postwar years Roger continued to paint, to lecture for the Audubon Society, and to write. He revised his first field guide. He wrote another on western birds and became editor of Houghton Mifflin's field guide series.

As the guides became popular, bird watchers no longer said, "Have you got Peterson's bird book?" They said, "Have you got *Peterson?*" John (Tex) O'Reilly, former nature writer for the New York *Tribune*, tells of the time when he was bird watching and came into the backyard of a large house. A woman came out and demanded to know what he and his group were doing on her property. They were obviously trespassing. They said, "Well, we are bird watching, and we're looking for . . ."

The woman interrupted, "Oh! Just a minute. I'll get Peterson," and she ran into the house and came out with Roger's little book.

Roger is delighted that the enormous sale of the field guides has made it possible for him to be "on vacation" ever since his first guide was published. "I have been able to do what I wanted to do because of the book rights." And for a man who wants to be free as the birds and do what he wants when he wants to, the wealth his books and paintings have brought him means more to him than just producing words and pictures. He says he is not money-minded, but "who could object to the money rolling in?"

Roger is also well aware of publicity and selling techniques, and Barbara, too, was adroit in setting up his appearances at key nature conventions as well as scheduling lectures at the right places. One Audubon cohort said that Roger told him that the reason he, Roger, did Audubon lectures was because "it sold books." The tours stimulated newspaper articles. There was feedback in "Questions and Answers." Constant interviews kept the books moving.

Writing them could be an awful chore. Roger said once, "I feel that doing a field guide is like doing a jail sentence. It is time-consuming and must be endured, a sort of penance. Therefore, in one lifetime there is not enough time to do all the field guides I would like to do or have been urged to do." His old Bronx County Bird Club friend Irving Kassoy says Roger writes in blood. One would never know it from the smoothness and effectiveness of his writing. But the long delays sometimes between dream and accomplishment reflect the tediousness of actual production.

The idea of *A Field Guide to Mexican Birds*, co-authored with Edward L. Chalif, was conceived in 1940. It was published in 1973. *A Field Guide to Wildflowers* took twenty years from the time Margaret McKenny, his collaborator, first discussed the book. And the complete revision of the first Eastern field guide lagged on in typical Roger fashion. "I have a bad reputation for not getting things done. I defer. I defer. I defer." When it comes to a painting or book to be published, Roger says he can't help worrying about the delay. "It is not just myself that is concerned," he says, "but the whole organization is depending on my work. It is the others that are inconvenienced by my not getting it done that bothers me. But I am not an organization. I am an individual, who must try to do all these things."

A lecture date cannot be deferred, Roger says, because a thousand people may be waiting to hear you, but a field guide, "where I'd like to be making progress, I can always defer it. Sometimes this goes on for years, which is bad. But my attitude about the pressure is that I've not merely got to cope with it, I've got to enjoy it, enjoy doing my work, without too much haste, without cutting corners. Cutting corners always makes one more frenetic. I think it's a matter of doing everything properly. If I'm bewildered with a really tough job, I just put it aside for a few hours. Meanwhile I do something."

Paul Brooks, his former Houghton Mifflin editor, once said of Roger, "Watching Roger Tory Peterson—never mind the birds—can be a lifelong avocation. He cannot be pigeonholed: *there are too many furiously moving parts.*"

The actual collecting of data, the field work, never was a bore to Roger. It might be hazardous and exhausting, but it was always exhilarating.

Guy Mountfort, P. A. D. Hollom, and Roger spent many days in the saddle in Spain getting material for the European guide. They flew, tramped, and drove from the Arctic tundra to the fringe of the Iron Curtain. Roger learned about Europe and European birds inch by inch, the hard way. Mountfort's text and Hollom's maps added the proper dimension to Roger's illustrations. The book, published in a dozen languages, is still Europe's best-selling field guide, according to Mountfort. It was first published in 1954 and went through nine "impressions" before revision in 1966. The European guide was dedicated to "our long-suffering wives," with a quotation from Shakespeare's *The Merry Wives of Windsor:*

> She laments, sir. Her husband
> goes this morning a-birding.

Chalif showed Roger the birds of Arizona while he was working on the Western guide and on a Texas version published by the Texas Fish and Game Commission. They became close friends. Chalif, whose father in Russia was Nijinsky's ballet master, had retired from his own school of ballet dancing, which he and his wife, Margaret, conducted, to Arizona to watch birds. Chalif, a past president of the Tucson Audubon Society in Arizona, returns to Martha's Vineyard each summer to lead bird trips and teach field ornithology. At the time of the Russian Revolution, Chalif was only two when his family was forced to flee Russia and "Eddie" was small enough to be put into a market basket. He grew up in New York. He was very active in the Boy Scouts, became an Eagle Scout, and pursued ornithology with all the fervor he had devoted to the dance.

The foreign editions posed many problems. One difficulty was translating the bird songs from one language to another. A bird song described phonetically in English might not be translatable to a German or an Italian. The translator had to know the song rather well himself in order to effect a proper phonetic translation; it could not be literal. For example, the chiffchaff, a small greenish leaf warbler that is found in most European countries:

In English, the chiffchaff sings chiff, chaff, chiff, chiff, chaff.
In Finnish, the bird sings til, tal, til, til, tal.
In German, the bird sings zilp, zalp, zilp, zilp, zalp.

In French, the bird sings tyip, tseyp, tyip, tyip, tseyp.

In Dutch, the bird sings tjif, tjaf, tjif, tjif, tjaf.

In Swedish, the bird sings tji, tju, tji, tji, tju.

In Spanish, the bird sings sib, sab, sib, sib, sab.

In Italian, the bird sings ciff, ciaff, ciff, ciff, ciaff.

In Icelandic, the bird sings tsjiff, tsjaff tsjiff, tsjiff, tsjaff.

In Danish, the bird sings tjif, tjaf, tjif, tjif, tjaf.

In only the Dutch and Danish does the rendition seem to be identical.

Many birds get their names from the sounds people hear them making. What people hear birds saying, however, depends very much on what country they live in.

It was in 1937 that Roger and Ed Chalif were on that trip through Arizona, but both men can recall details that belie somewhat the fact that memory always falters in the older years.

Chalif asked Roger, "Do you remember when we were pretty well up Madeira Canyon when we encountered a hummingbird which neither of us could recognize?"

"Yes, I do remember," answered Roger. "It was around some yellow columbines. At the edge of the stream. And there was a coral snake, actually, the false coral, a very handsome snake."

The two men were stumped by the hummingbird. Chalif said it must have been Mexican, and that maybe it might be a good reason to get started on the Mexican field guide.

On their first trip to Arizona, Mildred had been promised a ride by mule up Ramsey Canyon, a strange canyon in the Huachucas Mountains. There were, alas, no mules, no horses either. "This was, of course," Roger says, "a great disappointment to both of us—to Mildred particularly, because it was billed as the highlight of the trip. I had somehow failed."

During much of the Peterson-Chalif Mexican field work, I. Irby Davis was their guide. They traveled in his car to most sections of the country, except the Yucatan Peninsula, camping out in many wild places.

Roger acquired the intestinal "bug" so often attributed to eating salads and hot food in Mexico, but was told it was nothing serious, "simply something that was common to monkeys and hogs." Chalif says that one of Roger's problems was that Davis insisted they keep to a diet of "mashed bananas, oatmeal with condensed milk, and rolls." Roger lost a lot of weight on that trip. Chalif "noticed that Roger, at mealtime, would often hear a bird in the distance and walk off with his plate, and when he came back with it empty, commenting on how good the food was, I think it was for the birds."

Chalif remembers "a tremendous ceiba tree," a great umbrella-like tree, festooned, says Roger, with the nests of oropendolas, which were like long stockings hung from the outermost branches. Oropendolas are large black oriole-like birds with yellow tails. Roger wanted to photograph them, but while they went back to camp to eat, a truckload of men came by and cut down the tree. Roger was disappointed. "The oropendolas remind one very much of birds of paradise, the way they loop over and spread their wings, making gurgling sounds."

They did some butterfly catching. "At certain spots on the road," says Roger, "where a burrito had passed or a Mexican peasant had relieved himself, butterflies were attracted by the urine-impregnated mud. In one such place there were literally hundreds of butterflies, bright yellow sulphurs and zebra-striped swallow-tails. We referred to these gatherings as 'mud-puddle clubs.' "

The paintings in the Mexican field guide are some of Roger's best, so brilliant are the colors of the tropical birds. He was working on the Mexican field guide and the wildflower guide all at the same time, a juggling act of some proportion.

One thinks of Roger Tory Peterson as a bird man, but in the flower guide are 1,344 illustrations. It is no doubt this experience and knowledge that has made it possible for Roger to do the backgrounds so successfully in his gallery painting of today.

It was in 1964 that Roger had an automobile accident that almost ended his life. *The World of Birds* had just come out, and Roger was taking a copy of it to the Pettingills, at Cornell University, Ithaca, New York. He was alone on the seven-hour drive. It was on the way to Ithaca that Louis Fuertes' car had run into a railroad train and Fuertes had been killed. Was Roger remembering this as he drove along?

Roger took an unfamiliar road southeast of Ithaca. It was dusk. Heading into the setting sun, he went across a railroad overpass, misjudging the curve. The car took off three guard posts and plunged over an eighteen-foot embankment. Roger went through the windshield.

A farmer, patching his roof on a farm a quarter of a mile away, heard and saw the crash. If he had not, Roger would have bled to death. The road was used very infrequently, with few passers-by. Within ten minutes a state trooper came down the embankment, and an intern from a waiting ambulance helped Roger into it and rushed to the Ithaca Hospital.

Dr. Olin Pettingill, head of the Laboratory of Ornithology at the time, and his wife, Eleanor, were having a dinner party for Roger. Gardner Stout, president of the American Museum of Natural History, and his wife, Clare, were there, as was Betty Carnes of Scottsdale, Arizona (noted for her adoption of sick or injured wildlife and for her antismoking crusades).

"We were holding up supper for him," Dr. Pettingill tells the story. "Roger didn't come and didn't come—he was often notoriously late—so we went ahead and started dinner, when the phone rang. Roger had been in an accident and taken to the Ithaca Hospital."

The entire dinner party rushed off to the hospital. Roger was flat on the operating table. His face was torn wide open, but he was able to speak. "Isn't this a fine way to come to a meeting?" There was no plastic surgeon available, but a young man, Dr. Coates, said, "I'll do my best, if you want me to go ahead."

Gardner Stout made the decision. "I trust this man. Spare no expense."

It was after one o'clock in the morning when he got through.

Barbara, of course, rushed from Old Lyme, but before she arrived, the other wives had rallied to Roger's needs. Betty Carnes contacted a dozen or so persons to cancel Roger's appointments, and a special air-mail letter went to James Fisher, Roger's collaborator in England. He had heard about the accident over the BBC but didn't know whether or not Roger had survived.

A copy of *The World of Birds*, the book they had just written together, had been on the seat beside Roger when the accident occurred. Mrs. Pettingill had brought the book to Roger in the hospital. It was blotched with dried blood—Roger's.

"I thought you would want this, Roger," she said, and was amazed when he turned his head to the wall and did not answer.

Betty Carnes said, "Roger put his arm up over his head, kind of shielding his face." She did her best to cheer him up about how his face would look. "You have so much *more*, so much you have given to people of joy and happiness and interest in birds—all the things you have given them—do you think because you have a few scars on your face it is going to make any difference in the way people love and admire you?" Then Betty said, "And why didn't you want your book—that beautiful, beautiful book?"

Roger said, "You know, Betty, we worked so hard on that—James and I—and I had just gone through it and seen all the mistakes. And I have been lying here thinking if that were the last piece of work I were to do, I wish it had been *perfect*."

Eleanor had come back into the room, relieved to see Roger no longer staring at a blank wall. She picked up the bloodstained paper jacket of the book and started to throw it in the wastebasket. Whereupon Betty Carnes cried, "Wait a minute, wait a minute. Don't you throw that away! That book cover has Roger's blood on it! I *want* that."

"What's going on here?" Eleanor said, curiously. "What is Roger—Jesus Christ or something, that you want this?"

"No," Betty explained. "There are boys I know who work with birds who would love to have this as an award or something."

And Betty, says Mrs. Pettingill, went trotting back to Arizona with the book jacket with Roger's blood on it. She indeed gave it to a boy birder who treasured the unusual historic memento.

Sir Peter Scott and his wife, Phillipa, came to stay with the Petersons in Old Lyme for several days after the accident. "Peter," says Roger, "was licking his own wounds after the America Cup races at Newport. Peter was captain of the British team and their boat lost; one of the few times he has ever lost at anything. He is a formidable competitor. Peter frankly was afraid to go home where he would face the British critics. So, with us, Peter did not talk about boats, nor did I talk about cars. Instead we conversed about such eternal things as bird watching, fish watching, and the Galápagos Islands."

It wasn't for several months that Roger got his confidence back again about driving. He practiced in an empty parking lot. "How much physical damage accidents like this do is hard to say," he said, "but my hair became increasingly white."

A Field Guide to Wildflowers was not published until 1968. Twenty years earlier, when he had first discussed this book with Margaret McKenny, author of several nature books and executive secretary of the City Garden Clubs of New York City, Roger agreed to serve as editor only. This had been Roger's job for several other titles in the Peterson Field Guide Series. However, the artist who was to do the illustrations begged off; her publisher would not release her from another project. So Roger, in an unguarded moment, said, "Well, then *I* will do the drawings."

Such a simple thing to say, but such a staggering commitment! He made over 1,500 drawings of flowers. He covered thousands of miles by car in the eastern and midland states, trying to catch the brief period of bloom of various species.

In the introduction to *A Field Guide to Wildflowers*, he writes:

> My station wagon crawled at its slowest speed along back country roads while I kept one eye on the road and the other on the flowers; indeed, I became slightly wall-eyed.
>
> My battered vasculum [a tin box for collecting plants] was crammed with my finds, which I usually drew in the evening in some tourist cabin or motel. In the case of rare orchids, gentians, or other species where prudence forbade my picking them, I often drew them while lying flat on the ground.
>
> In my suitcase I carried a 200-watt daylight bulb that I often substituted for the weak 40 or 60-watt daylight bulbs in my quarters. To this day I am able to look at each drawing and bring back by association the place where I found the flower, the circumstances in which I drew it, and incidents—some pleasant, some trying. This odyssey was very educational.
>
> Birds have wings; they can travel, mix, and standardize their populations. Flowers are rooted to the earth. They are often separated by broad barriers of their unsuitable environment

from other 'stations' of their own species. Therefore, over the centuries, subtle differences have often developed, strains, as it were. Also, a flower from the same seed may be "depauperate" in a sterile soil and oversized in a rich soil or where lack of competition has favored it in some way. I found, as I zigzagged from Minnesota to Maine and from Ontario to Virginia, that a flower I knew well could, at times, look strangely unfamiliar. Sometimes it did not seem to key down properly even in the two standard technical works, *Gray's Manual of Botany* and *The New Britton and Brown Illustrated Flora*.

I became worried at first about my ineptitude, but later was reassured when I discovered that trained botanists to whom I showed such plants seemed frankly puzzled. Flowers are plastic; at least many of them are, particularly the flowers of late summer and fall. Furthermore, many of them hybridize; so we should not expect to score 100 percent on our identifications.

Roger used the same arrow system of identification for the most part and extended the analysis to general shape and structure. It was a visual, picture-matching approach, arranged not by families but under color of bloom. It was an exhausting job, and Roger threw out dozens of drawings.

In the wildflower book Roger included a charming essay on the survival of rare native wildflowers. "When a forest has been cut, its shade-loving orchids may also disappear, and half a century or more may pass before succession makes the forest suitable again for them. How can they return? Birds are mobile; they can return easily to their niche. And some seeds have parachutes or are carried by birds. But what about the others? Can seeds remain viable in the soil for half a century or more, until succession renders their habitat suitable again?"

And so the field guides grew, with Paul Brooks at Houghton Mifflin acting as gadfly and Helen Phillips, Roger's special editor, "the fine-toothed comb" for all the manuscripts. The other Peterson guides of the series were written (twenty-one of them, along with records and cassettes of the bird songs) under Roger's supervision and guidance, thus his title, "Editor" of the Peterson Field Guide Series.

While all this was going on, Roger was writing other things. His *The Bird Watchers Anthology*, published in 1957, is a collection of the selections Roger felt best "conveyed his enthusiasm for his science or his hobby." There are eighty-five stories by outstanding bird watchers "who were there." Roger wrote brief introductory paragraphs, classic vignettes, to introduce the author. His paintings and black and white drawings number nearly a hundred.

"If I could give but one book about birds and bird watching to my family," says one bird lover, "I would want it to be Roger Tory Peterson's *Anthology*. It is a classic, capturing the variety and the beauty of birds around the world and the *adventure* of bird watching."

Roger has been urged to do field guides of many countries. Prince Philip's suggestion for one, on Australian birds, was a temptation, but others have asked for bird guides of North Africa, the Belgian Congo, India, the Argentine, Antarctica, Colombia, and a wildlife guide of the Galápagos Islands. "In one lifetime," says Roger sadly, "there is not enough time to do all the field guides I would like to do."

Although doing them is laborious and tedious, Roger appreciates the fact that it is the field guides which make it possible for him to "fly free." Perhaps the writing that gave him the greatest personal satisfaction and happiness was the joint book project with James Fisher—*Wild America*—which came out in 1955, sandwiched in with all his other writing and field guides.

Roger had met James Fisher, his counterpart in Britain, in 1950, on his first trip abroad. There, on the island of Gotland in the Baltic Sea, the two bird watchers became friends. Roger's life was never to be quite the same again.

CHAPTER XII

The Adventures of Roger
and James Fisher

ROGER's 1950 meeting with James Maxwell McConnell Fisher, one
of England's foremost ornithologists, came about in a roundabout
way. Guy Mountfort, then secretary of the British Ornithologists'
Union, had been in the United States, at Hawk Mountain in Pennsylvania, in 1949, where he had come to watch "the raptorial birds
along the thermals rising from the Kittatinny Range." He had been
fascinated with Roger's Eastern field guide and impressed with
Roger. Immediately they decided to go into partnership in producing a book on European birds, which both had been contemplating. Later, Philip Hollom, a very fine field ornithologist,
joined them, at the suggestion of James Fisher, as a collaborator. A
year later, Roger and Mountfort both attended the International
Ornithological Congress in Sweden. And, of course, so did James
Fisher.

Fisher, at the time, was an editor at William Collins Sons & Co.,
Ltd., Roger's British publisher. Roger, naïve as he was said to be
about some things, was well aware of the importance of meeting
James Fisher. He wanted Collins to publish the *A Field Guide to
European Birds*. Roger admits that he was very brash to think he,

an American, could do a book on the birds of Britain and Europe. But he was young and the young can be brash. The problem was to convince a publisher. James was the editor at Collins who said "yes" or "no" about nature books.

Roger was a bit nervous when they met. He had heard about Fisher's sharp wit, which he could turn against a person to devastating effect, and he had other unpredictable qualities.

Traveling with Roger on the Swedish island of Gotland were Ed Chalif and his wife, Margaret. Roger told Ed that they had to handle James Fisher with kid gloves because "I was trying to woo him as editor of the British field guide that Guy and I hoped to write."

When the birders got into the crowded train that was to take them to the special birding place, there was some problem about how the conventioners would recognize fellow members. Margaret Chalif suggested that everybody put binoculars around their necks. "And so we did," she says, "and walked through the train finding others going to Gotland. James Fisher was the first person who spoke to us on the train. He was darling, and was just as friendly and sweet as he could possibly be."

Roger liked James at once, and promptly presented his case for the European field guide.

Meanwhile the naturalist studied Gotland's fabulous wildflowers and visited several seabird colonies, including those on Storo Karlso, a unique Swedish island sanctuary where razorbills, guillemots, and murres abound. James was especially interested in seabirds. The two men couldn't have been more congenial.

On the same trip they went to Swedish Lapland in the northern tip of Sweden, where four of the men shared a little cabin in the Arctic wilderness. They were Joselyn van Tyne of the University of Michigan, W. E. Clyde Todd of the Carnegie Museum, James Fisher, and Roger. James had his first good chance to look at the American field guide and to evaluate Roger's qualifications for the European guide.

Fisher did, of course, endorse the project, and Collins published it. *A Field Guide to the Birds of Britain and Europe* has since sold over 750,000 copies in thirteen different languages, and Roger thinks it is still the best-selling field guide throughout Europe.

James Fisher was about six feet, two inches tall, weighing 196 pounds ("fourteen stone"). He had a great shock of curly hair and a leonine head. Roger said with customary detail that James "wore a 6⅞ hat." Often he had a pipe between his rather wide lips. He and Roger made a handsome pair. Their backgrounds could not have been more different.

James was born in 1912 in Clifton, a suburb of Bristol. His father, Kenneth Fisher, was a master at Clifton College, later became assistant headmaster at Eton, and then headmaster at Oundel, another fine boys' school in England, but James attended Eton, where he was a King's Scholar. Later he went to Magdalen College, Oxford.

Roger says James Fisher liked to consider himself an old-fashioned naturalist in the mold of Gilbert White, author of *The Natural History of Selbourne*. James was incredible in his encyclopedic knowledge, an expert on British history. He was the greatest British interpreter of birds. He and Roger had planned to do a book together on seabirds, but James died, much too soon. The two books they did collaborate on, *Wild America* and *A World of Birds*, are still as classic as the field guides.

Fisher was also a radio and television figure. In the course of twenty-five years he participated in more than a thousand broadcasts, mostly on radio for the BBC. He had a regular talk show, comparable to the broadcasts of his friend Sir Peter Scott. Roger appeared on both their programs at various times, and after they made the Wild America film it was shown on the Peter Scott television show.

James Fisher was married to a New Zealand girl named Marjery, an Oxford student, the first female scholarship student from the colonies. They lived in a small town, Ashton, sixty-four miles out of London, near Northamptonshire, and owned a manor house with an old rectory and an old church (or chapel) where "Angus," as she was affectionately called, sometimes played the organ to a small audience of locals.

During the years when Roger and James worked on their books together, James and Angus lived in the old rectory.

James spent five days in London, where, in the evening, he would frequent the Savile Club, the distinguished gentleman's club. He saw to it that Roger became a member. Roger stayed there eight months while he worked on the European guide.

Roger's big problem at the Savile was the valet, who was indignant at the fact that he was so casual about his dress. "A valet can be quite a tyrant," says Roger, and he kept my clothing in the proper place, properly pressed, my shoes shined and what not, saw that I was awakened in time in the morning for a proper breakfast. More than once, the valet gave me a mild lecture."

It must have been more than clothes that upset the valet. At one time Roger had at least eighty bird specimens from the British Museum in his room! As it was virtually impossible to remove bird specimens from the museum, this "first" was again due no doubt to the great persuasion and prestige of James Fisher.

Two or three times a week Roger's co-authors, Guy Mountfort and "Phil" Hollom, would come over in the evening and they would have dinner together and review their progress. On many nights Roger would take a constitutional around the block. This was Piccadilly, and he would run the gauntlet of all the street-walkers. "I had not had previous experience with streetwalkers," he said, "and I thought it flattering to be accosted that way, singled out. But I resisted temptation and walked on."

From the outset Roger was accepted as a peer among the top ornithologists. His widely published Eastern and Western field guides served well as credentials. His friends in London soon included people like Sir Julian Huxley, who wrote the introduction to *A Field Guide to the Birds of Britain and Europe,* Lord Alanbrooke, chief of the Imperial General Staff, Prince Philip, Sir Peter Scott, Keith Shackleton, and Eric Hosking. The British class structure posed no problem for the boy from Jamestown. Roger took many trips with these naturalists.

Eric Hosking, in *An Eye for a Bird,* tells of one evening in the Hilbre Islands. Hosking, Alanbrooke, and Roger were sitting around talking about birds. Roger had been surrounded that day in the field with oyster catchers. He simply reveled in the experience, especially since he was working on the oyster catcher plate for his British field guide.

The talk gradually broadened and Alanbrooke recounted a tense scene in the Kremlin during the war. He described the night before the British delegation was to fly home. He and Churchill and Stalin were relaxing, sipping vodka, when "suddenly Stalin shook his fist at Churchill, swore, and demanded to know when the British were going to start fighting."

The effect on Churchill was explosive. He crashed his fist on the table and lit into Stalin with a burst of impassioned oratory. Stalin listened for a minute or two, then, with a broad grin on his face, stood up, stopped Churchill's interpreter, and through his own, said, "I do not understand what you are saying but by God I like your sentiment!"

The birders were hanging on Alanbrooke's words when Hosking happened to glance at Roger. "There seemed to be a glazed look about his eyes. He was not with us at all; he was still with his beloved oyster catchers. When Alanbrooke's story was done, and there was a slight pause, Roger spoke: 'Y'know, I guess these oyster catchers eat most any mollusc.'"

James Fisher wrote of those days, "Almost as vivid as memories of days in the field are memories of hours of talk: tea with Peter Scott at the New Grounds in Gloucestershire; dinner at the Cottrells', midnight at London's Savile Club, when the conversation begins to warm up by the fire; even breakfast—breakfast with the Petersons especially, for Roger, the obsessive, always wants to talk about birds. I have seen him many times, at an International Ornithological Congress—where the talk ranges wide—assume a faraway look when the conversation drifts away from ornithology, only to take it up at the exact sentence where he left off, when it comes back."

Their friendship grew. It was to culminate in their 100-day, 30,000-mile trip around the United States in 1953.

Roger had proposed the idea after Fisher had showed him so much of Britain and Europe. "If you come to America," he said, "I will meet you in Newfoundland and lead you around the continent. We will go as far as the Yukon Delta and the Pribilofs—by way of Mexico—and you will see a more complete cross section of wild America than any other Englishman, and all but a few North Americans, has ever seen."

Fisher became an eager victim of Roger's plan. Barbara and Angus spent long weeks helping to get the bird watchers ready for the expedition they could not join. They stayed at home with their families. Later the two of them typed at least half a million words of the manuscript Roger and James wrote together.

It was a unique book, published by Houghton Mifflin in 1955. Charles Poore, in the *New York Times* review, said it was a "friskily written and wonderfully relaxing book." Roger illustrated it with black and white drawings, sketches he had made on the trip. First, Roger would write a bit of introduction to a chapter, setting the scene. Then Fisher would take over the narrative, writing his journal under the dateline.

They had a "syndicate mind," says Lorimer Moe, who knew them both so well.

They could write about each other, too. And did. It is a wonder that their friendship could survive so intimate a fourteen-week period. Neither of them had dispositions of the milquetoast variety.

Although James had a delightful sense of humor, "there could be barbs in it," as Chalif had said. And Roger has always admitted his own temper.

They had Roger's new, shiny green Ford country sedan, seventeen feet long, loaded with gear. In Arizona, where the road twisted through an endless series of outcrops, small ranges, and flats, the two men changed places at the wheel every fifty miles. Switchbacks and hairpin curves made the driving hazardous. At one sharp bend Roger slammed on the brakes to prevent hitting an oncoming car. James, his nerves frayed thin by the heat, nearly blew up. "What's the idea of hugging the middle of the road when you should have been on the outside?"

"And go over the precipice? I once lost a friend in just that way—forced over the edge."

"Well, have it your way," finalized James. "I think you're a bloody bad driver." (But it was Fisher who was killed driving in England in 1970.)

Roger says this was the only time tempers flared. Not even when they went down the Grand Canyon on muleback. Nor when Roger slipped when he was filming on a steep slope in Newfoundland and fell, straining a muscle. Limping in pain, James said, he went into the icy waters of a river "by mistake on purpose" to cool his wound, "always cheerful, never complaining."

During the long 100-day trip for the book they covered the periphery of the United States, taking side trips into Arizona and Mexico.

The Grand Canyon, from Navaho Point, filled Fisher with awe. When he first saw it, he was silent for ten minutes. So was Roger. Then Fisher said, drying his eyes under cover of Roger's handkerchief, while pretending to dry his forehead, "I shan't want the big lens; I wish I had a wide-angle."

James, in the United States, was "seeking the differences and finding the similarities" between the British and Americans, especially how they regarded bird watching. Roger said he was rather amused because at home he had always seemed scornful of mere bird listening—or "tally hunting," as he called it. That was boys' play; Fisher was interested in the more scientific aspects of bird watching—such things as population dynamics, geographic distribution, and ecology. But, secretly, the truth of it is that he had run out of "new" birds in England. He was even more diligent than Roger in keeping his score up to date on the little white checklists Roger had furnished. Every time he got a new bird he shouted "Tallyho."

When James Fisher saw the California condor with its monstrous ten-foot span, he watched it catch a new thermal and soar into the southeast until it became a tiny speck, then turned to Roger and said, "Tally—*most incredibly*—ho!" It had been worth traveling ten thousand miles to see.

James pulled a fast one in Anchorage. While Roger stayed in the hotel to work on a drawing, James went into the mountain with Ed Chatelaine of the U.S. Fish and Wildlife Service and came back with five new birds on his list.

He retained this margin until he returned to England; and so, for a month, an Englishman held the record list of birds seen in one year in North America. It was not until Roger returned home that he caught up. Always competition and one-upmanship for Roger. His list, at that time, 1953, was 572 species not counting 65 Mexican birds. Fisher's was 536, plus the 65 Mexican birds, plus 117 others seen in Europe, a total of 718.

It was not until eighteen months later that the two men had time to think about their book *Wild America*, to sort it out a bit and start writing. Roger finished a color movie of the journey that millions have enjoyed on television and has twice packed London's great Festival Hall. James Fisher showed it in Leningrad, too, at Russia's first ornithological congress in 1956. It was the first time a color film on American nature had been shown in Russia. He showed it later in Moscow.

Of his American experience Fisher said that he never had seen such wonders or "met landlords so worthy of their land. They have had, and still have, the power to ravage it; and instead they have made it a garden."

As an indication of the value of his work in the United States, James Fisher was given the Arthur A. Allen medal of the Cornell Laboratory of Ornithology in 1968 for his outstanding contribution to the popularization of ornithology.

In the years that followed *Wild America* he and Roger made many other trips together through Europe, fifteen countries, for the material in *The World of Birds*.

Barbara typed the entire book (James wrote in longhand on long legal sheets, like Roger). She did much of it in England when they stayed with the Fishers at Ashton. "As you know," Barbara tells of the experience, "April can be very chilly in England. I was given the nursery as the room in which to type, a fairly large room with a fair number of windows. There was a fire, and you know the English fires are about 'so big.' I had an electric heater on either side of me. And then I went out and bought thermal underwear and the heaviest slacks I could find. By mid-morning I could get so I was uncongealed. My fingers would finally manipulate." Barbara told Angus she would do all the typing for both James and Roger if she would do all the cooking, "which worked out nicely."

Fisher gained weight, lived a too sedentary life, and developed arthritis and deterioration in one of his hips. He suffered severely. Roger feared that he drank too much because of the pain, but the doctor permitted it. Roger felt he was having difficulty financially, also, and was overdoing in general.

On the night of September 30, 1970, after a convivial evening at the Savile, James drove home for the weekend at Ashton. "Although normally he was one of the best drivers I have ever known," says Roger, "with the reactions of a racing driver, he took the turns on the country roads near his home literally 'flying low.' He had a fatal accident near Hendon. He was only fifty-eight." It was a shock to the entire ornithological world, but Roger had lost his most valued friend. His visits to England were never again the same. "For me," he said, "its nerve center is missing."

James told Roger once that he had only one fear—of dying before his time. There were several books that he wanted to write and Roger says James was more qualified to write them than any other person.

Roger wrote James' obituary for *British Birds* and also gave the eulogy at Copinsay, the 270-acre island in the Orkneys north of Scotland, which was to become the James Fisher Memorial Conservation Island. Complete with a working lighthouse and an old crofter's cottage, the island was dedicated in 1973. Roger said in the memorial ceremony, "There has never been anyone quite like James Fisher, nor is there likely to be."

CHAPTER XIII

Barbara—and Farewell

MOST of Roger's friends say Roger "wouldn't be where he is without Barbara." One says, "The capacity was there, but would he have developed it without Barbara?" Another: "Every time Roger receives another award for his greatness, Barbara should be given a gold charm for her charm bracelet." Another: "Without Barbara —Roger can't say 'no' to invitations to speak and to social engagements—Roger would have burned himself out at both ends."

Paul Brooks wrote that she was "a combination of platoon leader and chief of staff." He tells a fascinating story of how he first became aware of Barbara:

"Roger had stopped in my office [in Boston] with a suitcase full of old clothes and new nature books. As he dug down for a Swedish flower guide, I noticed a large and battered alarm clock attached to the inside of the case by a string. 'Barbara's doing,' Roger explained. No longer did Roger leave his clock behind in his motel room as he concentrated on timeless matters. Barbara, I thought, must be quite a woman." The alarm clock was better than the Western Union telegram to get Roger up in the morning.

Another time, Paul remembers, when they were all on a birding trip in California, "our outboard motor sheared off a cotter pin. Where did we find a spare pin? In Barbara's tool kit in her handbag of course!" Barbara is adept in carpentry, painting houses, plumbing, all kinds of handyman's jobs. Not Roger!

Barbara said one day in 1975, "You know, Roger classifies people in two categories. One, as engineers, which is creative, which he is. And then there are the mechanics. I am a mechanic. I keep the factory running. I don't initiate or cannot initiate to the extent that Roger does. I am not creative in any way. But I can paint the house"—she laughs—"and I can keep it running."

Paul says that Barbara, remarkably, always realized that "every artist must get away from his drawing board, and that she had resignedly quoted the example of Captain Cook, who said to his wife, 'You're the joy of my life, though oceans may roll between us. But I must be off the Isles of the South to observe the Transit of Venus.' "

Roger was always aware of Barbara's understanding and acceptance of his absence and her contribution to his work. He wrote in the introduction to the second edition of *A Field Guide to Western Birds* this note of appreciation: "To Barbara my wife, who, doubling as secretary, virtually became an ornithological widow when I was in the field. She took in stride the months of pressure when her husband found it expedient to work around the clock. To her, more than to any other, I owe the completion of this book." In this edition all text and illustrations were new.

(When Roger prepared the earlier edition it was Mildred who accompanied him on two of the field trips. In tribute to her he wrote in the preface that she "spent altogether too many lonely nights at home while I burned the midnight oil in my study.")

John Livingston, one-time president of the Canadian Audubon Society, has said that the involvements, the obligations, the responsibilities Roger had were sufficient to submerge any man. But with tact, unending energy, and spirited good humor, he said Barbara invariably managed to maintain order and balance, even in the most potentially explosive situations.

Barbara's efficiency might frighten a novice assistant, for her quick action and knowledge may turn to briskness and even brittleness, which unnerves underlings—even Roger. Jane Kinne of Photo Researchers, Inc., who had worked with Roger at Audubon and has followed his photographic career for more than twenty-five years, says, "There's nothing retiring about Barbara. She's very definitely her own woman. She has devoted endless hours and time and patience not only to Roger and what he's doing, but to all of the people who are concerned with his work in various ways. She's like the president of a small corporation; she's keeping track of everything that's going on."

When Barbara was called once for an appointment with Roger, the telephone conversation went something like this:

BARBARA: Hi, dear! Just got Roger off at six A.M. to England. Am in weakened condition.
CALLER: How long will he be gone?
BARBARA: It depends on whether he can find some puffins to photograph. I hope you're not planning on coming up here this month. Let me get the calendar: May 16th—National Wildlife Federation, here. May 22–25—Mount Pelee, Michigan. P E L E E [forcefully]—great migration point. May 28–20—Germantown, Pennsylvania. International Conference of Bird Preservation. Or something like that [giggles]. June 5–9 —Earth Care Week, New York Hilton.
CALLER: May?
BARBARA: No! Not May, not June! Then I have Roger scheduled to go out to Wilson Ornithology—Montana. Wheuuu! Back to Jamestown—fiftieth high school reunion, June 25th. Never again am I going to drive to Jamestown in one day. This morning—what a scramble. Roger forgot to get travelers' checks, no money. By the way, I am told there is a European ruff at Guilford marshes. Roger will miss it. Also Robert Pyle. He's the man who started the Xerces Society. Butterflies. One of the greatest guys in the world. Great long beard. You never saw such a beard in your life. Sorry, but Roger is going to be tied up all through May, June. He's supposed to get that damned bob white painting finished . . . and Bob Lewin is coming up with prints to sign. Miserable weather. Glad I have the flowers planted. A new tree. . . . No, I have not yet told Roger of Peggy Nord's death. He's got enough on his mind. Yes, I had to laugh yesterday. Lee [the younger son] turned to Roger, who had made some crack about how slow Lee was coming with his edible wild plant book, and said, "Really, Dad, you're getting to be an

old nag!" And I really can't forgive Roger because, you know, it took him twenty-eight years to do the *Eastern Flower Guide*. . . . (I don't really think he'd like that in print.) Bye, dear.

Roger, with his "mechanical drawing" mind, saw life as picture segments, Barbara has said. So many objectives to be accomplished in so many years. He has said that he knew he would accomplish "certain things at certain points in my life." Barbara believes that women should have "planned achievement" also.

All kinds of extracurricular activities fell in Barbara's lap. One time, Roger's mother—aged eighty-four in 1963—turned up from Ventura, California, where she was living with Roger's sister, and said she was on her way to see Europe. Roger's niece, Rosalinda, nineteen, was to make the trip with her. They had booked ship passage, but had not the remotest idea of what they were going to do when they got abroad. No "booking" whatever. "Babes in the woods," said Barbara.

She scurried around and made arrangements for them, and got them on their way. Then, not much later, she flew over to give them a helping hand. "And a good thing, too. London and Europe were crowded because of the Shakespearian year." They went to England and Holland and had a marvelous time. "Another joy of growing older," says Barbara, "is that changing relationship to one's parents—they become more friends than parents."

Barbara was always flying off—or driving off—to come to the aid of Roger, bringing his films or his cameras or his projectors. At Las Vegas, one year, where Roger was to be speaker at the annual National Wildlife Federation luncheon, there was some fear that Roger wasn't going to be able to get there from wherever he was, and Barbara flew out West, prepared to deliver the commentary with his *Wild Europe* film. As projectionist, she had seen it so many times she knew it by heart. Actually she had shown it and other films to women's clubs and garden clubs in many places.

For Roger, Barbara typed fourteen of his books during their marriage. Under "Acknowledgments" in *Wild America*, Roger and James Fisher wrote, "To our wives, Angus Fisher and Barbara Peterson, we are deeply in debt; they not only spent long weeks getting us ready for an expedition they could not join, but also had the task of typing at least half a million words before the manuscript was boiled down to a book."

Handling Roger's correspondence alone was a massive chore. People wrote in for all kinds of information about birds, and Barbara answered these letters over Roger's signature. She called them her "dickey-bird letters." People asked all kinds of questions—"I'm writing a bird book. How?"—"I'm sending a pine cone. Will you please draw the face of an owl on it?" Many such.

Roger says Barbara was a good organizer, but had no mind for figures or finance at all. There is room for argument.

Roger, as he reached the peak of his career, became increasingly loquacious, and Barbara had heard and reheard his accounts of his difficult childhood and his climb to success more times than they could interest her. Once she turned down a weekend invitation to the home of one of their best friends because it wouldn't be any fun for her, "listening to Roger talk about himself."

It would have been difficult for any person, overcoming as many handicaps as Roger had, not to become slightly dazzled by the sensational worldwide recognition he has received. Most men would have become egomaniacs, and Roger has been accused of leaning in that direction. In the later years more and more things that Roger did were "turned inward." Barbara must have been, frankly, bored: drinking perhaps more than she should, some of her friends said, and spending more and more time in Seattle with her mother, a good excuse to pass up some of the trips with Roger. There were plenty of girls to carry his cameras, plenty of girls to listen, goggle-eyed, to his stories.

Modest, poised, but not exactly withdrawn, Barbara has always been a little surprised when people invited her for "herself" when Roger was away. "You mean it?" she asked Carl Buchheister once when he and Harriet had invited her to dinner. "You mean you want me to come *without* Roger?"

The Petersons finally took on a joint secretary, "Pidge" (Mrs. Cornelia Eastland). But when Roger came back from a trip and discovered that somebody else besides Barbara had been opening the mail and sorting it and sending off certain kinds of answers, "he was physically ill," said Jane Kinne. "I remember Barbara calling us in New Canaan and saying, 'He's disappeared into the bathroom, and Lord knows when he'll come out.'"

He did become adjusted to outside help, of course, and looks to Robert Lewin of the Mill Pond Press to manage his painting schedule and exhibits and tours.

Barbara also screened out portions of books, magazine articles, and newspapers that she knew he would want and should see, marking them with a large red pencil. One friend of the Petersons said Roger got "fed up" with Barbara's "managing his life, almost bossily." Barbara, he said, didn't have a color television in 1975, lest Roger watch it too much and not meet those deadlines.

But Barbara is a woman in her own right too. So many women, sometimes, at bird meetings, smothered Roger with attention. Asked how he missed being an old roué, Roger laughed and said, "I never—Barbara says I never recognized the opportunities."

Barbara always kept people from bothering Roger: "He's made himself available to students, writers, everyone who wants to know about birds or nature. Someone has to run interference." This was especially true at meetings or on field trips. Barbara learned to protect Roger's time and energy as much as possible. "Roger can't bear to disappoint anybody," she says.

Barbara's only relaxation was horseback riding. She was an expert. She owned several Morgans. The Petersons' New Year's letters are full of her hobby: "The Vasiloffs [who owned the stables where she rode] and I took part in a number of trail rides this year and climaxed by joining a thirty-five mile fall-foliage ride in Vermont. My little black mare had a chestnut filly, named Curley (1966) and this year (1967) a black colt, named Black Hawk. . . . This fall I helped the Morgan Versatility Show."

Her pride and joy were her last two Morgans—La Beau and Whippoorwill Melody. Barbara has won many blue ribbons. Roger did not ride at Old Lyme. He's not much of a horseman, Barbara said. "He just sits on a horse, he does not ride."

Barbara has spent much time in conservation work with and without Roger. From the time Roger began working with the declining population of ospreys in Old Lyme in 1955, it was Barbara who was up and down the inlets and estuaries, climbing up to the nests, checking and counting the eggs. Roger wrote Herbert

Mills, New Jersey conservationist and authority on ospreys, in 1960, "Barbara is at present marking osprey nests here and has more than thirty numbered and tagged now out of fifty or sixty that we have in this area." Early in the spring Peter Ames, a Yale naturalist, was tackling the osprey project with Roger. Barbara writes in the Petersons' annual New Year's letter, "We sank three four-by-four oak posts into the marsh with platforms on top. We ferried these out on a lovely spring day. Ospreys had already arrived but quickly adopted the new sites. A total of six young were successfully raised (a poor showing for the number of adults we have in the area, but better than last year). We also rebuilt the nest in Copp's apple tree and the birds had four eggs, later destroyed (by raccoons, we think). Later in the summer, a two-story four-by-four bird blind was built. Towing this monster and setting it up was a herculean task. Our plans for next season call for twenty nest poles and platforms and we hope more birds can be raised next year." The next year's letter says only three young were raised in spite of their efforts. And the eggs had traces of DDD and DDE. In 1975 there were none. Today they are beginning to come back in nearby areas.

On a more ambitious scale, Barbara recorded the Antarctic Adelie penguin count for the Office of Polar Programs of the National Science Foundation in 1973. "Total adults, plus adults on ice headed for Royds, 2,976; total chicks recorded, 1,604; five flipper bands recorded." She was on the *Lindblad Explorer* with Roger, who was coordinator of the project. A Certificate of Appreciation came from the Bird Banding Laboratory of the U.S. Department of the Interior, Bureau of Sport Fisheries and Wildlife.

Barbara has been to the Antarctic eight times. Only two women have been there more often. She knows her penguins.

There's a lovely little story about Barbara and the satin bowerbird, an Australian bird noted for its elegant color and display. The delightful, shiny blue-satin male courts a female with a selection of blue ornaments placed in front of his "bower," a sort of nest with a parting of grasses as an entrance. At the New York Bronx Zoo, in the large, open exhibit "World of Birds," there is a bowerbird that Barbara has admired especially. She decided to bring it some matching blue ornaments to put in front of its bower.

A Milk of Magnesia bottle is the exact shade of blue she wanted, so she went down to the Old Lyme town dump and found bits and pieces of broken blue glass. She took these to William G. Conway, the Petersons' good friend and general director of the New York Zoological Society, and the blue tokens were placed at the entrance of the bower. Whereupon Bill Conway wrote the following letter to Barbara:

Dear Barbara:

The bowerbird blues are so pretty I almost took them home to set before my own front door. After all, I'm not as old as I look.

Many thanks for another example of that very special brand of thoughtfulness, a proprietary brand peculiar to yourself.

As ever,
Bill

In January 1976, Barbara was given an award by the women's committee of the New York Zoological Society, of which she is an active member. It was the fifth Vera Award. Howard Phipps, Jr., president of the New York Zoological Society, presented the gold hornbill pin (a really ugly bird, the hornbill) to Barbara Coulter Peterson, in appreciation for her work. "She excels in her own right," he said. And Barbara said in her acceptance speech, "More often than not, the behind-the-scenes efforts are a shared endeavor, and we, as wives, more often than not, just fast on reflected glory!"

The award read, "To Mrs. Peterson, a lifelong naturalist and ecologist, as well as an accomplished wildlife photographer and world traveler."

Though not exactly "gung-ho" for women's lib, Barbara says, "This is my woman liberation pin."

No one realized how liberated until the annual Peterson New Year's letter was received in February 1976. The last page ended:

At the close of the year Roger and I arrived at a decision that we had pondered for some time—that it would be best for each of us to go our own way. Therefore this will be the last letter that will be signed jointly by us.

At this juncture I am driving West and will live in Seattle, where I shall be able to keep tabs on my mother, now in her ninety-seventh year. Roger, because of his work base, his studio facilities and library, will stay in Old Lyme.

We will remain as friends and continue to face the future with optimism.

With our best wishes for 1976,

Barbara and Roger,
Old Lyme, Conn.
January 1976

Part III

CHAPTER XIV

Call Me *a Bird* Watcher!

WHEN you see people, young and old, out focusing their binoculars on birds in the field or along the shore, are they "birders" or "bird watchers?" They can be very pedantic about the correct identification of themselves.

The distinguished, fairly new American Birding Association, whose president is G. Stuart Keith, a research associate in the Department of Ornithology of the American Museum of Natural History in New York City, prefers the terms "birder" and "birding."

His old and good friend Roger Tory Peterson, however, says, "Call *me* a bird *watcher!*" According to Roger, a bird watcher by any other name is still a bird watcher, and no apologies are needed. The term, he says, is a good one, for it covers everyone from enthusiastic aficionados of the sport (sometimes called "ornithological golf") to behavioral scientists like Niko Tinbergen and Konrad Lorenz; to ecologists like Joe Hickey and John Emlen, and to wildlife technicians and administrators like Ira Gabrielson and the late Clarence Cottam. Even the white-breasted nuthatch type of bird watcher, who sees most of his birds from the kitchen window, is a bird watcher. They all watch birds and, to paraphrase E. B. White, the birds also watch them.

THE WORLD OF ROGER TORY PETERSON

"I suppose there was a time," Roger says, "when the term 'bird watcher' brought to mind either 'an absentminded ornithology professor or a Helen Hokinson dowager,' but so popular has bird-watching become that these are but a minuscule minority. Generals, admirals, governors, senators, prime ministers, cabinet secretaries, kings, and presidents can be counted among the Field Glass Fraternity. Nehru was a bird watcher. So is Prince Philip, who uses my field guides constantly. Of eight princes of my acquaintance, seven are bird watchers. Among my bird-watching friends I count captains of industry as well as innumerable ordinary people."

Roger believes the common denominator, if there is one, is probably curiosity. These people are more aware of life than most. It is no accident that the bird-watching clan produced Darwin, whose study of Galápagos finches resulted in one of the greatest theories conceived by man, the origin of species. The bird watchers and ornithologists were the ones who first developed such concepts as ecology, behavior, territory, and animal navigation. They have been among the leaders in systematics and genetics. Rachel Carson, who warned us of the dangers of the pollution of our environment by insecticides, got her clues from watching birds. "Birds are far more than quail and pheasants to be shot or chickadees and cardinals to brighten the garden," says Roger. "They are indicators of the laws of life."

But while Roger prefers to call himself a "bird watcher," and does not quarrel with those who prefer to be called "birders," he just can *not* stand the often-used term "bird lover."

"I don't *love* birds," he says with spirit. "I am obsessed with birds. I have always been obsessed with birds. But I don't love them. Loving demands reciprocation, or at least the promise of reciprocation. Birds simply do not reciprocate. We might enjoy them, watch them, and study them, but to 'love' them—that is being *too* anthropomorphic."

Many a fine argument has been started on the subject of "loving birds." W. H. Hudson, the English naturalist and novelist, author of *Green Mansions*, once wrote, "It is impossible for us not to love whatever is lovely, and of all living things birds were made to be beautiful . . . [and] the birds, too, I love." Also there was Dr.

Frank Chapman's own *Autobiography of a Bird-Lover*. The term did not worry *him!*

Despite Roger's being so emphatic about not loving birds, he once got caught in saying the opposite of loving—hating birds. But only once! On the record is the following story, which Alexander Sprunt, Jr., related to his son Sandy:

"It was in the summer of 1936 at the Audubon Camp in Maine. From July 24 to 28, I joined Bob Allen, Roger Peterson, and Allan Cruickshank on a survey of nesting seabird colonies off the rocky coast of Maine in one of the camp boats. And it was on this trip that Roger voiced the classic remark that he has probably regretted ever since.

"Roger, the poor fellow, had a case of trench mouth and was pretty miserable. I regret to record that our sympathy was not exactly overwhelming. We isolated him as best we could in the stern of our little boat, the *Osprey,* and made him use the same knife, fork, and spoon and wash them himself. We practically fed him on a stick. And we paid him rather scant attention. As we came up to the various ledges and islands where the gulls, guille-mots, and terns and other seabirds were nesting, and we noted the numbers of each species and other details, Roger paid no attention whatsoever, his head sunk down between his knees. Finally we came to a ledge that held a large concentration of cormorants, the rocks being black with them. We exclaimed at the sight and shouted to Roger to rise and look.

"Roger lifted his head from his knees, gave a bleary glance, and dropped it again. As he did so, he growled distinctly—'I hate birds.' From that date on we never let him forget it. And I daresay he never has."

As general interest in birds increases, the question comes up: Just how many bird watchers are there? Roger estimates, for North America, that the number varies from twenty to forty million, "depending on how one defines bird watching."

Roger says that there are at least fortyfold the number of bird watchers there were when his first field guide was published in 1934. There can be no doubt that the publication of that book has had a lot to do with this proliferation of bird watchers. Furthermore, bird tours and nature tours to every place in the world have expanded bird watching internationally.

Webster's dictionary defines bird watchers under two categories: those who observe birds and those who identify birds—in other words, those primarily interested in the lives, habits, and abilities of the birds, and those primarily interested in their names. It is impossible to pinpoint the number of bird watchers, but Roger has tried to define or list the various levels of intensity:

1. The Window Watcher—or "white-breasted nuthatch type of bird watcher," the person who simply enjoys those species that are attracted to the window feeding tray with sunflower seeds, suet, and cracked corn. This must be a very large group indeed. Certainly upward to ten million, if the sale of birdseed can be used as a measure of this. Birdseed is now "big business," and in a community like Old Lyme, there is hardly a house up or down the road where the tenants do not feed the birds.

2. The Sportsman—the duck hunter or grouse or quail hunter is certainly a bird watcher, although the number of species that he is interested in is usually limited to the few that he is allowed to "harvest."

3. The Typical Bird Watcher, who has a field guide and enjoys weekend birding, primarily as a recreation. He can identify most of the birds that occur in his neighborhood—or hopes to someday.

4. The Hard-core Bird Watcher, whom we also might call a birder, or lister. Actually lister is a more restricted term than birder. In England they use the term "tally hunter," or "ticker." These are the people who work very hard to see how many they can check off on their life checklists. The hard-core birder or lister is, in a sense, the lineal descendant of the sportsman, substituting the bird on the list for the bird in the bag. However, the hard-core birder has the advantage of no bag limits, no restricted species, no season. The ultimate in the hard-core listing game is a group that calls itself the 600 Club, whose members have a life list of more than 600 species seen north of the Mexican border in North America. Joe Taylor of Rochester, New York, leads the pack with a North American life list of 716 birds.

Then there are those hard-core listers who do not confine themselves to the continent, but who travel to the ends of the earth for their birds. The man who leads this pack, according to *Birding*, the official publication of the A.B.A., is Stuart Keith, who lays claim to a world list of 5,200—a very large percentage of the 8,600-plus species of birds known to exist in the world.

5. The Bird Photographer or nature photographer demands something a little more tangible than the list, and he, too, might be termed a lineal descendant of the sportsman, only in this instance using a 400-mm lens instead of a rifle or shotgun. Nature photographers of one sort or another—not strictly bird photographers—must now number in the millions. The invention of color film has expanded the whole interest in nature photography; more and more people are taking pictures of birds and the outdoors.

6. The Armchair Birder, who is very well read on birds of distant parts of the world but spends little time in the field. He is very well informed about all kinds of birds, but enjoys his birding—or his science—among his books and periodicals. Many of those who religiously attend the Audubon Wildlife Films fit into this category.

7. The Print Collector—a new breed, probably numbering only a few thousand because buying prints is expensive. Some print collectors may be ornithologically inclined, but others are basically collectors of bird prints as one would be a collector of bird stamps or coins.

8. Finally, there are the Academics and Advanced Amateurs, who hold memberships in the A.O.U., the Wilson Club, and the Cooper Ornithological Club. They subscribe to such magazines as *The Auk*, the *Wilson Bulletin*, and *The Condor*. These people would number not more than five or six thousand in all.

Topping the Academics would be such Nobel Prize winners as Niko Tinbergen and Konrad Lorenz, who delve into that most esoteric of ornithological fields—bird behavior, part of the growing science of ethology.

Aviculturists, those who keep birds in cages and those who watch birds in zoos, run into the millions. They cannot be thought of in the usual sense as being birders, but they cannot be excluded from the overall total number of people who enjoy watching the beauty and behavior of birds.

Roger has some ties with nearly all of these levels of bird watching. "I have always been a Window Watcher and feed the birds at my home. While I work I enjoy the constant activity outside the window. Much of my bird watching is of the recreational sort, but I can also be called a Hard-core Bird Watcher—lister." (The ivory-billed woodpecker was the "toughest.") His list for North America is 668. His world list is somewhere between three and four thousand. "I am also a Bird Photographer, exposing at least 10,000 transparencies every year; and I am a print collector, too, in a modest way. As for the Academics, I am more of an interpreter than a researcher, but I hold memberships in the A.O.U., the Wilson Club, and the Cooper Ornithological Society. I have been president of the Wilson Club and first vice president of the A.O.U., and have won the Brewster Medal of the latter society."

In addition to the specific categories of bird watchers, there are those who have a broad interest in conservation and the environment. A large part of the Audubon membership would fall into this category, as would much of the membership of the National Wildlife Federation and other conservation groups. "I regard myself primarily as a bird watcher *and* a conservationist," says Roger, adding that "bird watcher is really a very good term because it is so general that it covers all levels of the observation of birds at all seasons."

An ornithologist has been described by Sir Peter Scott as "one who clears his throat uneasily when he is called a 'bird watcher,' " just as a biologist is "one who clears his throat uneasily when he is called a 'naturalist.' "

Joe Taylor is perfectly content at being a "listing" bird watcher. He says he uses the terms "birding," "birder," and "bird watcher" interchangeably. He once made a 4,600-mile round trip between Rochester, New York, and Big Bend National Park in West Texas just to spot a rufous-capped warbler, his 716th bird. He flew back from Africa to see the Ross's gull.

"I am a bird watcher," he says, adding, "Some people who don't like to use the term 'bird watcher' just don't know what they're missing by not going out with the little-old-ladies-in-tennis-shoes type of bird watcher."

The well-known radio and television wildlife and pet specialist Roger Caras went to the defense of the bird-watching little old ladies in tennis shoes. He said on a CBS broadcast:

> There was a time when it was almost an insult to describe bird watchers that way. People seemed to think of them as bleeding hearts and Bambi-lovers. But what actually is their stance?
>
> Well, they don't think very much of leg-hold traps. They don't think hurting is a "kick." They don't like rodeos with calves being terrorized and bruised. Most of them fed birds and studied birds in their environment long before the hot-shot ecologists came along and staged rock concerts in tribute to gentle, singing creatures.
>
> Those little old ladies in tennis shoes formed garden clubs and fought for the aesthetic integrity of their communities in the face of name-calling and rock-throwing.
>
> They fought against roadside animal slums used as come-ons for junky gift emporiums.
>
> They fought the destruction of wetlands. They got endangered wild flowers legal protection.
>
> They fought to save trees and to build humane animal shelters. They paid veterinarians to care for stray dogs and cats and adopted them by the millions. They fed those they couldn't adopt. They had their pets spayed.
>
> They wrote their checks, large and small, and supported the very organizations and societies we all are now so proud to join.
>
> In short, those little old ladies in tennis shoes were there first. They cared first. They understood first. In fact, they were the first of us to graduate from people to human beings. Times have changed. Now it is an *honor* to be identified with these *ladies with the human conscience.*

Richard H. Pough, now of the Natural Area Council, would agree, for it is such ladies who have done so much to help preserve sanctuary land. But Pough disdains the "nature-trail school" of bird identification. "It smacks of environmental stamp collecting," he says. Pough believes that people should get the whole picture of the dynamics of nature from fungi to cloud cover. Pough likes to think of the forest as a chemical factory powered by the sun. His three-volume work for the National Audubon Society—*Audubon Water Bird Guide*, *Audubon Land Bird Guide*, and *Audubon Western Bird Guide*—is designed to give the reader insights into each bird's role in the ecosystem. Unlike the Peterson field guides, they are carefully compressed encyclopedias.

Close birding friends, Pough and Peterson have made many bird trips together. Shortly after World War II they toured Europe together to inspect the Camargue, the great marsh at the mouth of the Rhone in the south of France. Both men were so preoccupied with their exploring that they kept pushing farther in. Suddenly they came upon the newly exploded carcass of a cow. They realized they had ventured into an area that had been mined by the Germans. The birders expected to be blown sky-high at any minute. Roger, who had spent part of his war years as an army draftsman on camouflage and worked with enemy mine techniques, knew something about mines and explained to Pough that this gave him some insight into the German military mind. The Germans, he said, would have planted the mines beneath the tussocks rather than in the surrounding mud. Pough disagreed. Peterson, he feels, is sometimes vague about nonbirding matters, and Pough argued that his friend had it wrong. The Germans, Pough said, would have mined the *mud*, not the tussocks.

The two men were unable to reach an agreement, so they gingerly retraced their steps, with Peterson taking the mud route and Pough going from tussock to tussock. Dick Pough laughs now, "but it was no joke then."

James Fisher once said that bird watchers have many different drives and directions. Some like to work alone, to discuss things with few. Roger liked to bird alone when he was a boy. He still likes to bird alone, but he is more gregarious today and enjoys being with others interested in the same pursuit.

Belonging to a birding group intensifies the pleasure for many bird watchers. "Some," James Fisher said, speaking largely for his British birders, "have lost count of the clubs they belong to. To be quite clubless is to be on the bank, with the streams of warm companionship, benign freemasonry, scientific criticism and encouragement, flowing ever more deeply by. . . . The brotherhood of the bird club has contributed more than a little to the cause of international understanding and friendship. Our hobby knows no more political boundaries than the birds. Its devotees exploit nobody, compete only in excellence and thoroughness, take little, give much."

The A.B.A. was organized "to promote the hobby and sport of birding, to educate the public in the appreciation of birds and their contribution to the environment; to contribute to the study of birds in their natural habitat; and to contribute to the development of improved methods of population studies of birds."

The A.B.A. works with other organizations, such as the Nature Conservancy, to preserve birding habitats. Members are asked to suggest such areas, and there is the magazine *Birding*, a bimonthly devoted to birding activities. Many joint trips are arranged for birders, including international field trips.

There are, of course, a variety of ways to compile lists of birds seen. They may be daily, yearly; by locality, state, North America, or the world, or any other variations.

"I remember when I was a boy," Roger recalls, "I was not really interested in any bird that occurred outside of Chautauqua County, New York. I never had seen a night heron before at that time, but one day I crossed a little stream called Silver Creek into Cattaraugus County—and there I found a night heron on the other shore. So I chased it back into Chautauqua County and put it on my list." When a bird watcher tells you he or she has a new "lifer" or "life bird" it means that the individual has spotted for the first time a species new to him or her.

Since birding has no referee or judge, the question may be asked: "How can one know that everyone is playing the game honestly?" The answer is that even in simple day-to-day birding, a player's level of competence and self-discipline can't be hidden. Any birder who reports a species he is unable to show his fellow birders soon destroys his own credibility. Rare sightings are seldom officially accepted unless they are confirmed by other competent observers.

Ludlow Griscom, in the early days of bird watching, shot the bird to prove his identification was correct. That was the custom of the day. Fortunately, that practice is now rare.

The goal of the A.B.A. is to uphold the integrity and simple pleasure of birding—as an antidote to the snobbery sometimes displayed by the academicians, says Roger. He is an active member but says that he has never pursued listing as a personal game or goal. The late Allan Cruickshank and Joe Taylor, who birded competitively with Roger and knew his intense one-upmanship, would deny this.

With the years, Roger's travels tend to be more and selective; not to build lists, "though I have seen the bluethroat in Japan, not in Alaska where it also occurs; and I have seen the Aplamado falcon in Mexico, but not north of the Mexican border in Arizona where it is sometimes seen." Roger has seen over 100 birds that are on the A.O.U. checklist, but he has not seen them within our continental limits.

Roger indulges in "Big Days," "Christmas Counts," and special sightings, but he prefers to emphasize his capacity as a naturalist—a generalist, actually—and an interpreter. And, he says, frankly, he is really the one who, through his field guides, has stimulated birding more than anyone else.

Notwithstanding all the birds Roger has seen, he is currently most anxious to see and photograph the kagu, a bird native to New Caledonia that looks something like a plover and a heron, and New Zealand's notornis, a big gallinule-like bird. The latter was thought to be extinct until, reportedly, seen recently.

Stuart Keith first became enthusiastic about Roger, whom he had never met, when he read *Wild America*. He was a young Englishman new to America, and when he read of the Peterson-Fisher 30,000-mile trip around the North American continent, he wanted to do it too. So he and his younger brother, Anthony, bought an old station wagon and set out, with *Wild America* in one hand and Roger's field guide in the other. The trip took seven months.

Afterward, Keith wrote Roger and told him about the trip. Roger was delighted, and invited Keith to Old Lyme. And what was Keith's first impression of Roger when they met?

"Awe"—Keith smiles as he recalls the day—"awe. I was in the presence of a great man. He was such a big name in birds. And physically he made an imposing figure. I did feel a little embarrassed, too, because I had seen more birds on my trip than he had with James Fisher. But he did not cross-examine me."

The two men became great friends, birding together in many places: Japan, Greece, Africa, Scotland, the Pribilofs, and elsewhere.

Joe Taylor is another staunch birding companion, who has known Roger for at least thirty years. It is a friendship that permits Taylor to speak of Roger with frankness and affectionate criticism.

"I can forgive Roger for sometimes rambling on and on, and not always being cohesive at lectures, but there was one meeting where Roger's talk was complete reminiscence and he held the audience spellbound. This was at the first national meeting of the A.B.A. at Kenmore, North Dakota, in 1973."

At the dinner Roger did something that surprised Taylor no end. He explained:

"After twenty years Roger had finally finished, with Edward Chalif, *A Field Guide to Mexican Birds*, and he wanted everybody to know it. He had brought with him leaflets printed by Houghton Mifflin describing the new book. He walked through the dining room and placed the brochure about the book at each table. This did not upset anybody."

According to Taylor, "Nobody can get away with things like Roger. Everybody was so pleased that Roger had finally finished the book that he got cheers! Anybody else might have been run out for self-advertising."

Taylor is not hesitant to say that Roger's *original* field guide is "antiquated" and "not the best by a long shot when you compare it with the Golden Press guide." [*Birds of North America* by Chandler S. Robbins, Bertel Bruun, and Herbert S. Zim, and illustrated by Arthur Singer.] Taylor says Roger's old field guide "is especially difficult on a cold day when you are wearing gloves or mittens." He eagerly awaits the new one.

Asked if bird watching would be as popular today if there had been no Roger Tory Peterson, Taylor replied, "Good Lord, no! The fact is that the general interest in the whole outdoors and the environment had been growing, and Roger has provided his piece of the movement."

Taylor recently told a reporter that he had become interested in birding at the age of ten. "It was an excuse to avoid filling the coal furnace." At that time he did not want to have it generally known that he was so active "because it was a bit sissy."

It was certainly not sissy. Many of our finest ornithologists were bird watchers from the age of ten or eleven. John James Audubon, Frank Chapman, Alexander Wetmore, Ludlow Griscom were bird watching even earlier than that. Apparently ornithologists have always felt bird watching was something young boys could do in perfectly masculine fashion. (Professor Arthur Allen of Cornell University, as director of the Laboratory of Ornithology, sent out a questionnaire to the fellows of the A.O.U. to find out their ages when birds became an interest and "every last one of them was launched before he was out of his teens and 90 percent by the age of ten.")

National organizations, such as the Royal Society for the Protection of Birds, in Britain, and the National Audubon Society, in the United States, represent large and well-organized forces for conservation and preservation of birds. But, like the new A.B.A., they, too, encourage bird watching for the *fun* of bird watching.

No bird watcher who attended the 1961 annual Audubon convention in Corpus Christi has forgotten the fun and thrill of seeing the whooping cranes at Aransas, or the cowboys at the King Ranch.

A most amusing incident occurred on the trek to the King Ranch. There were about 1,200 members there, including Roger Tory Peterson, Carl Buchheister, John Baker, Rosalie Edge, and other leaders. Bus after bus set out one morning to the King Ranch, a long dawn-to-dusk trip.

All of the sightseers had been having a most delightful time—shouting "Bird! Bird!" as they trained their binoculars out the windows of the buses. But enthusiasm began to run out in the normal course of things. There were no rest rooms on the buses, no rest rooms out on the rolling prairies. The bus arrived at the King Ranch at noon. The "facilities" were quickly overtaxed. A goodly number of the birders, predominantly older women, began drifting off as inconspicuously and as rapidly as possible down to an arroyo with a few small trees and shrubs and rocks.

This was all fine until a leader suddenly had a worrisome thought. King Ranch cowmen confirmed his fears. Picking up his bullhorn, the leader called out:

"Ladies! Please be aware! There are apt to be rattlesnakes down in a place like that!" There was a remarkably quick exodus from the gully.

There is another story about the enthusiastic birding ladies going to Texas during the migration season. Rockport is one of the best places to go to see this fabulous display, and for years many birders have stayed at the Rockport Cottages, which were run by the well-known birder Connie Hager.

One season a guest arrived late, when the cabins were all filled. Mrs. Hager told her she would have space a little bit later. One was being cleaned up at the time. "Dr. Peterson has just checked out," she said.

"Dr. *Peterson?* Not *the* Dr. Peterson—Roger *Tory* Peterson?" exclaimed the excited lady.

"Yes, indeed," replied Mrs. Hager. And the birder looked at her and said, "Do me a favor. *Don't* change the sheets."

The story has been told by Sandy Sprunt and others. Roger does not deny it.

Roger is not what is usually described as a "ladies' man." There is no doubt, however, that women flock to his lectures and sign up for his birding trips like migrating birds themselves. He has a gentle, exceedingly patient way with women. It is partly due to his own endless enthusiasm about birds which he wants to share with everyone who wants to know about birds, whether they are small boys or old men or women of any age. But his eye is quick to spot a pretty face or figure. It is not always a bird he is looking at so intently through his binoculars. "When I see an attractive woman," he admits, "I may even have a flirtation," but adds quickly, "Nothing ever happens."

Although men and women have always been fascinated by watching birds, it was not until about 1900 that bird listing in an organized way began. Dr. Frank M. Chapman, of the American Museum, organized what was then called the "Christmas Census," which is now known as the "Audubon Christmas Bird Count." Chapman first had the idea at a time when gunners took to the woods and fields on Christmas Day to see how many wild creatures of any sort they could shoot. These included songbirds, which at that time were not protected by law.

That first bird census on Christmas Day, 1900, saw twenty-seven observers take to the field and Dr. Chapman received twenty-five reports from across the country which he published in *Bird Lore* magazine.

Sixteen years later the project was set up so that each group of observers would be limited to an area fifteen miles in diameter on any one of fifteen days during the Christmas season, starting December 16.

Today there are more than 27,000 Christmas-list bird watchers in 1,100 or more areas from the West Indies to Alaska reporting on eighty million or so birds. A special bimonthly Audubon publication, *American Birds*, in collaboration with the U.S. Fish & Wildlife Service, is over five hundred pages long and is an overwhelming document, a source of bird information that staggers the mind. Tucked in it are occasional comments, little items, like the one in 1971 by Henry N. Halberg on "How We Counted Forty Million Blackbirds." "It is to be noted," he says, that "40,000,000 blackbirds would require 17.50 million ounces of food per day, or 1,100,000 pounds (550 tons); a sizable daily intake from one foraging area, and a whopping seasonal total."

But the bird lister may not be thinking of that; or he may not be watching at all, but rather listening, making his count from the songs and sounds of the birds. Roger says that "in wooded country and around farms and in marshes and swamps, I do more than 90 percent of my own field work by ear."

The person who has a good ear, he says, can do the bulk of his field work by ear. But he must do his homework with birdsong records and cassettes. Roger often plays these records and cassettes as he works. They relax him. And he enjoys them.

One of the thrills of a lifetime is to see a rare bird like the ivory-bill woodpecker or the Ross's gull. And in March 1975 a Ross's gull *did* turn up off the shores of Salisbury, Massachusetts. It was a bird that Roger had never seen. Bird watchers from all over the

United States came with the wildest enthusiasm to see "the Bird of the Century."

The Ross's gull is so rare that it is seldom seen even in its normal habitat along the rivers of Siberia, and Roger says no one is quite sure where they spend their winters.

Ross's gull is a small, gray-winged sea gull distinguished by rosy chest markings, a wedge-shaped tail, and red feet. It is named for Sir James Clark Ross of the British Royal Navy, who collected one by shooting it in June 1823.

"It has always been the glamour bird to the hard-core bird watchers," Roger says, "so when this bird turned up next to Salisbury at Newburyport Beach, it was great ornithological news."

Word of the sighting of the rare bird reached Roger at work in his studio at about 8:30 in the evening of Saturday, March 3, 1975. Within fifteen minutes he had had three calls. Thanks to a grapevine, hot-line telephone-notification program called Rare Bird Alert, or just R.B.A. (a national, highly reputable service sponsored by state Audubon societies), the word went out to hard-core birders with instant speed. The Ross's gull had been spotted by a group of four bird watchers, among whom were a young man from Vermont, Paul Miliotis, and a local couple. The group sighted it at eleven o'clock near a boat ramp at Black Rock Creek at Salisbury Beach State Park.

Their first word went to the birder Davis Finch and to Noble S. Proctor, an assistant professor of biology at Southern Connecticut State College. Paul Buckley of the National Park Service in Massachusetts had confirmed the sighting. That was about 8 P.M. Proctor, who lives at Branford, Connecticut, telephoned Roger at Old Lyme and invited him to accompany him to Massachusetts to see the gull. Branford is only about twenty-five miles from Old Lyme, and Proctor arrived at Roger's home at 3:30 A.M., Sunday.

"Roger was having breakfast," he says, "spaghetti and a cup of hot cocoa. His schedule is so busy and constant that I assumed it was his supper and that he had been working through the clock."

Actually Barbara had been up, too, most of the night helping Roger with cameras and his binoculars and winter parka—"the *Lindblad Explorer* bright red parka."

"We loaded his gear," says Proctor. "There were two Nikon

cameras and lenses ranging from 50, 135, 400, and 600 mm. Lots of film. Also tripods and binoculars."

By 4 A.M. the two men were on their way. They arrived at Salisbury Beach at 7 A.M. They went to a diner for coffee and found Miliotis there. Within a few minutes the group headed out for the shore and the boat ramp.

The sun was just rising on a very cold, bleak, and windy March day. Proctor's diary describes what happened:

> During the next three hours we milled about. More people arrive, swelling the crowd to some forty or more. Roger, Paul, and I go over to the entrance side of the harbor to scan the area, drink coffee, and worship the sun's rays.
>
> People continue to arrive and now reporters from *The New York Times* and the Boston *Globe* are on the scene. Main focus is Roger, for his impressions. He explains he just may have missed seeing one off Spitsbergen. Sir Peter Scott had identified it but Roger didn't get a good look and bird has never really been confirmed as 100 percent good. Therefore this was a "life" for Roger to add to the spirit of the occasion. Few more people arrive.
>
> 10:15: Miliotis nudges me and tells me to get a scope on a gull out in the cut. [At this time Roger had wandered back to the parking and boat-launch area with his longtime friend Don Alexander. This area was some three hundred yards from us.] I put the scope on the bird just as it banks and can see the pointed tail. I yell, "It's the bird! No question!" We yell to the other group.
>
> Roger, bedecked in his Antarctic parka, is seen outrunning the entire group to our area. I have the bird in the scope and Roger takes over. He confirms it. "That's it for sure." He watches it at length. The crowd watches the bird as it flies about for some five minutes, dipping to water and up in air. Then it disappears into the inner harbor area. All satisfied and talking, we mill back to the parking lot and head over to the village of Newburyport where the bird has been seen on the mud flats behind the coal yard—a longtime birding spot for Massachusetts and visiting birders. We snake our way to town in a long caravan. About six miles.
>
> At the harbor the people all set up scopes. Ranks of them.

An optical battalion. The gull is quickly found sitting on the flats with Bonaparte gulls. It is studied at length as it flies, feeds, and preens. Quite far away for photos, but people try.

Roger is just as excited about photographing people and runs about taking all sorts of snapshots. (I took one for Roger with him in the group and the ranks of scopes. I used his camera.)

We mill about exchanging views. The group follows the bird up the road as it moves about the flats.

12:30: The crowd breaks up as the edge of the mud flats are mid-harbor. At 1:30 the tide should push the bird back in closer. Roger and I go to Don Alexander's house for a nice fish chowder, tea, and scone lunch.

1:30: Roger and I return but no gull in sight. Crowd now has moved back to Black Rock Creek area. We circle around. On way into park see a group of my friends. They had just seen a tufted duck in the creek. Roger needed this for his U.S. list. We quickly locate the area where it was last seen and plunge headlong across the light snow cover of the marsh grass and the few inches of water. This is really hard-core for Roger as he has sneakers on and the first step his feet are thoroughly soaked. We walk some one hundred yards in this and sight up the ditch. There sits the tufted duck (a drake). Roger is elated. "Good to finally pin down that European one for the U.S." (I believe that was his statement.)

The bird finally flushes and heads out over the marsh. We go back to the car and drive on to the group at the point. We take some pictures of Bonapartes. Roger talks with *Times* reporter [John Kifner of Boston] and photographer runs numerous pictures of Roger in several poses as well as while he photographs.

We decide to call it a day at three o'clock and head back to Connecticut.

At Roger's home the calls are starting to dribble in. Several papers call for his opinion on how the bird got there. We filter through books in Roger's massive library, lining up all the information ever written on the bird. We then go up into his magnificent studio and another full library of books. Calls continue and Roger patiently repeats for each person the events of the day and his feelings on the birds.

11 P.M.: I head home. Quite an adventure!

Roger had no sleep for twenty-three hours and was overstimu-lated. "I don't have to take drugs," he said once. "I get my 'kick' from birds."

How the Ross's gull happened to be so far from its native haunts can only be conjectured. One assumption was that it had simply been caught unexpectedly in a jet stream of air and carried thousands of miles across polar vasts from Siberia to Greenland, perhaps. However, Roger had a different theory:

"I believe that the bird was wandering around along the Arctic coast of Alaska, and found itself at the mouth of the Mackenzie River and followed it straight up as it would a straight river in Siberia, then got mixed up with a flock of Bonaparte gulls that live in Alaska. The Bonaparte gulls, when they leave their nesting grounds in Canada, come in great numbers East by way of the Great Lakes to our Atlantic coasts. In other words, it came over-land with the Bonapartes rather than taking the long way around. It had no way of knowing." Other ornithologists had other opinions but everybody agreed that seeing the Ross's gull "really was something." "When we reached the beach to see the gull," Roger said, "there were already fifty-nine telescopes trained on the Merrimack River. More and more people came." Roger counted fifty-nine people, twenty-nine with tripods, lined up aiming at the gull! In fact there was such an army of assorted bird watchers, local police became concerned about what was going on and came out to the dune to investigate.

When one policeman was told the people had come to see the gull with pinkish tinges, he said, "Well, if I had seen a pink sea gull, I wouldn't tell anyone about it."

CHAPTER XV

Photographer and Film Maker

PHOTOGRAPHY has been a persistent and inescapable preoccupation with Roger, and at one point a number of years ago, he said that he was even more enamored of it than painting.

"I don't think I really meant it that way," Roger qualified the statement recently. "I don't *prefer* photography to painting. I *enjoy* photography more. But I *am* an artist. Painting has always been my first ambition. Painting is sweat and blood—and pleasure mixed with agony. It is extremely hard and demanding work. I find in photography a kind of relaxation. It has a kind of therapeutic effect on me. I enjoy it. Painting is so demanding. I do not do it easily. Furthermore, photography is not as confining as painting."

The boy who sought the open fields and envied the birds their freedom of flight still becomes restless after prolonged concentration at his easel and must fly away to other lands every so often, always with a load of camera equipment to add to his pleasure. "I go to India for a whole month of it, and that will last me for a while and then I'll get itchy feet again."

Photography is not as frustrating as painting, Roger believes. At times, of course, photography *can* be frustrating, due to the fact that the bird will not always cooperate or the equipment malfunctions.

Roger once traveled a thousand miles to photograph a Kirtland's warbler only to have his camera shutter jam. And he has never forgotten his embarrassment that day at the opening of the Audubon Camp in Maine when he photographed the first arrivals—with no film at all in his camera. Many an expert photographer has suffered similar frustrations.

"It is frustrating and discouraging, too," Roger says, "when you're doing a book and submit six hundred photographs and have only four or five accepted." This happened when Roger Peterson co-authored *The Birds* for the Time-Life Nature Series. Yet thousands of his photographs have appeared in books and magazines.

Roger has about 100,000 transparencies filed in his Old Lyme studio. He has over 10,000 on penguins alone for his full-length book on penguins.

Though thousands of Roger's photographs have been taken for publication and illustration for his writing, most of his pictures are taken for the sheer joy of photographing. Also, Roger uses his photography for reference material for his painting, not that he paints from the pictures, but to check detail and accuracy. Where many photographers throw out their less successful pictures, Roger saves most of them. He has found that even some of the worst ones can be useful as research material for certain drawings, depicting, for example, "how a bird holds its foot, or the way a leaf turns, or the way light comes through the trees or over water."

The problem of photography, Roger feels, is that while it can record what the camera sees, it does not intellectualize or edit. Roger in his painting uses his eyes and experience to accomplish this. "Photography can be as much of a personal expression as painting if the photographer is aware of the limitations of the camera and uses it in such a way that conveys exactly what he has in mind, the feeling he wishes to portray. It is basically a matter of seeing and *then* using the camera in such a way that the impression is captured—*and in a moment in time*. That is the important thing. A photograph is a permanent record of a bird at *that given instant*. A photograph can only freeze one aspect of a bird."

Roger has taken a great number of pictures that might be called "straightforward portraiture," with the bird filling up a large part of the frame. Others are "documentary"—behavioral.

Jane Kinne says that the minute you look at one of Roger's photographs you know that the person who took it knew what was important in the subject. Roger knows so well that it is behavior which is important in the bird or animal.

Robert Hernandez, a young naturalist and bird student who works with Roger at his studio, says that Roger, when he is photographing, doesn't simply see the bird, but sees the bird in its environment. "By moving from one side to the other, by waiting a few minutes, he perhaps sees it a little bit more than I would see it. For instance we were once out in a marsh in Old Lyme where I had been hundreds of times, and Roger was seeing things, he was feeling things that I hadn't seen before—leaves drifting in the water, patterns in the sand, or even the general overall pictures of patterns of behavior within a given bird. It was quite extraordinary." Robert explains it "as a sort of esoteric quality of perception" rather than just scientific thoroughness.

Now Roger is beginning to explore "in depth, the truly aesthetic, visual impressions of the living things in relation to their environment." His photographs, he says, are becoming more behavioral in the documentary sense. He tries to see things not only as an arrested moment in time, but also as a part of a continuum. This, he says, is what Andrew Wyeth gives us in many of his paintings—"an awareness of time." Roger explored this "awareness of time" in his painting of the snowy owl, where the background of glacier and lichen on the rocks offers a "mood" of the continuity of life.

Recently Roger has shifted, in his photography, from a very literal front-lighting approach, which, he says, would be comparable to a Fuertes drawing without casting shadows, to more side lighting, which gives a more three-dimensional feel. Front lighting, he explains, is a very literal approach, and easier to do.

"I am doing more with back lighting, too, in my painting, even though it does require a bit more control and compensation. Sir Peter Scott has been at his best in his painting in back-lit subjects." Roger says that both side and back lighting provide more "gut feelings" in both photography and painting.

For mood and three-dimensional activity Roger prefers natural light, but when there is no other way to document his subject, he does use strobe lighting equipment that takes flashes up to a thousandth of a second, and which in nature exists "only in lightning." About 95 percent of Roger's camera work is done in color.

Roger has owned so many cameras he can hardly remember them. There was that first Primo Number 9, which he bought with his newspaper money when he was a boy in Jamestown. Later Roger had a Graflex, a Graphic, and some smaller reflex cameras, then two Leicas and several Nikons, two Hasselblads, which he says he finds harder to use than the Nikons. His old four-by-five Graflex had been one of his favorites. There were bellows you peered down through from the top to focus. On the West Coast, Roger was pleased with the "fine photos of albatrosses and nice white pelican pictures" he had taken with the Graflex. It had a seventeen-inch lens. "The equipment weighs a ton," he wrote Clarence Beal in 1940, "but the pictures are worth it." It was this Graflex that got Roger in trouble during World War II on the south shore of Long Island, New York, when he and Edwin Way Teale were checking out a report that a first European goldfinch, a rarity which had not yet been sighted by Roger, had appeared in the area.

When they spotted a "likely-looking bird" darting into a maple, Roger hurried over, "and there, its red face peering at me from amongst the green leaves, was my first European goldfinch, sitting on a nest." The species had never been photographed on this side of the Atlantic. An old door placed across two sawhorses made a platform for Roger's tripod and Graflex. Standing on a tall stepladder, he focused on the nest and wired a remote-control release to flash equipment. Two patriots driving along the Sunrise Highway reported his suspicious operations to the local police, and a patrol car pulled up just as Roger was waiting for the bird to come back. In those early war years everyone was nervous about spies along the south shore. Only a week before several German spies had been captured after landing from a submarine a few miles to the east.

When Roger told the officer he was after goldfinches the policeman asked, "British or American?"

"British!" Roger gasped in astonishment. The policeman had heard about the bird and even had a field guide with him. Peterson and Teale got the picture.

Ever since Roger started taking his own moving pictures for his Audubon lectures he has relied on six movie cameras—two Bolex, a Bell and Howell, an Aeroflex, a Beaulieu, and a Kodak Cine Special.

Roger has enough filters and lenses, ranging from close-up to 1,000-mm telescopic models, to fill a wheelbarrow. He has a reputation for taking too much of it on his trips.

Sandy Sprunt says that as long as he has known Roger, "he has always been slung about with so much gear."

On one occasion when Sandy Sprunt and Roger were in Trinidad photographing oil birds the two men were "dripping equipment all over the place." They had strobe lights and flashlights because the cave where the oil birds were was pitch black. It was also wet. They had to follow a stream into the cave. "Roger"— Sandy laughs as he recalls the picture—"had taken off his pants at the entrance of the cave and was absolutely festooned with camera gear." Sandy was pantless too, trying to hold the flashlight so Roger could see, when Roger dropped his glasses. Roger wears glasses only when he is working with cameras or painting, and here in this black cave, he had to have them.

The worst of it was that the bed of the stream was full of the pits of oil nuts, which is what the oil birds eat mostly. "They are about the size and shape of marbles," says Sandy, "and they are slimy to boot after they have gone through the oil birds. Well, here Roger and I were practically down on our hands and knees at the bottom of the creek hunting through these oil bird pits." They found the glasses and the photographs turned out to be very good indeed.

There's hardly a person who has traveled with Roger who hasn't told of his overloading himself with equipment when he's on a photographic safari. There's not a companion who hasn't said he'd been conned into carrying some of Roger's equipment. How else could Roger get it to his destination!

Barbara, Jane Kinne has said, refused to go on many trips with Roger because she always ended up carrying tripods and extra cameras and lenses. Barbara was "always sixth or eighth in line and loaded down and couldn't see anything."

It has been reported that on the *Lindblad Explorer* Roger's stateroom was so full of photography equipment that Barbara preferred a cabin below. And once when Roger was photographing storks in the Rhine Valley he went to forty belfries. Barbara said "there wasn't enough room in a belfry for a guide, Roger, me, and all the camera equipment. So after four belfries, I waited in the car, knitting. Besides, belfries are dusty."

Stuart Keith was in Greece once with Roger and a birding group and, as they were going up a mountain, Keith once again noticed Barbara wearily lugging a heavy camera case. "What are you doing with that thing?" he said. "Oh, Roger thought he might want to take a picture," Barbara answered, "so I am carrying it for him."

Keith says he had to prove he was a gentleman. "I couldn't see her carrying the thing, you know, lugging the heavy thing. So I said, 'Let me carry it for a bit,' expecting Barbara to collar Roger ahead and say, 'Why don't you carry your own case?'" Keith ended up by carrying it the whole way.

Barbara Hurst, the attractive young photographer and scuba diver, was on the *Lindblad Explorer* one time when Roger had help—not unintentionally—from willing fans.

"There were quite a few younger people aboard," Barbara Hurst says, "and they all worshiped Roger—from afar mainly—and then one day he said, when they were out on a trip, 'Oh, I wish I had someone to carry my cameras.' Four of us volunteered. We tossed coins to see who would win. We even thought the person who won had cheated somehow!" The winner was Kyra Stephens, an attractive blonde from California.

It has always seemed quite natural to borrow pieces of equipment from other photographers on trips. Russ Kinne, the expert wildlife photographer who is Jane's husband, says that Roger not only borrows equipment, but he is "terribly absentminded about it."

Once in the New Hebrides a woman following Roger's course found a light meter. "Oh, Dr. Peterson," she said, running up after him. "You left your light meter behind at the last place you stopped." Roger thanked her and turned it over and looked at the name on it. "Son of a gun," he said, "how did Russ Kinne beat me to the New Hebrides? I didn't know he'd ever been here." Roger had forgotten that he had borrowed the meter from him about a year before and was still carrying it around.

Kinne says Roger does have trouble with his equipment, partly because of his absentmindedness or preoccupation. He may forget to put the camera strap on when he has the camera on his lap, and when he stands up, it sometimes gets "bashed up."

Roger isn't exactly handy with mechanics or tools, and he often calls Russ Kinne, who is an expert with camera equipment, for advice. One middle-of-the-night, Russ was awakened out of a sound sleep by the telephone. It was Roger.

"What's up? Who's dead?" the startled photographer said, then remembered that Roger often didn't know night from day when it came to working.

"Nobody's dead," said Roger. "But what's the matter with this darn camera?"

The next day Russ drove to Old Lyme, about seventy miles from his home in New Canaan, Connecticut, and fixed the camera. "Roger is not the type of fellow who would—or should—venture into the inner workings of his camera," Russ says. "He'd take the battery out and clean it and take a lens out and maybe knock it gently a couple of times or shake it or something and say, 'Well, the mirror's hung up,' but he wouldn't dare try to fix it."

There has always been a surprising camaraderie between Roger and his fellow photographers. "Surprising," some say, because of his intense competitive spirit usually present in such fields of endeavor. Allan Cruickshank, who many critics thought was a better photographer than Roger, was an intimate friend, but they were always in neck-and-neck rivalry. Jane Kinne says she became aware of the one-upmanship between Allan and Roger when Allan was systematically photographing in four-by-five still color every bird species in the United States and Roger promptly followed suit.

Perhaps noticeably intense today is the competition between Roger and George Holton, who, Roger says, is one of the world's better nature photographers. Holton is the Lindblad official photographer and is also with Photo Researchers, Inc. He and Roger are always meeting in the Antarctic or some other exotic place throughout the world. In South Georgia, on one trip, Roger tells of the handsome, lively, colorful George Holton trying to photograph one wandering albatross that was walking away from him. "Don't do that!" shouted George. "Go that way! Turn this way!" Roger, attuned to animal behavior, just waited until the bird came his way "while George was getting into a tizzy hot-footing after it." The albatross deliberately stopped and looked at Roger, and posed as Roger got "a half a dozen excellent shots," then took off before George made a shot. "Thank you, George," said Roger.

Certain countries appeal to Roger more for bird photography than others. Particularly sensitive to color, Roger likes especially the birds of Australia. "They are big and colorful. They are exciting. They are fairly tame." Many areas of the world are heavily wooded and in such places, rain forests, for instance, it is difficult to see the birds. But in Australia and in the African veldt, "You can really photograph and show people birds."

In Africa, Roger thinks of the average tourist on safari as a lineal descendant of the big-game hunter interested in the so-called big four—the lion, elephant, rhino, and buffalo. But there is a difference! A single lion may yield a thousand photographic trophies, but only one head for the den wall of the gunner. As the late Aldo Leopold, the great conservationist and author of *A Sand County Almanac*, said, "the camera industry is one of the few innocuous parasites on wild nature."

Roger is insatiable when it comes to taking photographs, especially of penguins. Francisco Erize, the Argentinian ornithologist, who is working on a field guide of South American birds, was a nature leader with Roger on the *Lindblad Explorer* in 1974. Erize said they spent five days camping in the penguin colony at Punta Tombo, Argentina, fighting very strong winds most of the time. Normally under those circumstances "you don't feel like taking pictures at all, and you don't give a damn for the birds either," said Erize, "but you have this Magellanic penguin colony of about a million birds or something and a very interesting cormorant colony. Walking from the base camp a mile away, you are unprotected from the windstorms bringing a lot of sand into your face and clothes and into your cameras. And bursts of rain. Roger would take pictures as long as there was film in his camera. I would see him standing up against that wind shooting cormorants against the edge of the sea or composing them with the whitecaps of the waves which might make nice patterns. A couple of evenings he said he still felt that he hadn't taken enough pictures of those Magellanic penguins and he would put his strobe on his camera and go on taking pictures at night. He must have taken fifty spools in five days."

His film making is being limited these days as Roger concentrates more and more on his painting, although in that medium his artistic talents come through with great finesse.

According to Ellen Lank, wife of David Lank, Roger, in his prize film on the Galápagos, didn't use the motion-picture camera to show motion. He "used it more as a brush, as an artist would. He lingered on long, long shots. One in particular was a long shot of black volcanic rock." Roger confirmed this idea and went on to suggest that as an artist he often started "shooting" with the head of the bird and then went on to the whole bird. Roger said he was a very sensuous person and he said he used the camera sensuously.

Is photography art? Lank has heard it argued both ways. "Really what photography is, is seeing; trying to make the camera record what you see. You're not doing it with the dexterity of hand, you're not translating in that way. So you can argue that it's a mechanical translation of what your eyes see. Painting requires not only the ability to see, but also the ability to translate somehow through your hands to the paper." Some photographers and others would argue this point, Lank admits. Others say, "Is it not Roger's ability to make his camera capture the behavior of the animal in its environment, sweeping his camera slowly as a paint brush—is that not art?"

In any event, Roger has found photography fun and recreation and "therapy," and, in addition, "the best way of preserving a record of my bird adventures."

One of the most exciting and difficult of these adventures was in the South American Andes where Roger had accepted an assignment from *Life* magazine and the Peabody Museum at Yale University to photograph the "lost" nesting grounds of the James's flamingo. The James's flamingo, a rosy-red bird with dark red legs and eye patches, had been believed to be extinct since 1906. Three expeditions were sent out, in the second of which Roger participated, in December 1957. The altitude in Bolivia was fourteen thousand feet or more, the location nearly inaccessible. Breathing was painful. Even lifting one's feet was an effort. A strenuous way to spend Christmas.

Furthermore, the flamingos, several thousand of them, had established their nests about three miles out, almost in the center of Laguna Colorada, "the Red Lake," which is more salty than the sea. The lake was of Plasticine-like mud of varying depths. Roger and his Chilean entomologist companion Señor Luis Peña, who had confirmed the presence of the flamingos there in the first expedition, got to the colony twice, but it took five attempts in five days to do so. So high was the altitude that a half inch of ice kept them from starting early. Wading through red mud, and using aluminum poles to test the depth of the lake, the men wore hip-high rubber wading boots to protect their legs somewhat from the salt crystals, which cut into the flesh. Once in the quagmire, Roger lost his red cap, which was the only identification the native guide could spot; he thought the photographer had been swallowed by the mud. But Roger made it. "I had a full hour to photograph," he says, "using the 400-mm lens." Then came rain, hail and snow. Retreat to the camp on the Bolivian border was even more horrendous through the viscous, rubbery mud.

A most spectacular telescopic photograph was taken by Roger of hundreds of James's flamingos with their conical mud nests of eggs in the foreground, one egg to a nest. The flamingos actually incubate their eggs with snow on their backs. Roger was hidden in a mud blind, and beyond were the great awesome blue mountains of the Andes. The picture was a double-page spread in *The World We Live In*, published by Time-Life several years later, in 1960.

Roger was quite certainly the first naturalist to see all of the six species of flamingos in the world in the wild. From his first acquaintance with flamingos in the Camargue in southern France to the Andes and to Africa, from the Marismas in Spain, from the Galapagos to the Bahamas and to Miami's "Flamingo Derby," Roger photographed the "corny-looking bird." His film *Flamingos of Four Continents* was shown in Finland at the International

Ornithological Congress and was on Canadian Broadcasting Corporation television as well as at countless Audubon Society meetings.

Roger has been very active in documentary film making, especially in Canada, where he has acted as cameraman, as consultant, and actor-participant for several television series. The first full-length film he became involved with was a four-hour installment on the Galápagos Islands. It was the first color television show in Canada. Parts of it are still being shown in the United States and Canada. In fact, at the 1975 Royal Art Museum worldwide wildlife exhibition, so many people came to see Roger present the film that the building overflowed and they had guards lock the doors to keep out the crowds, causing a minor near riot.

Roger had been on the Galápagos International Scientific Expedition before, in 1964, representing the National Audubon Society, and so was well prepared to do the filming for the CBC. To Roger, the Galápagos Islands, in the Pacific six hundred miles west of Ecuador, have been a sort of Eden "before the fall" and have enchanted him more than any other primitive island area, except perhaps the Seychelles in the Indian Ocean—"a different kind of Eden."

The cluster of jagged cinder cones, tortured lava flows, and basalt cliffs look, he wrote, as if they might belong to the moon. Iguana, cacti, mockingbirds thrive on the arid terrain, and, of course, the giant tortoises, the Sally lightfoot crabs, and the especially rare Galápagos penguins and flamingos. A reporter for the San Francisco *Chronicle*, David Perlman, who was with Roger on that scientific trip, says there was no limit to Peterson's curiosity and scientific interest. "We came upon some unusual flamingoes one day, and Roger suddenly burst out, 'I've never seen this species of flamingo copulating before—and I don't think anyone else has either.' "

It was here, from the H.M.S. *Beagle* in 1835, that Darwin stepped ashore to begin his studies of finches that were to result in the publication of his revolutionary book on evolution, *On the Origin of Species by Means of Natural Selection*, published in 1859. And it was the *Beagle II*, a fifty-five-foot square-rigged vessel with the silhouette of a tortoise on its sail, belonging to the

179

UNESCO-sponsored Charles Darwin Research Foundation, that took the 1965 CBC television crew from the airport to Academy Bay. Aboard were John Livingston, who was then director of the English-Canadian CBC nature unit; Dr. William W. H. Gunn, "the world's best recordist of natural sounds"; James Murray, the producer; Rolph Blakstad, cameraman; George McAfee; William Banting (son of the insulin discoverer, Dr. Frederick Banting); and Terry Shortt, the Canadian artist, who had come along to get material for a habitat group of the Galápagos for the Royal Ontario Museum in Toronto.

They had 80,000 feet of film available and shot 50,000 feet of it in the six-week period they were there. Gunn recorded about 40,000 feet of sound tape. They had two and a half tons of equipment in thirty-two wooden crates, and with this went hopping from island to island. They even had a refrigerator to keep the film cold.

When Karl Angermeyer, captain of the *Beagle II*, heard how much film they had, he was impressed, but said, "We had a German photographer here last year. He only shot a hundred feet." Roger was incredulous. "Well," Angermeyer said, "*he* knew what he was doing."

It is often difficult to explain why one must shoot so much footage, says Roger. "An Audubon lecturer, on the average, may use only one foot of every three that he shoots, providing he is on a shoestring budget, as most lecturers are. By television standards, one might use only one foot out of ten—or fifteen."

Blakstad was good at mood pictures, landscapes and animals that had a sensuous quality. Roger, being the naturalist, was more aware of behavioral significance.

Gunn became dehydrated by the excessive dryness of the islands and had to go home. Then something happened that occurs in a cycle of seven years. Torrential rains. The cactus forest was covered with millions of diamonds. "We rushed out to film the event." In fact the desert sprouted fresh grass and new flowers, new insects. Where Darwin said the insects were few, drab, and disappointing, Roger did not find them so. "I saw things that Darwin never saw, nor William Beebe of the Bronx Zoo on his brief visit."

Roger was fascinated by the finches. One of his favorites was

Scandens, "the climber"—the cheeky one, the clown. Terry Shortt, in *Not As the Crow Flies,* wrote, "I was giving Roger a haircut one day and as quickly as the silvery locks fell on the gravel between his feet, a hen *Scandens* gathered them by the beakful and carried them to her nest. How appropriate that a Darwin's finch was lining her nest with hair of the high priest of bird-watching!" The same finches came into Roger's cabin and pulled horsehairs from the mattress on which he was lying. And they unraveled the towels on the clothesline. "Resourceful," says Roger.

Because of the unusual rains, the mosquitoes became a nightmare on that trip. Livingston was driven nearly to despair and said he would never set foot on Hood Island again. They had gone there to film the Galápagos (or waved) albatross, which has its only nesting colony in the world there. The mosquitoes had erupted in such numbers that most of the birds had deserted their eggs. It was a miserable situation. Terry Shortt says that Roger has an amazing capacity to ignore all extraneous matters, even mosquitoes.

When he was concentrating on taking a photograph of a sulphur butterfly sipping nectar from the Opuntia, a cactus plant as high as some trees, "Roger seemed not only unconcerned but actually unaware that his neck and arms were black with fiercely biting mosquitoes. Nothing in the world existed for him save the butterfly and his viewfinder."

Bill Gunn and Roger actually spent a night on Hood Island "to see what it was like after dark." They found a spot on the lip of a sea cliff where there was a good updraft and, by using a mosquito net and plenty of repellent, kept reasonably comfortable. "We saw frigate birds (man-of-war birds) hovering over the cliff edge all through the night, whenever we turned our flashlight beams upwards. And the bird we were most desirous to know at night was the fork-tailed gull, a nocturnal feeder—a bird with huge eyes and a curious clicking call."

On Duncan Island, where they were filming the rare Duncan tortoise with its saddle-shaped shell, Livingston fell among the rocks and broke his cheekbone, "a nasty accident, but it did not inhibit his work on the trip."

And Roger, trying to get a close-up photograph of a Galápagos tortoise at Academy Bay, had a curious episode. "It was during the breeding season," wrote Terry Shortt. Roger was leaning over. He was wearing shorts, and did not see another tortoise coming up behind him, "his rheumy eyes fixed on Roger's bent-over figure. With gestures like a dog, the tortoise marched right up and bit Roger in the calf of his leg. His calves looked like overripe papayas to the tortoise." No tetanus shots were given, but Roger wore long pants from then on.

They filmed the marine iguanas, which live on the islands by the tens of thousands. A three-foot land iguana scampered from under Roger's bed one day. And, of course, there were Roger's penguins to photograph endlessly, as well as the flightless cormorants. They photographed many other things that demonstrated Darwin's principles.

They also told the conservation story as it ties in with tourism. The Galápagos need tourism to help support conservation programs. The $6.00 tax brought by each visitor goes directly to the islands' wildlife protection projects. The entire archipelago is now (since 1965) a national park under Ecuador's jurisdiction. The park has twenty-four wardens and guards. Although only about four thousand people live on the Galápagos, its three thousand square miles must be protected if the wildlife is to survive in some semblance of the state in which Darwin found it.

Photographing in the Galápagos was one of the most difficult assignments Roger has ever had, because of the color contrasts. It was either black lava or white sand, and the birds tended to be dark and match the lava or white and match the sand. One needs the contrast of bright green water and the silhouette of birds against it in some way, Roger explains. On the other hand, the tameness of the birds and wildlife made close-up photography a complete joy.

Roger acted as cameraman and advisor for the CBC in the making of two African films, one of which won an award as the best Canadian documentary of the year. It was especially important because it dealt with the conservation of African wildlife at a time when most of the emphasis seemed to be on social problems.

With Bill Gunn doing the sound recordings, they drove their Land Rover down into Ngorongoro Crater, following three lions half the night, three big males, that swaggered across the plain and sent the herd animals into a panic. "It was an eerie thing," Roger says, "seeing all the herd animals in the headlights of the car, only their eye-shine showing, the zebras running along, their eyes like so many tiny lights, and the eyes of the wildebeest bouncing up and down as their heads bobbed up and down, and the startled fixed stare of the tommies [Thompson's Gazelles] all nervous in the fearsome hours of the night. We carried floodlights down into the crater to film the hyenas make a kill of the wildebeest."

Photographing the very colorful Masai was a problem because of the flies, a special kind of insect that completely covered the close-cropped pates of some of the Masai. The flies stuck like glue to the photographers and their Land Rover. Another tribe, the Molo, at Lake Rudolph, liked to have their pictures taken with flash bulbs—"because" Roger explained, "we would hand them the still warm but burned-out blue flash bulbs. These made good ornaments for their ears."

Canada and Great Britain excel in their natural history programs. According to Roger, both the British Broadcasting Corporation and Anglia present natural history programs in depth. Roger has appeared on many of these programs, many times, with James Fisher and Sir Peter Scott. The United States lags far behind. "Except for Marlin Perkins, Lorne Green, and one or two others, the public has been shortchanged when it comes to natural history documentaries," says Roger. He has no complaints about book publishers. We have some of the best nature books—and magazines —with the best photographs, among them the *National Geographic, Audubon* and *National Wildlife.*

Roger once came to the aid of one of the NBC television shows, *Wild Kingdom*, when his old friend Marlin Perkins was forbidden to take movie footage at Cape Crozier. Roger was already there in the Antarctic, camping in a hut with the scientists of Operation Deep Freeze. He was taking stills of the emperor and Adelie penguins. "No room for camera crew" was the word sent to Perkins, who then suggested "maybe Dr. Peterson could do the filming for him." So for three days Roger "received union cameraman's wages." Without his crew, Perkins joined Roger in Antarctica, where they visited penguins snowed in by a blizzard; Perkins even chopped one out of the ice with an ax. "I did enjoy those three days with Marlin," Roger says. "He does get around, as I do. I ran into him in such far parts of the world as Nairobi, Argentina, and the Falklands."

Roger says photography on any trip is one of the best approaches to natural science there is. The camera to Roger is as essential as his binoculars, whether he is in the marshes and hills of his own Connecticut or down in the Antarctic on the *Lindblad Explorer*. And he likes to think that in spite of his own personal pleasure in photographing he is making the public aware of "our wonderful heritage which could so easily be lost if it were ignored."

CHAPTER XVI

Conservation— and Man's Survival

WHEN Roger Tory Peterson and Guy Mountfort went to south-ern Spain in 1952 to see some species of birds they did not have for their European field guide, they were accompanied by a young man named Mauricio Gonzalez of the famous sherry-making family. While they were riding on their donkeys—Peterson and Mountfort on one donkey and Gonzalez, six feet four inches tall, on another—they started talking about conservation, Roger's favorite subject, next to birds.

"How can one expect people to preserve wildlife in Spain," said Mauricio, "when they do not even know the names of things?"

That has been the basis of Roger's conservation efforts from the beginning of his field guides and teaching years at Audubon. "Recognition is the first step toward preservation. Every birder becomes to some degree an ecologist. In political terms he is a conservationist," he has said repeatedly.

So when he suggested to the Spaniard that it would be fine for nature educators in Spain if a proper scientific body were formed —a Spanish ornithological society—Mauricio took to the idea, but he suspected that not over fifty members would join. A society was started. It grew to three hundred members in two years. The entire conservation movement in Spain came from that double-donkey ride in 1952. Furthermore, Mauricio Gonzalez translated the European field guide into Spanish—and with distinction.

Spain today continues to show more interest in environment and preservation than many countries, according to Roger. Conservation lags in other Mediterranean countries. "It is pretty good in Australia, and I think there is a lot of interest in Japan, but it is incomplete. They certainly don't think very much of whales. In Europe it is on the upswing, as it is in the United States."

Not long after Roger and Guy Mountfort were in Spain, they were able to get the ball rolling through the World Wildlife Fund to preserve the Marismas, the marshes near the mouth of the Guadalquiver River. This sanctuary serves as a nesting ground or way station for birds flying from South Africa to Scandinavia.

With Peter Scott and Ira Gabrielson, Roger was involved early with World Wildlife Fund in 1962, and was on its board of directors until 1976. He received its Gold Medal Award in Spain in 1972, the first American to be given this award, which was presented by Prince Bernhard with Juan Carlos at his side.

Royalty, Roger has said, as it still exists in the world, seems to be almost universally interested in wildlife and preservation. "Perhaps they know all too well what it means to be an endangered species."

Roger had been awarded the Geoffrey St. Hilaire Gold Medal for conservation by the French Natural History Society in Paris in 1958—"for doing more in France than anyone else to interest people in birds; and, for nature conservation, more than anyone else in the world." And there have been other conservation awards—the Audubon Conservation Medal in 1971 and the Green World Award of the New York Botanical Garden in September 1976 for public leadership in environmental affairs.

Conservation has become such a broad term today that it needs defining in terms of nature and wildlife. Barbara once clarified it in a speech she was giving to a Connecticut women's club: "Conservation is not, as many people would like to assume, complete and total isolation of an area or of a species. Conservation is broader than that. Conservation *can* be wise land management. It *can* be total protection for a very endangered species." Conservation,

Roger adds, is more than preserving wildlife. He believes it certainly goes beyond the dictionary definition of "the act of conserving; protection from loss, waste; official care and protection of natural resources." Conservation includes pollution control—halting air and water and land contamination by pesticides, for example. It is also population control.

From the time he was a child, Roger was always something of a reformer. He could not bear the pain of even a trapped skunk.

Years later, when he was sent by the National Audubon Society to Cape May Point to observe the practice of hawk shooting, one can imagine his consternation when a family who had invited him to supper served him hawk pie. They did not realize that a single season's sport by the Cape May gunners could drain the sharp-shins from thousands of square miles of northern woodland.

The National Audubon Society has now established the Witmer Stone Wildlife Sanctuary at Cape May. Hawk shooting is illegal.

Roger started a flamingo conservation project that twenty years later remains of major importance, not only to East Africa, but to the rest of the world. The famous salt lake, Lake Nakuru, is a national park, and at its head, Baharini, a research and educational center has been established to study and protect the flamingos. In *Audubon* magazine, Roger wrote of this extraordinary thirty-two-square-mile saline lake with its "staggering" millions of delicate flamingos and pleaded that it be made a sanctuary. The article reached the Nakuru press and the town council, which then did designate the entire lake a sanctuary. A year after his article appeared, the Ministry of Tourism and Wildlife in Kenya received more requests for information about Lake Nakuru than for any other tourist attraction in the country, and it became a national park in 1967.

In other countries—France, in the Camargue at the mouth of the Rhone River, the French protect the only active colony of flamingos in western Europe; the Bahamas, where he was helpful in getting the National Audubon Society to give guidance—and elsewhere, Roger's influence has been felt. Even the salt companies that own lands and lakes with flamingo colonies (Camargue, Lake Magadi, and Inagua) have cooperated with Roger in his crusade to protect the flamingos.

Roger was not always a subtle politician when it came to bird conservation. Roland C. Clement, a vice president of the National Audubon Society, says Roger's only instinct was to "save the birds." There was the time, he recalls, that Roger went to Japan to the International Ornithological Congress in 1960 and on the way back stopped at Midway. He was terribly distressed about the albatrosses.

The Navy had found the birds' breeding grounds were not only a nuisance but dangerous to the planes. They had tried all kinds of ways to get rid of the birds, even striking them with heavy wooden clubs at the base of the skull. They had actually killed 30,000 nesting Laysan albatrosses in one year. Now they wanted to expand their airport and take over the birds' breeding grounds entirely. The Fish and Wildlife Service objected. The Navy put out its memorable "gooney bird" propaganda film with the admiral saying at the end, "I don't want to be in the position of having to tell some mother that her boy lost his life because of this," and he pointed to the albatross, "deadly enemy of defenseless aircraft." No wonder Roger was distressed.

He went to Clement and found that he had already written John Baker to say that Audubon should take a hand in the situation along with the U.S. Fish and Wildlife Service and counterbalance the Navy's propaganda.

Roger asked to see a copy of the memo. Clement, knowing he shouldn't, showed the memo to Roger because they were "good friends."

"Well, dammit," says Clement, "Roger took that memo to Harold Coolidge in Washington, the key man in the International Union for the Conservation of Nature program. And Coolidge took the memo to the U.S. Navy! It was very indiscreet of Roger, but he is no politician."

Baker, unaware of this exchange, had received his copy of Clement's memo. "Clement has something here. I'll go to Washington and see the Navy," he said, and did.

The admiral handed him the copy of the memo Roger had sent to Coolidge. "You should harness some of your staff people," he told Baker. "This is not very complimentary to the Navy."

Baker was nonplussed. He called New York and got Carl Buchheister, who happened to be in the same office with Clement at the moment. Buchheister cupped his hand over the telephone and said to Clement, "How many copies of that memo did you distribute?"

Clement said, "Only two—one to Baker, one to the editor of *Audubon* magazine. And I, well, I *did* give a copy to Roger."

"My God. It was Peterson! He wouldn't be diplomatic about a thing like this."

Clement was caught in the middle. He went up to the American Museum and saw, among others, Gene Eisenmann, who called a public conference on the albatross problem and invited the Navy to come up and justify itself. There was so much criticism that it backed down on the new airport. The Navy instituted a program of research. The dunes at the end of the runways that created the updrafts were leveled so that non-nesting birds (Roger says "unemployed" birds) would not fly in concentrated spots, on collision course with the aircraft. The albatrosses were saved at Midway.

Clement says Roger is usually "very delicate" but when he is concerned with a mission he "doesn't fool around much when he sets out to accomplish it."

"There is a terrible finality about the extinction of a species," Roger wrote in the *National Geographic* in 1962.

Ever since he and Barbara had moved to Old Lyme in 1954 he had watched the ospreys decline. Bitterns, kingfishers, night herons —whole colonies of fish-eating birds were disappearing from the Connecticut River. Even the bald eagle was in serious trouble along the Atlantic Coast.

Insecticide poisoning by man was said to be the cause. DDT (dichloro-diphenyl-trichloro-ethane) and its derivatives were believed to be the chief destroyers. Sprayed widely over farms and orchards, these chlorinated hydrocarbon pesticides build up in the food chains, and at the top of the biological pyramid are birds, which feel the cumulative impact. Roger describes it this way:

"Traces of poisons ingested by little fish upriver—either in the runoff or through poisoned insects—make them easier prey for larger fish. Numbers of affected fingerlings compound their poisons in the predators, and it is the large fish that is wobbly, swimming near the surface, that is most likely to be caught by the osprey, which transfers the accumulated poisons to its own tissues. Natural selection becomes unnatural selection."

Although the birds laid eggs, most failed to hatch; in some the embryo started to develop, then died. The eggshells were so thin, they broke under the weight of the nesting bird.

Rachel Carson, in her best-selling book *Silent Spring*, published in 1962, had blown the top off the pesticide scandal, but others were to prove that DDT in the eggs could explain the high egg breakage. Joe Hickey, of the University of Wisconsin, was one of the first to show the definite relationship between the chlorinated hydrocarbon pesticides and the thickness of eggshells. The U.S. Fish and Wildlife Service and other scientific groups were active. Paul Spitzer, a neighbor of Roger's and a graduate student at Cornell University, made endless studies on the Connecticut River (and Barbara helped in the surveys). Spitzer brought young ospreys from Maryland, where the ospreys for some reason did not seem to be so affected, and the foster parents accepted the eggs of the Connecticut River ospreys and many of the babies fledged and flew.

In the midst of the DDT uproar Roger was given the opportunity to address a U.S. Senate investigating subcommittee in Washington. That was in 1964, and Roger, as happens when he is angry, pulled no punches about where the blame for pesticide poisoning came from. He was no stranger to pesticide research, having been assigned to DDT studies by the Air Force in 1945, shortly before the U.S. Fish and Wildlife became involved. In those days conservationists did not suspect the residual effects—that a bird only slightly poisoned by these stable compounds might increase their concentration until a lethal threshold was reached. "It is these residual effects that are much more subtle and sinister than the immediate results of spraying," he told the senators.

As to the blame: "The manufacturers of the hydrocarbons ask, 'What would agriculture do without these pesticides?'" Profit-making for industry is inevitable, but some industrial wildlife research laboratories, like Dow Chemical, Roger said, were trying to find less harmful chemicals and still make a profit, "fighting the research battle and also the economic battle."

Roger took on the government: "There is very little effective coordination among the different federal departments and bureaus. . . . The Pest Control Review Board, established by President Kennedy, has exercised no influence over the policies pursued by the Department of Agriculture in the registration and labeling of pesticides in interstate commerce. The Department of Agriculture has been almost arrogant in tending to ignore, even to scoff at, the proven damages to wildlife resources and the potential hazards to human health. The Public Health Service has been ambivalent. With one voice it has warned of the increasing pollution of our streams by the persistent agricultural chemicals. But with another voice it has encouraged the broad-scale use of DDT for the control of nuisance insects—programs aimed at mosquitoes, black flies, and other insects that merely annoy people." He said the Fish and Wildlife Service was not above reproach. Roger recommended that it do advance screening of new chemicals to determine their potential effects on fish and wildlife resources.

And he backed up the recommendation made by Rachel Carson a year before her death in 1964 that Congress create a federal control board and vest it with the powers to regulate the distribution and use of chemical pesticides. "Congress can help by amending the pesticide laws," he challenged them.

That same year Roger told an Audubon group, "Birds are my life, and I cannot sit by while the highly paid public relations men of industry tell the public that there is no pesticide problem, or that it is overstated."

In 1972 DDT was banned in the United States.

And in 1976, Paul Spitzer reported that, due to conservation "transplant" programs, the "reproduction of ospreys is on the upswing for the first time in twenty-five years." A "bumper crop" of 130 young ospreys was found between New York and Massachusetts. The transplanting of uncontaminated eggs and chicks from the Chesapeake area had indeed paid off, and the residues of DDT and other chlorinated hydrocarbons elsewhere are being reduced to levels permitting normal reproduction.

At the time of a gypsy moth and leaf loper infestation in Connecticut in 1971, when trees were stripped of their leaves in areas that could be measured in miles, the sprayers moved in en masse.

Roger saw the butterflies and other Lepidoptera go, as well as the whippoorwill, because there was nothing for it to eat. The area still feels the effects of that one mass spraying.

But Roger thinks that the pests would have gone, even without the spraying. "True," he says, "we went through an unpleasant year—defoliation, and all. The *environment*, however, survived. There's a natural cycle. Various things go to work on the gypsy moths. Not parasites, but natural checks of some sort. The gypsy moths move on—to the next county. A sort of natural pruning takes place. The dangerous thing is that by spraying you knock out some of the natural checks and you could prolong the cycle, the infestation difficulty, rather than help it."

Others have played a vital part in preserving birds and wildlife, of course, but as Edwin Teale expressed it, "If Roger says it, people will pay attention." And Clarence Allen, writing in *The Florida Naturalist*, said that Roger, "together with his good friend Rachel Carson, shared the urge to point the way to fellow Americans on how they can help save the wildlife and the environment on which it thrives." Allen continued, "In his writings, pleading for the cause before congressional committees, serving on leading conservation commissions and boards, Roger has gradually taken his place with world leaders in this vital awakening of public and civic conscience to the effects of pollution and the upsetting of the life cycle."

The effects of pollution on land, sea, or the air disturb Roger. In 1969, at the dedication of the heronry at Stone Harbor, Charles Lindbergh and Arthur Godfrey were both speakers, along with Roger, Ira Gabrielson of the U.S. Fish and Wildlife Service, and Herbert Mills. Bird preservation was the keynote of the meeting, but the ever-growing problem of air pollution came up. Lindbergh commented that if he had to choose between airplanes and birds, he would opt for birds, and, turning to Godfrey, said, "Arthur, someday we might have to give up planes if air pollution tends to accelerate at the rate it has."

Godfrey agreed, and added that when he first took up flying he could often find the city he was headed for simply by sighting the patch of smog over it. This was no longer possible, he said, "because the blanket of smog frequently is so continuous." Lindbergh concurred. Furthermore, he added, aviators, for this reason, are quick to notice what pollution and encroachment of civilization are doing to the land they are flying over.

(Godfrey and his staff had arrived in two helicopters; Lindbergh had driven down in an oldish car, with a sandwich and a cardboard carton of milk for lunch.)

Water pollution concerns Roger—from the nearby Connecticut River to remote Greenland. There he has seen sheets of plastic washed ashore and cans and bottles that simply will not sink. They are signs of man's insult to the environment, possibly thousands of miles away from the place they had been tossed into the sea.

Strolling along the banks of the wide Connecticut River one day, Roger pointed with disgust to the rusting beer and soft-drink cans, and some made of long-lived aluminum. With his companions, he rolled over a log and buried some debris in the sand. There was too much to carry off to a town dump.

His friends, who were yachtsmen, told him of a day's sail on Long Island Sound, and a picnic with a bucket of Kentucky Fried Chicken. The skipper, finishing a drumstick, had tossed it into the water, and then apologized to his ecology-minded daughter who was aboard. "Darn it, I shouldn't have done that! That's polluting." But the teenager reassured him. She piped up, "Oh, that's biodegradable. It will disintegrate and provide food for marine life." Roger beamed. "One more optimistic strike for the future," he said, and added, "Young people have to be optimistic. Young people have more vitality and a life ahead. An older person, he becomes pessimistic—you've got to guard against this."

There has been a "tremendous renaissance" in nature study in recent years, Roger says, but when people speak of a recent breakthrough in conservation and environmental protection, the roots go back much further. "A lot of it was in the Audubon Society work in the early years. It has been cumulative. Finally we have seen the breakthrough to the point where almost everyone knows what the word 'ecology' means today—biology dealing with the mutual relations between organisms and their environment."

In the course of cleaning up an environment, Roger admits that we are losing a special bird environment. "I have always taken the view that some pollution may be a good thing—provided it is organic pollution. Chemical or industrial pollution is more damaging. Very often the best spots for water birds in the lower Great Lakes are the harbors of the cities, rather than in the broad stretches between. Sewage-treatment areas are often very good for shore-birds and other water birds. In fact, what are known as sewage farms in England are always the best places for rare transient waders.

"Conservation must be a positive thing—not approached just from 'No, we mustn't do that' and 'No, that is wrong.' There are times, of course, when we must take stands against such things as indiscriminate dredging or filling in of marshland, but more often we must approach the problem positively, by campaigning *for* open spaces, green belts, preserving marshlands and wildlife."

Shocked by sheepherders and goatherders, and what overgrazing had done to create the Sahara and "wipe out much of Italy, Greece, and Turkey," Roger said he refused to eat lamb chops because of his strong feelings! (But sometimes Roger, paying little attention to what he is eating, doesn't know lamb from veal.)

In Ethiopia in 1974, Roger saw firsthand what hundreds of years of land abuse had done. The great famine had wiped out 100,000 people. With a young man, Tom Tischler, from Texas, who was trying to set up the organization of the country's Simien National Park, Roger was alarmed to see the local tribesmen burning the slopes of their last bits of native vegetation. High on the plateau at nearly 15,000 feet, they saw little wildlife, "a few very rare ibex on the almost inaccessible crags." But he found the view was al-most as spectacular as the Grand Canyon.

"The man-made deserts make the landscape look almost like moonscape," Roger said, depressed by the mutilation of the land. "I have never seen a country in my life that was so completely ruined ecologically. During the last fifty years more than 85 percent of the forest of Ethiopia had been removed." Because of the wasteful methods of threshing, rats were plentiful, as were vultures and birds of prey, including the "elegant" large lammergeir.

Roger has argued against the use of the expression "undeveloped countries" in the belief that there are no such things in terms of renewable resources. "They have already pushed things to the limit with forest lands denuded, marshes drained, and every bit of arable land is under pressure. They are actually *over*developed in this sense. If they possess oil or other mineral resources, they are lucky. If not, they may face ultimate poverty and starvation."

Traveling in Nepal, the independent kingdom between India and Tibet, in 1975, Roger visited a forest, "the last of its kind, a subtropical ecosystem of limited extent with serpent eagles screaming overhead, parties of babblers and titmice trooping through the undergrowth and rare barbets and woodpeckers in the trees." He saw more than seventy species of birds, fifty new to him, and a tremendous variety of butterflies. And then he came upon men hacking away at the trees and undergrowth, women trooping past with great sheaths of leaves to put on the fields.

How long could the ecosystem of Nepal survive such attrition? All over the world Roger has seen vulnerable ecosystems, and in the United States also. He has called it a "universal dilemma, a mutual tragedy involving man and nature—a tragedy from which no country is exempt."

Although it is largely due to overpopulation, that is not the only cause for this dilemma, Roger believes. Nor can population control solve it. But it can help.

Since the time Roger and William Vogt were young men together, the problem of overpopulation had been a prime concern to Roger. Vogt spent years at the Pan American Union and was president later of Planned Parenthood. It is said that Roger took Vogt's cry for birth control so seriously that when Lee was born, Roger was hesitant to report it to Vogt.

Today, with the realization that the world's population may double to eight billion in the next fifty years, Roger is violent in his denouncement of unlimited population, especially in underdeveloped countries. He says man is one of the few animals in the world that has constantly increased over a period of two thousand years, adding, "There have been a few explosive populations in the animal world—usually satellites of man, such as pigeons, chickens, rats, cockroaches, starlings, and things of that sort."

Medical science is partly responsible for man's overpopulation, by bringing about "massive death control," prolonging longevity. For example, Roger says that in Iceland a "young" man of sixty-five is looking for his third wife, and he is still looking for some real action at seventy. In Bangladesh, if a man is thirty-five or forty, he may be called "Grandpa" and is amazed that he has lived all those years. Civilization has brought its own peril to survival. "We have the ability," Roger stresses, "to consciously limit our populations." He believes we must. "But man *can* become extinct" Roger has emphasized in the hundreds of speeches he has made to various conservation meetings, colleges, and institutions. "Man is the dominant animal on Earth and literally can eliminate most of the other forms of life by his own proliferation until he may eliminate himself."

Roger has, as lecturer-leader on the M.S. *Lindblad Explorer*, proselytized on all phases of conservation—wildlife preservation, air, land, and water pollution, and population control. Sometimes his results have been both large and small. Passengers—tourists—raised over $20,000, for example, for the Cousin Island sanctuary on the main island in the Seychelles. Roger, as American chairman of the International Committee for Bird Protection, which bought the island for a sanctuary, was influential in raising thousands of dollars for the Charles Darwin Research Station in the Galápagos. And one lovely Italian lady, who had never thought of preservation before her exposure to Roger, told him one morning, "Today I found a moth in my desk, and I didn't kill it."

Many of the "tourists" on the Lindblad nature tours who have gone just for the ride or just for bird-watching have inevitably become conservationists. If one of them does not observe the rules—"don't pick the plants"; "respect the right of the sea lions" —the fellow passengers quickly reprimand them.

The fundamental theme that Roger continues to preach is that man ultimately is the endangered species, and the extinction of a wild species is a milestone or a road marker of our own decline. "Each one of us is a mine canary," he said at the American Association for the Advancement of Science in 1974. "Like the canaries that miners used to bring down the shafts with them to warn of lethal gas leakage. If we create the political, chemical, physical, and moral environment that other forms of life cannot survive—by what insane arrogance do we think *we* could survive? The animals use the same air, the same water, the same space. Animals use protein, carbohydrates—and if the animals around us are dropping dead we had better take a look—a careful look.

"Birds," he told the A.A.A.S., "are far more than cardinals and jays to brighten the garden, ducks and grouse to fill the sportsman's bag, or warblers and rare shorebirds to be ticked off on the bird watcher's checklist. They are indicators of the environment— a sort of ecological litmus paper. Because of their furious pace of living and high rate of metabolism they reflect subtle changes in the environment rather quickly; they warn us of things out of balance. They send out signals when there is a deterioration of the ecosystem. It is inevitable that the intelligent person who watches birds becomes an environmentalist."

And Roger told the Earth Care Conference in 1975 in New York that while man, as a species, may survive for a long time, there are hundreds and thousands of animals and plants—even entire ecosystems—that are already gone.

"Most people still fail to appreciate the real meaning of extinction. Extinction is not simply the vanishing of the whooping crane. It is not the vanishing of the Andean flamingo, nor the vanishing of the vicuna. It is the termination, the abrupt termination, of a long line of evolution."

In an essay in *This Week* magazine, Roger wrote:

> We are too close to ourselves, much of the time, to see our proper relation to the natural world on which we depend for survival. Watching birds and other animals seems to clarify my perspective; I see demonstrated the natural laws that regulate not only the lives of lesser creatures but also of men, for we are not apart from nature but a part of nature.
>
> Man is only one of more than one million named forms of animal life on this planet, from one-celled protozoa to huge whales. But we, alone of all creatures, have it within our power to ravage the world or make it a garden. Men have already rendered uninhabitable large areas of the world, but they have restored others. Inevitably, observing cause and effect, I have become a conservationist. My fervent desire is to see the soils safeguarded, the waters unpolluted, the forests

and grass lands properly managed and wildlife protected. To attain these ends means not only self-preservation but also a better future for the race. Conservation is plainly a moral issue.

In Roger's philosophy, man's role in nature and conservation can be summed up in these three words: "reverence for life."

CHAPTER XVII

The World's Most Traveled Field Ornithologist

"IF you had your life to live over, how would you have changed it?" Roger was asked in 1974, on the fortieth anniversary of the publication of his first field guide and on the day he announced he was going to devote the rest of his life to gallery painting.

There was not even a pause before Roger gave the answer: "I would have traveled more—and begun sooner." From the time this once mischievous boy of Jamestown rebelled against his father's stern discipline at home and the chiding of his school companions at his "nuttiness" about birds, Roger has longed to be "free to fly away."

In his early youth, lack of money made it impossible for him to go very far. Not until he was to start making lecture tours for the National Audubon Society did he really begin to fulfill his dreams of travel. He went to all fifty states in the United States and all the provinces of Canada when he was lecturing for Audubon. Now he has been to eighty countries and to each of the world's seven continents—Africa, Asia, Australia, Europe, North and South America, and Antarctica. In one year, 1973, he visited all of them and the Arctic as well.

199

It is not surprising that the Explorers Club in New York City, at its seventieth annual dinner in 1974, awarded Roger its prestigious Explorers Medal "in recognition for his being the world's most traveled field ornithologist."

Some of Roger's friends have likened him to the Vikings for his love of travel and, when one commented on "Roger's itchy foot," another quipped, "You mean itchy *wing*."

The amount of time Roger has spent traveling has ranged from four to six months a year, including not only his field work, but also lecture tours, ornithological meetings and conventions and conservation congresses. "I find this amount of travel results in so much grist for the mill that I can scarcely make use of it all," says Roger. He can't begin to accept all the invitations from friends who just want to go birding with so entertaining a companion.

Roger has been to the Galápagos six times. As a nature leader he has traveled so often on the *Explorer* that they call him affectionately "Roger the Lodger." And he has been to the Antarctic so many times that one associate called it "Roger's winter home."

It would take a five-foot shelf of books to report on Roger's accomplishments and birding experiences in Mexico, parts of Africa, ten trips to Europe, ranging from Spain and Gibraltar to Scandinavia, to Scotland, to Iceland. He now wants to go to places in Central America, Madagascar, Southeast Asia and China, Russia, West Africa, tropical South America below the Amazon River, and western Australia, "places I do not yet know," he says.

First trips abroad always seem, somehow, to be especially significant or memorable even for insignificant incidents. This was the case when Roger went to the International Ornithological Congress in Sweden in 1950, most important to him, perhaps, because he met James Fisher. But he remembers a side trip they took with Ed and Margaret Chalif. They were all at the same table in the dining car of the train, which made so much noise rattling through the country that they had virtually to scream at the top of their lungs to be heard. They were discussing birds when the train made an abrupt stop. There was absolute quiet just as Roger was shouting, "Well, my favorite sewer outlet is in Brooklyn at Fifty-ninth Street."

Another of the side trips that the world's leading ornithologists took while they were attending their ornithological meetings in Stockholm was to Lapland. They were anxious to see the northern phalarope. The party left the train and started afield when they came to a wide stream. Roger and the men could leap across, but not the ladies, though a guide did carry petite Margaret Chalif across. Meanwhile, some of the other ladies disappeared behind some trees, took off their hats, coats, blouses, skirts, "some knickers underneath," corsets and bras, and carrying their clothes on top of their heads, waded across, dressed, and proceeded as if nothing unusual had happened.

Sir Peter Scott, the waterfowl artist and conservationist, was on this memorable Swedish trip too. Scott acquired a pair of lesser white-fronted geese to take back to the Severn Wildfowl Trust in England. But as luck would have it, the crate got misplaced in the railway station in Stockholm and he amused the locals by going through the crowded station making geese calls until the birds responded and were rescued.

Another highlight of that trip came when the group was taken to Gamla Upsala, the old town where the first Christian church in Sweden is situated. Knowing his grandparents had come from Upsala, Roger was curious about the names in the little graveyard behind the church. He found one that read "Anna Sophia Peterson," the same name as his grandmother, who had died in 1926 in Jamestown.

Roger, an ardent botanist, also went to the Linnaeus home and saw the twin flower *Linnaea*, the plant named after Carl von Linné, who was responsible for the binomial system of naming plants and animals—that of the genus to which it belongs and that of the species itself. It was his favorite flower, and one of Roger's.

In 1957, Roger was on a four-month safari in Africa, and the next year found him heading the Yale-*Life* expedition into the Bolivian Andes to photograph the rare James's flamingo, "lost" since 1906. The next year he was on another expedition for Yale, to the Straits of Magellan and the Beagle Channel, just below the Antarctic Circle. Then came a journey to Japan and a visit to St. Kilda in Scotland.

On the way back from Japan, Roger and Eugene Eisenmann stopped off in the Hawaiian Islands, principally to acquaint Roger with some of the Hawaiian birds for his Western field guide. They were lucky in seeing the akepa, the palilo, and the ou, which was seen for the first time since 1953, on the slopes of Mauna Kea and Mauna Loa. They were also tossed out of bed by an earthquake. And at Kauai, Roger hired a pink jeep with a fringed canopy and with Dr. Frank Richardson hiked to the edge of the great Alakai swamp to hunt for rare birds.

Roger's many trips to the Antarctic were always special but he treasures that first one, which was his real introduction to the penguins, the bird he has most photographed. He was a member of a team of scientists participating in Operation Deep Freeze, a project organized in 1961 by the National Science Foundation and the United States Navy to make recommendations about the conservation of local wildlife. Roger's principal purpose was to work with Dr. William J. L. Sladen of Johns Hopkins University on the population dynamics of penguins. Others in the ornithological group included Robert C. Wood, an associate of Dr. Sladen's, who was interested in skuas, a rapacious gull-like bird. The team was flown in to McMurdo, where they lived in a Jamesway hut, a strong and tough shelter resembling a World War II Quonset hut. It had a roof and side of canvas laced to wooden frames, with a window at each end. It was about twelve by twenty feet and had a diesel-fuel stove for cooking and heating.

All of the men in Operation Deep Freeze had been given special survival training. They learned how to get out of a crevasse with ropes and ice picks, how to build a snow cave or an igloo with ice blocks. And with very good reason, for the Antarctic, roughly the size of the United States and Mexico combined, has been described as the world's highest and coldest continent; it has an average elevation of six thousand feet and contains about 90 percent of the Earth's ice and snow. Happily all went well, despite the cold and sometimes very violent winds. Sladen, who had been a medical officer on a British expedition some years earlier, had had two colleagues cremated when fire consumed their hut, and Roger's group was constantly aware of the possible danger.

In 1962, Roger attended international meetings sponsored by the International Union for the Conservation of Nature in Africa, with field work in Uganda, where he was made an honorary trustee

© Roger Tory Peterson — '73

CARDINAL
Richmondena cardinalis

Published by permission of Mill Pond Press, Inc.,
Venice, Florida 33595

BOBOLINK
Dolichonyx oryzivorus

Published by permission of Mill Pond Press, Inc.,
Venice, Florida 33595

BARN SWALLOW
Hirundo rustica

Published by permission of Mill Pond Press, Inc.,
Venice, Florida 33595

Roger Tory Peterson – '76

ROADRUNNER
Geococcyx californianus

Published by permission of Mill Pond Press, Inc.,
Venice, Florida 33595

MEXICAN QUAILS

Color plate #9, from A Field Guide to Mexican Birds

Published by permission of Mill Pond Press, Inc.,
Venice, Florida 33595

SHOWY WAYSIDE FLOWERS
From A Field Guide to Wildflowers

Published by permission of Mill Pond Press, Inc.,
Venice, Florida 33595

WOOD THRUSH
Hylocichla mustelina

Published by permission of Mill Pond Press, Inc.,
Venice, Florida 33595

of the Uganda National Park. He also went to Kenya and Tanzania. By 1964 he was off on his first trip to the Galápagos.

Roger had always wanted to go to the Galápagos, but had concluded they "were inaccessible unless one owned a yacht or mounted a full-scale expedition." His opportunity came when Harold Coolidge asked Roger to represent the National Audubon Society at the dedication of the Galápagos International Scientific Project of the new Darwin Research Station and participate in a six-week research project sponsored by the University of California Extension Program and supported by the National Science Foundation. Fifty scientists from numerous countries were invited.

Flying over the highlands in a helicopter, he sighted his first Galápagos tortoises. "They glistened like huge black bubbles in the green swales below."

He camped out one night with Dean Amadon, curator of birds at the American Museum, on Point Espinosa, on Fernandina Island. They left their folding cots and sleeping bags high upon the shingle of a beach where the breezes would be cool while they were trying to sleep.

"This was fine," Roger recalls, "but in the middle of the night a big bull sea lion that felt he owned the stretch of beach mistook our prostrate forms for invading sea lions. It was with horror that I found a great face with whiskers leering at me from the foot of my cot. Dean and I made a hasty retreat back to the tent camp and the other scientists."

Roger, loaded down with photographic gear as usual, patiently hauled it from island to island to make a film record of all possible birds in flight, resting, eating, mating, and nesting. It was fascinating, and the film one of his best. He was excited to find a colony of flamingos nesting in a salt lagoon near the north coast of Florena Island, the first time they had been reported nesting there. He counted thirty-six in the colony of nests on a flat piece of land in the center of the lagoon, "the rarest and most endangered birds on the Galápagos archipelago." Flamingos are now protected in the Galápagos by laws of Ecuador, but local residents apparently sometimes shoot them for their feathers and for food.

The finches, of course, intrigued Roger especially. He recalled that Darwin had recognized thirteen species on the Galápagos, the same number still currently recorded, although classifications have changed. "They all looked very much alike—little dusky-brown or blackish birds with stubby tails. They differ mainly in their bills, which vary from small, thin beaks resembling those of warblers to huge, thick ones like those of grosbeaks."

Roger says today it is generally accepted by scientists that all finches in the Galápagos came from a common stock, from some lost mainland finches marooned there long ago, and "their descendants, pioneering further, became isolated on various islands" and, "adapting to local conditions, they developed physical differences. Those with larger beaks could crack larger seeds; those with longer bills could probe the deep cactus blossoms; those with smaller bills could exploit the tiny insects. Genetic traits that have survival value were preserved."

When traveling is done for as many years and in as many countries, there are bound to be some unusual, ticklish, and even dangerous moments. Apparently thriving on adventure, Roger has had his share.

There was a lion episode in Africa when the first Pan African Ornithological Congress was held at Victoria Falls in 1956. On a field trip to Wankie, two busloads streamed out along the road to look at guinea fowl and hornbills when one of the women saw a bateleur eagle with a snake. "We got out for a better look," recounts Roger. "Looking at tracks in the road, the guide commented that there was a lion nearby with a jackal following it. We were more concerned with the bateleur eagle. Suddenly an older British woman, Clem Ackland, a fine photographer, quietly said, 'Lion!' Our native drivers got back in the buses faster than any of us. It was only after we were down the road a little that we found a pride of seven lions hidden in the deep grass scarcely more than two hundred yards from where we had been. They were in a great semicircle, probably watching us."

Margaret Chalif, who was on the trip, said the lions were ready, absolutely ready to spring at the unsuspecting ornithologists. "If Clem hadn't warned us, we would have had a tragedy. And the lions would have had a beautiful meal."

Roger sent Clarence Beal a postcard: "I have photographed lions at ten feet and ten species of antelope and many birds. *I must come back* to Africa." And he did, not only to photograph but to help establish sanctuaries and parks to conserve the magnificent wildlife.

In another adventure, in Patagonia, Roger nearly lost his life.

It was in 1961 when he was asked to join a Yale University expedition led by Dr. Philip Humphrey, then of the Peabody Museum, for the purpose of exploring the birds of Patagonia and Tierra del Fuego, on the southern end of South America. The museum was collecting, but Roger was along simply as an observer, paying his own way.

Upon arriving at a little town called Camarones, where a lettuce-like seaweed was harvested and shipped to Japan for breakfast food, Roger asked the proprietor of the inn where they were staying about seabirds. He was told that there was a fine bird island called Isla Blanca about three miles offshore, and arranged to get Roger and Dr. Humphrey out to it.

They were there at four the next morning. The boat turned out to be simply a rowboat, but the boatman looked quite powerful and inspired confidence. He took the oars and then on a relatively calm sea, with the breeze behind them, they were soon on the island. The morning was spent observing and photographing Magellanic penguins, nesting, as well as shag and other birds. At midday the boatman began getting apprehensive about worsening weather and said they must try to get back to the mainland.

Heavy seas began to build up so big and so fast that both Humphrey and Roger had to lend a hand with additional oars. "The waves were rolling past and cresting at six feet, and they were breaking so that often we found ourselves shipping water. For a long time we seemed to make no progress at all. Raw blisters formed even on our skipper's horny palms. For five or six hours we kept trying to make those three miles. Finally the wind and seas dropped somewhat as we got in the lee of part of the mainland, and we made it. After the boat was hauled up on the cobble, I was so exhausted I collapsed on the beach."

That night he relived his experience in a nightmare. But he tells of the narrow escape quite philosophically. He said he and Humphrey had paid the boatman five dollars for the trip to the island and back, "but we came so close to losing our lives that we gave him ten. To lose one's life for only five dollars seemed too little." He grinned. It was one of his most grueling and unpleasant experiences, but he says he would not have wanted to miss it. "To take a chance once in a while and get away with it is to feel alive." Then he paused. "How many lives does a cat have? Nine? Well, I've lost at least three, almost, anyway."

On another trip to Patagonia in November 1974, Roger set up his tent at Punta Tombo. There was a colony of an estimated million Magellanic penguins, which Roger wanted to photograph for his penguin book. Strong dry winds upset his tent and Roger was nearly blown away. But the next day, when he was returning alone from the tip of the point where a shag colony was located—a two-mile walk—Roger saw a mirage in the distance. It wasn't a mirage, but a group of figures that looked larger than penguins, a straggling group. They turned out to be people. They proved to be a group of bird watchers from the Massachusetts Audubon Society. They were as surprised as Roger. "This is how one builds a legend, I suppose," he says. "The omnipresent Peterson in the wilderness."

Despite his travels over the years, it was only when he became a lecturer for tours sponsored by Lars-Eric Lindblad that Roger found himself exploring a new way of life for himself. He has made more than twenty trips for Lindblad, most of them on the beautiful ship *Explorer*. On shipboard, Roger discovered a social life entirely new and fascinating and exciting.

Roger and Lars first met at a National Audubon dinner in 1965. Roland Clement, an Audubon Society vice president, introduced them. Roger was showing some of his films taken on the Galápagos when he was on the Galápagos International Scientific Project the year before.

Lars said, "We simply must go to the Galápagos together," and he asked Roger to be the leader of the nature group. The two men were instantly attracted to each other. Lars is an ebullient person, and Roger is pretty ebullient himself. Roger said, "Lars is a man of action. To him nothing is impossible. In the year 1000 he instead of Leif Ericson would have found North America."

Lars' specialty is to take people to rarely visited places, people who have a genuine interest in "exploring" rather than just a ride and a rest on a ship or a beach.

The Motor Ship *Lindblad Explorer*, a one-class, 250-foot-long, husky craft built in Finland in 1969 is especially designed to operate through ice fields and to go into waters too shallow for big ocean liners. The ship is operated by Lars and the Swedish-American Line, has fifty outside cabins, can accommodate ninety-two passengers, travel at better than fifteen knots with a cruising radius of six thousand miles. Lecturers and leaders on the cruises have included, besides Roger, such nature notables as Sir Peter Scott, Keith Shackelton, Dr. Lyall Watson, M. Lorimer Moe, Francisco Erize, and Dr. John Livingston. The trips have ranged from the Arctic to the Antarctic and way points at sea as well as partway up the Amazon River. Lars offers land trips as well, such as the one to Ethiopia and another to Bhutan, eighteen thousand feet up in the eastern Himalayas between Tibet and India. Roger "scouted" both of these land trips, to see if they were feasible for tourist travel.

The passengers on the trips differ considerably. According to Roger, on trips to the Antarctic at least a third of the people "are nature oriented in some way; about 50 percent or more are intelligent citizens who have no basic knowledge of natural history but want to learn, to try to extend their more-than-average intelligence or they wouldn't be on such a trip. Ten percent might be what are called 'travel snobs.' They have been everywhere and they want to tick off another country or two on their world checklist." Then there are the occasional ones who are so confused they do not really know where they have been, or where they are going, or why they are on the trip in the first place. Such a person might go to the Antarctic and ask, "Why haven't we seen any Eskimos?" Or, "Where are the polar bears?"—somehow confusing the two poles of the Earth. One locomotive engineer simply wanted to go someplace where there were no trains. But those who sign up for the Galapagos, Roger says, are very often oriented in a somewhat different way. They are interested in Darwin, evolution, islands, tame wildlife, snorkling, and so forth. These passengers are rarely the frivolous kind that one would find on a typical Caribbean cruise.

Life aboard ship at sea is leisurely, with evenings usually devoted to movies, nature lectures, and orientation talks, and discussions after the day's exploration in the "zodiacs," the rubber shore boats.

Of course there is swimming aboard, a library, a lounge for games and drinks. There is often romance. As on most sea voyages, passengers removed from reality and responsibilities feel romantic.

It was on the *Explorer*, when he was sixty, that Roger discovered dancing.

When it came to dancing, Roger, as a boy in Jamestown, had been "pretty sad," he said, "about grappling with girls, but it was the one-step, two-step, and step-and-a-half routine that bugged me. I simply didn't seem to have the rhythm or at least I couldn't get the rhythm if I had to think about the steps. So I quickly gave it up. I am sure the girls didn't like me anyway—I was too skinny, had too many freckles, and I preferred to be in the woods north of town watching birds." Roger tried dancing again in New York when he was going to art school, but that hadn't been successful either.

On the *Explorer* in 1971 an attractive New York City divorcée, Barbara Hurst, finally taught Roger to dance. After a week or two at sea, she says, Roger decided he wanted to dance. She tells of his "conversion."

"He came up to me. I was very honored."

Roger said, "I'd like to know how to do this modern stuff, and you seem to know how to do it pretty well. I've been watching."

Barbara Hurst said she'd be glad to teach him.

"Shall I take my shoes off?"

"Sure. Would you be more comfortable that way?"

"Yes, I think so."

"The ship is rolling. O.K. But if you take off your shoes, you had better take off your socks, too, because you might slip on the floor."

So Roger took off his shoes and socks. "Now what do I do?" he asked.

"Well, you know what the mating dance of the birds looks like?"

"Sure."

"That's what you do."

With that, Roger "did his own thing."

He relaxed. "In fact," the young lady said, "he was better than many other people, even Keith Shackelton. Once I explained it—

think like a bird dance—Roger got it right away. It clicked. He was very uninhibited."

Roger says, "I found that I *did* have rhythm and paired up with a pretty girl who didn't give a damn what I did. So I could dance. I would improvise special dances such as the albatross mating dance, and the blue-footed booby dance. I did the Adelie penguin in ecstatic display. It was great fun. I regret all those years of non-dancing."

But it was the trips to the island that Roger enjoyed most of all on the Lindblad tours. Sometimes he would slip away from the others to photograph a rare bird. He enjoyed, too, giving the orientation talks and showing films in the evening. Francisco Erize, who was frequently aboard, felt that Roger's influence on the public was his outstanding achievement. He emphasized that "if you don't get people interested in wildlife, you won't have any conservation. Roger can't see an animal species without being concerned about its future. Many people, including many wildlife photographers, are satisfied with just seeing the places they have gone to—not being concerned at all about its future. Many passengers on the *Explorer* are influential. They come from many countries. Roger has started a sort of tidal wave on these trips that spreads internationally through the passengers, stimulating conservation projects in other countries."

Erize explains that many Americans, though inclined toward conservation, may be provincial about supporting wilderness areas outside of the United States. They may give to Audubon or the Sierra Club, but spend very little outside on preservation. On the Lindblad tours, because of the atmosphere created on board through lectures, the horizon is widened. They are prepared to help outside their own immediate areas.

Lindblad's nature and exploring tours are not the only travel programs that have expanded the interest in wildlife and bird education and conservation. The National Audubon Society, the American Museum of Natural History, Wonder Tours, Bird Bonanzas, and many other agencies have stimulated interest in birding all over the world. Such trips have helped swell the "bird industry."

Not all of Roger's nature evenings on the *Explorer* have been successful. On one of the Seychelles trips he revealed a seldom-seen side of his character. He tells it himself: "There were several difficult passengers, not nature-oriented—swingers, you might call them—who found bird watching a bit boring and actually booed me in the lounge when I was about to give my evening talk. I can be very articulate when I am angry, and in spite of the fact that they were paying passengers, I really gave them the facts of life. This quieted the ship considerably, and the next day when it came time to raising money for Cousin Island, the passengers forked up a total of $8,000. I have found on several occasions that my articulate anger produces results—a sort of 'psychological goosing.'"

Lars recalls the incident very clearly: "Roger tore the people apart, became very abusive," he says. "He said the passengers were very ungrateful, stupid, shallow. The reason Roger acted the way he did was because he felt they were being unfair to me, Lindblad, their host, by inattention and so forth. He was defending me, Lars."

To Lars the episode was contrary to Roger's general image. Lars sees Roger as "modest, reticent, and self-effacing. But to a degree that is an act. Being modest is good for his image. Roger's self-image is that of a Lutheran prude, charming, a bumbling, lovable sort of a character; never hates anybody; very patient. But—scratch the surface and you find that he has strong dislikes and a violent temper. And, as I say, I love Roger with all his faults and Roger knows I know the real Roger, tantrums and all."

Trips are almost never dull and some are the scene of special adventures. In 1972 on an Antarctic trip they nearly collided with an iceberg during a gale near the Briscoe Islands when the ship was trying to make its way into the Palmer station. For shelter it put into a big fjord filled with icebergs. Roger and Keith Shackleton were on the ship's bridge, heard the captain call to the helmsman to turn the ship to port, or left, only to have the confused man at the wheel turn the vessel the opposite way. The captain then ordered engines reversed, and as the *Explorer* stopped and backed away, Roger said he "could have almost touched" the berg, which was twice as high as the ship. It was a "terrifying" episode, he recalls.

Later, Keith Shackleton made a painting of the storm with a snow petrel flying past an iceberg, and Roger, after seeing it in

London on the artist's wall, purchased it for the Peterson residence in Old Lyme.

Roger once grew, during a month in the Antarctic, what he has described as an Ernest Hemingway-type beard but he decided he did not like it and shaved it off. He left the mustache on, however, which he liked because "I thought it made me look rather distinguished, rather British." He happened upon Sir Peter Scott in Christchurch in New Zealand. The Englishman did not recognize him at first and commented, "I liked you better the way you were." Next Roger ran into Sewall and Eleanor Pettingill. Eleanor told Roger the mustache made him look ten years older. That almost did it. However, he kept it on until he returned home and "Barbara's comment was it made me look cruel. So off it came, and I have never tried to raise a mustache or beard since."

Actually, Roger's full head of hair, prematurely white, does make him look distinguished and mature. It led to one unhappy incident that showed his vanity. On a Lindblad trip a passenger made the mistake of saying she thought Barbara Peterson was not his wife but his daughter. Roger never spoke to the woman again.

On one of his many trips to the Galápagos Islands, Roger, the horseman, had a bad mishap while riding. Lars Lindblad had bought about thirty western saddles for the use of his clients on the *Explorer* to go by horse—or donkey—into the highlands to see the famed tortoises.

The horses were miserable little creatures, most of them. They were wormy, ate cactus, and had no shoes. One felt that he would rather not ride them. There were not enough to go around, so, being staff, Roger chose to walk into the highlands, about five or six hours uphill over rough rocks and lava. He had done it before, but Miguel Castro, the conservation warden, insisted that Roger use his horse, which, actually, was one of the best on the island.

"I accepted and got on its back and was about to go up the rocky trail when the horse reared violently. Apparently it had never felt a crupper under its tail before. I'm not quite sure why it acted the way it did. I yelled, '*Whoa!*' which apparently was the wrong word to the horse's ears, attuned to Spanish, and horse and I went over backward. I landed on the back of my head on the lava rock and saw constellations that are not in Dr. Menzel's *Field*

Guide to the Stars. My first thought was 'I'm dead!' Then I realized I was not and I scrambled out because the horse was lying on its side and kicking toward me with its hoofs. I limped to my feet while Miguel Castro beat his horse for behaving so badly.

"Then I noticed my watch had exploded. The band was there but the watch was gone, although my wrist was not broken. I was in pretty sad shape with bruises on my legs and a bad headache from my fall, but no fracture."

The group, with Roger limping along—no more riding—made the trip up the mountains as scheduled and spent the night in a camp at the tortoise preserve. Back on the ship Roger discovered that his legs were swollen badly and he was in considerable pain for the rest of the voyage. He decided the reason he felt so bad must have been because he was probably "out of condition" and it was then that he decided to take up jogging.

It was on a trip to Ethiopia that Roger had a narrow escape in an encounter with four hundred gelada baboons he was photographing.

Roger moved up to get some close-up pictures of some great big males—"they have a mane like a lion, a great big cape," he says, "and are enormously fierce. Four of these got to pulling back their lips and chasing each other. All of a sudden one peeled off from the others and came right toward me. If I had run, well . . . but I just stood there and I guess he suddenly decided I was just another baboon. Anyway, I held my ground, and he went back with his friends again."

An Ethiopian who had been watching from the distance told Roger he had done "just the right thing. If you had run you would have had it. You would be dead."

Roger said, "Sometimes you do these things instinctively. It was not a matter of thinking there. I am afraid, though, on certain other occasions I would have run. I am never quite sure how I will react. It's not a case of being a coward. It's just being sensible. You never know what you are going to do. Sometimes running is the wrong reaction. The better thing is to stand there and see what happens. It takes a little bit of courage."

He cited as an example a slightly different experience one night as he was walking in the Canadian north woods in the moonlight.

Suddenly he saw just ahead of him a big wolf. Roger's immediate and impulsive reaction was to growl at it. The animal scooted off and Roger's comment was that "I acted more wolf than it did."

Roger's lust for travel finally got him and Barbara in March 1971 to the Shag Rocks, islands 170 miles west of South Georgia, far in the South Atlantic, which have probably been seen by fewer human eyes than any other islands in the world, according to the late Robert Cushman Murphy, famous naturalist and curator of birds at the American Museum of Natural History.

The cluster is named for its cormorants, or shags. There are five of the islands and they look like hag's teeth or discolored sugar lumps jutting out of the gray ocean. And, once more, Roger was in for a little adventure.

Inasmuch as the sea was quite calm, a lifeboat was lowered from the *Explorer* (then operated by the Norwegian Line), and the Petersons, Dr. Murphy, and about twenty-four others set off to circle the rocks with their maelstrom of birds—shags, cape petrels, and a few albatrosses. The weather worsened and the *Explorer*'s whistle called the party to return to the ship. Then came trouble. As the boats banged together, Roger snatched Murphy's hand away from one gunwale just in time to keep it from being crushed.

The hoisting gear was attached to the lifeboat and as it was being lifted aboard one end came loose. Roger vigorously pushed one white-haired woman down in time to keep her head from being hit by the swinging hoisting gear. The group started to tumble down into the lower end of the boat as it tilted, on top of Barbara, who found herself waist-deep in icy water with her new Rollei camera soaked. The higher end of the lifeboat was lowered immediately before anyone could be washed overboard. The skipper saved the day by swinging the *Explorer* around to provide a smoother patch of water, the lifting gear was refastened, and the party was lifted back aboard safely, badly shaken, cold and wet, but unharmed.

Many of the passengers who have made trips with Lars are members of a travel group called "The Intrepids," which meets once a year somewhere in the world. They publish a handsome illustrated quarterly, *The Intrepids Magazine*. Lars is club chairman of the Intrepids, and Roger has been its president for two years. He says, "Inasmuch as a large percentage of the members are senior citizens,

I have sometimes referred to the club as the 'Decrepits,' which is not a very diplomatic thing to do." And Roger, past Social Security age himself, has been called by one member of the female bird-watching sorority "the dreamboat of the geriatric set."

There are only so many hours in a day. How long can Roger travel and write and paint and be a man of so many careers? It was Barbara who said that Roger saw life as "picture segments, so many objectives to be accomplished in so many years, certain things at certain points."

Now Roger says, "I have to cut down on my lotus-eating travel existence and spend more time writing and painting. I have much to tell with my pen and brush."

But he sounded almost wistful as he added, "Travel is the best part of it."

CHAPTER XVIII

Wildlife Painting—and Painters

ROGER was being congratulated warmly one day for his having been described in a newspaper story as "a second Audubon" when he raised one hand, stopped the speaker, and said quietly but very firmly:

"I don't want to be known as 'a second Audubon.' I want to be known as 'the first Roger Tory Peterson.'"

Although fame and fortune may have come to Roger through the Peterson System of flash identification of birds for his series of field guides on nature subjects, his ambition—to be an artist—has never waivered. In his later years he has become increasingly determined to concentrate on that ambition. Furthermore, he wants to be his own man—Roger Tory Peterson, artist.

His decision to devote his energies to what he calls "gallery-type painting," as opposed to what some have described as "those little decoys" illustrating the bird guides, was disclosed in *The New York Times* in 1974 on the fortieth anniversary of the publication of his first field guide. Since then Roger has produced four pictures a year of "gallery-type" painting, in addition to new paintings for the revised edition of his Eastern field guide.

Opinions differ as to Roger's art.

John Henry Dick, the South Carolina artist, warbler expert (and owner of an Audubon elephant folio), feels that Roger's drawings in the field guides themselves have "arrived at a new art form." Dick never tires of them and hangs them on his walls. "Roger's drawings are out of this world."

Dick prefers these to Roger's recent "artier" bird portraits, adding "Roger's placement of the birds in the guides, the brilliance and clarity and accuracy are absolutely exquisite. And nobody in this century has communicated to so many people the fascinating and wonderful subject of wildlife."

Others have called Roger the finest living bird painter of this century. His latest paintings are selling in the $20,000 range, and his limited edition bird prints are already becoming collector's items.

The Carnegie Museum of Natural History in Pittsburgh has purchased a complete set of Roger's signed and numbered prints produced by the Mill Pond Press, and the Metropolitan Museum of Art has acquired two of his recent prints—the bald eagle and the great horned owl.

Recently an art expert viewing the prints at the Metropolitan Museum said, "Without reservation Roger is a contemporary Audubon." The comparison inevitably is the subject of stimulated discussion at every gathering of wildlife artists. Roger may not want to be a second Audubon, but Irving Kassoy says, "You should have seen Roger's eyes light up when I told him he had out-Audubon'd Audubon."

Roger, the perfectionist, has always been sensitive about his paintings, including the older ones. He has been quoted as saying he is so unhappy with some of his birds in the very first field guide that he will not show them to anyone.

A typical example of his almost supersensitiveness is told by Betty Carnes, the ardent birder, now of Phoenix, Arizona. One time several years ago when she was attending a meeting of the A.O.U. in Canada, the late Robert Cushman Murphy said in a speech that there had never been a really fine bird artist since Audubon.

Later in the day when Betty and her husband were driving to a restaurant in the country some distance from the meeting, they passed a man walking along the road alone. He looked familiar.

It was Roger. He was all alone, his hands behind his back, his head dropped on his chest just like Napoleon. And he was not watching birds, did not even have his binoculars, just walking, apparently terribly depressed. They stopped the car and called to him. He turned and, almost in a dazed fashion, said, "Betty, did you hear what Bob Murphy said? Did you hear him say that there had not been a great American bird artist since Audubon?"

"My husband and I dismissed the Murphy remark. 'Oh, fiddle-dee-dee, Roger, that's just Bob Murphy,' I said. 'You know how he talks. So what.'

"And Roger said, 'You know when I was a boy and used to go to the American Museum, Robert Cushman Murphy was one of my idols. Now my idol has said to me, 'You're no good as a bird artist. There hasn't been a great one since Audubon.' "

They hustled Roger into the car and took him to dinner and arranged for him to sit beside a pretty and vivacious girl, who soon had him in better spirits.

It is to be remembered that Roger's paintings were not limited to field guide didactic, created specifically for the purpose of field identification of birds. Roger did cover illustrations for *Audubon* magazine in the late 1930s and 1940s and he painted the pictures for twelve issues of *Life* magazine's bird series, as well as illustrations for other magazines and books.

But there has always been a dividing line between illustration and what some critics call "fine art." Roger knew he could always make a success of illustrating and commercial art, but he has never wavered from that childhood dream of being a "real" artist.

"The fact that Roger's book illustrations are useful does not in any way detract from their aesthetic qualities," says Dr. John. A. Diffily, director of education at the Amon Carter Museum in Fort Worth, Texas. "Many are 'fine art.' Very definitely paintings in the Mexican guide are fine art." (Dr. Diffily explains "fine art" as art that exists only for aesthetic reasons: "There is no other reason for its being.")

Roger says certain drawings in his books are "highly successful," but does not speak of them as fine art. He singles out the black and white drawings in *Wild America, The Birdwatcher's Anthology*, and *The World of Birds*. He describes these as basically illustrations, but other critics call them "art."

David Lank has said, "To me, the greatness of Roger is only equaled by two other people. One is Gilbert White. The other is Thomas Bewick. In White's case, he never did a sketch. And yet his *The Natural History and Antiquities of Selborne* [1789] has never been out of print. It is the pastoral classic which started the popularization of appreciation of nature. Thomas Bewick invented wood engraving as opposed to wood cutting. A consummate artist. One of the truly great. In terms of everything I consider important, he far surpassed Hogarth. There have never been bird drawings or animal drawings at their very best that surpass Bewick's miniatures, although they were black and white. He was the number two man in popularizing wildlife. Roger is the number three man but on a greater scale than ever before. Here are three great men who have very little in common except great genius."

Whether doing illustrations or easel paintings, Roger's procedure is relatively the same. For illustrations, he makes pencil sketches on a number of tissues. Then by tissue overlays, he modifies his concepts until he arrives at positions he likes. These are then transferred to drawing paper. Or he might cut out the sketches with scissors and assemble the cutouts. Barbara calls these "Roger's paper dolls."

"For example," Roger explains it, "if there were three birds involved, I would make a number of open outline sketches which I would then juxtapose or superimpose until I arrived at my composition. These would then be transferred or scaled up or down, depending on what was involved. The perfected penciling would then be done, followed by painting.

"I tend not to paint too strongly in a direct manner, but to build up my tones in the traditional English watercolor fashion. First light washes of Windsor Newton watercolors, becoming heavier and bolder as I work. For control, or to get the desired effect, I often resort to so-called tempera or opaque watercolor."

Recently Roger has been painting with a combination of transparent water color, designer's color (opaque water color), and then finishing with acrylic glazes. He explains that acrylics dry in almost the exact tone that they are laid on wet, whereas watercolor or designer's colors do not and one can be thrown off by this. There is the constant problem of making mental adjustment between the wet paint and the dry, end result. There is no such adjustment with acrylics.

As for the paintings for limited edition prints, Roger follows almost the same technique—first the small sketches of the subjects involved, and then an assembly of the tissues until he reaches a conclusion he likes.

"I like to do my bird subjects in the exact size of the bird," says Roger, "the bobolink the size of a bobolink, for example. The snowy owl was done the exact size of the snowy owl. If, in the final painting, the composition would be too large for the sheet size in reproduction, a certain reduction would take place, by 10 percent or whatever." Roger says he finds it very difficult to draw a bird's head in three-quarter view or straight-on.

Roger prefers watercolors for small birds. He says that there is an incisiveness about a small bird that watercolor handles better than oil. But if it is a moving bird in a landscape, such as a duck in flight, then he prefers oil. "Oil is a medium where you can get the feeling of atmosphere, of activity, movement in space, better than in watercolor. Oil is a rather juicy, flexible medium. There are men who can handle watercolor in a moody brilliant landscape, but I find that oil is my medium for that. Often I mix three mediums in the same painting—transparent water color, gouache, and acrylics."

Roger paints all the backgrounds for his birds. At one time (1950), he admitted they were a problem, "for they have to be handled with a certain amount of freedom if they are not to look static."

Roger uses only fresh botanical material for background. Bob Lewin reports that "Roger told us in the spring—after we agreed that he was to do the barn swallow for us—that he couldn't do it until the fall of 1973. I asked why and he said he wanted to paint it when the phragmites are dying."

The phragmites, a tall, plumed marsh grass, are a natural habitat for the barn swallow. But Roger had to wait until the phragmites turned to their autumn brown-gold-reddish color, which would accentuate the cinnamon-buff breast of the barn swallow. Roger feels the rugged barn swallow is one of his best paintings.

Lewin says Roger feels very strongly about doing the complete painting himself. "Otherwise," he told Lewin, "it wouldn't be a Peterson."

Some artists do let others help out. Audubon had others who filled in the background at times—Maria Martin among them. But David Lank says "Audubon could have done it if he had wanted to."

Roger does not use pictures or photographs "to copy" for his painting. He does, however, take hundreds of Kodachromes to use as reference for background or detail. Where he was to portray sea ducks in a painting, he would not have been able to remember just how rockweed grows on the rocky boulders if he had not taken photographs. Another example is the color of the lichen, a plant that grows on bark and rocks, which Roger has painted in the background of his snowy owl painting. Roger had not only seen it grow—in six trips to the Arctic—but has many pictures of snowy owls on just this kind of lichen. "Roger," says Bob Lewin, "paints with a knowledge of geology, botany, and ornithology. Any of the good bird artists today can paint faster than Roger. And all of the good ones paint beautifully. But Roger goes a step beyond."

Many artists rely on their sketching in the field to provide detail both for the birds and the backgrounds. Roger prefers the "mirror of the camera," though he has done some sketches on birding trips in the past.

"You can't do both sketching and photography in the field," Roger says. "You either sketch or you take photographs. I have elected to photograph. It's faster. A sketch may take me half an hour."

The only time Roger uses pencil and paper "in the field" is in a zoo. He has always liked zoos, the Bronx Zoo especially. "I used to go there on Thursdays. You had to pay a quarter on Thursdays and a lot of people didn't go for that reason. I liked Thursdays because fewer people would be looking over my shoulder as I was sketching."

Most people do not realize that Roger can paint animals and

humans as well as birds. Once he did a lion for Evelyn Allen, which she treasures, and Guy Mountfort, in England, has a grizzly bear in a forest setting. Lars Lindblad has a picture of a musk-ox in his office. (And there are those nudes Roger painted in art school that his sister has hidden away.)

In spite of the fact that Roger does not use photographs for anything other than checking detail, some of Roger's paintings have been criticized as being "too photographic." To these critics Roger replies, "They are not really photographs at all. You hear that simply because a painting may be very representational. In other words, as it would appear logically to a person's eyes. It's not fantasy, although you can have fantasy sometimes in representational painting. It would have to be quite literal as the artist remembered or as he saw it. But it is contrived by the artist even so. Painting can be more poetic. It depends on the artist to produce to what extent there is a feeling of poetry in it. When a painting is called 'photographic' it never really is unless it's a direct copy of a photograph."

Roger has frequently pointed out that a photograph can freeze only one aspect of a bird. It records a permanent record of only one given instant.

Lank says, "If you have a photographer like Roger, who has taken photographs of tens of thousands of birds, he is not going to, as some artists do, project it over his shoulder on a white canvas and trace every line. Roger would look at how a bird may sit on a branch, and then from his vast experiences and his incredible retentive memory, come up with a whole bunch of ideas in his head which in fact are a composite. He can recall from memory whether that shadow is too purple or not purple enough. If the artist had done it too purple, you know he has copied a Kodachrome. It tends to be on the blue side. Roger would never, never trust a slide for true color fidelity. He would rather trust his written field notes."

In addition to the transparencies Roger may have taken of birds in the field and pictures in books and magazines, plus any sketches or notes he has made himself, he checks his own knowledge or memory of the bird with specimen material which he may borrow from the American Museum or the Peabody Museum of Natural History at Yale.

As for his pencil sketches on the tissues, Roger destroys most of them. They are functional but irrelevant to the final painting. "People somehow expect one's simplest sketches to be rather brilliant, but they are not," he says.

Many of the commercial artists who paint wildlife do not have field experience, certainly not the half a century of field experience Roger has.

Many wildlife artists have what are known as files of "swipes, or morgues" in which they deposit useful clippings out of magazines such as *Life, National Geographic*, and so forth. To avoid the stigma of direct copying they often "flop" their drawings—reversing things from right to left—and sometimes copy mistakes.

Once, Roger, driving outside of Detroit, saw a huge billboard with a meadowlark about ten feet high which had been taken from a drawing of a meadowlark he had done a few years earlier for *Life*.

Roger has also detected every manner of derivative use of his art work, even on candy boxes and Christmas cards. "However," he says, "in most cases this kind of 'slurping' is flattering, providing, of course, it is not of a competitive nature. All artists tend to be subconsciously influenced by the work of other artists."

It is very difficult for a bird artist always to be dead right. If a painting is 90 percent or 95 percent right, that *is* something, he says. He never allowed himself to forget how *he* painted four toes on a woodpecker that should have had only three.

"I recall one of the problems that Fuertes had," Roger says, "when he was painting years ago, being trapped by systematists like Oberholser and Chapman and others. These scientists insisted on putting calipers on Fuertes' work even when he had drawn a bird in a foreshortened position, not taking into account what foreshortened meant. Arbitrary opinions would also impose restrictions. For example, if a painting were to show two birds, they each would have to be totally visible—no bird could partially conceal the other bird. This, of course, meant restrictions in attractive composition. Whereas another artist might criticize Fuertes for doing that, it should be remembered that Fuertes was often under pressure from the people who were commissioning these special works."

Roger wrote many years ago in *Audubon* that to produce a drawing that is ornithologically correct is difficult enough, but to add to this the more intangible assets of good craftsmanship and good painting is something few ever achieve. Yet, of all subjects in the field of wildlife painting, birds are the most popular.

Roger has asked himself why he ever aspired to be a bird painter if "nothing can be more difficult to paint than birds." His answer: "An artist strives with his brushes and his pigments to create the illusion of form. Nature, in coloring the birds, whether with patterns or by countershading, attempts to obliterate it. How, then, can the artist succeed? First, he builds the basic form of the bird. Then he destroys it by superimposing the bird's pattern. He winds up with a zero. That is why the most successful bird painters have not attempted to interpret nature literally. Either, like Frank W. Benson, the American painter of turn-of-the-century prominence (his murals are in the Library of Congress in Washington, D.C.), they paint three-dimensional birds, completely ignoring detail, or, like Fuertes, they have painted feather patterns, overlooking the natural play of light and shade on the bird 'in the round.' "

Roger had caught this three-dimensional activity in some of his very early paintings, those that were exhibited at the American Museum of Natural History at the A.O.U. meeting in 1933. But these were to be the last of that sort for many years, as he was sidetracked by his field guide drawings, "strictly patternistic, strictly schematic." Roger does not wish to be remembered only for his "little decoy birds." Roger said, at the opening of the 1975 international exhibition of "Animals in Art" at the Royal Ontario Museum in Toronto, in the keynote address:

> For my own self-respect, I have had to free myself from this field guide type of drawing. I am not entirely free, but I will be. The recent things that I have done as limited edition prints are a transition stage. They fall into the category of decorative portraiture in the Audubon tradition. I fully intend to paint more expansively, to get back into oils and canvas again. To play with mood and color and light. To paint more sensuously.

And it remains to be seen how successful I will be in making the switch. I like to think that an artist can change direction if he chooses.

Some people do not realize that Roger has this other background as an artist. "I've never had a chance to give it full play," he says.

In his work Roger thinks about a project for a long time, waiting for concepts to evolve before starting to develop them.

"I may have a good idea," he says, "for a snowy owl being mobbed by a raven [there is one in a Royal Ontario Museum diorama exhibit], and the idea might be splendid, but on the other hand it might simply not work out. The difference between an idea, a concept, and the handling is very considerable. Once it is nailed down, the technicalities of painting it—that is just a matter of time. And to put it in quotes, 'artistry.'"

Roger hesitates over the word "art." "It presumes too much. It is not a matter of being modest. I think the thing is that a person is either a photographer, or a painter, or a sculptor, or what not. To use the term artist is like using the word 'scientist.' It is a loosely used term, so I tend to use it rather carefully."

He contends that there is no right way or wrong way to paint or draw or sculpt. "The important thing," he says, "is to *see*. The artist sees things and wants you to see them. In viewing each piece, ask yourself whether the artist managed to do what he set out to do. Does it grab you? If it doesn't, perhaps the artist had something else in mind."

It is Roger's view that nature "should be interpreted by those who know something about their subject and feel deeply about it. A painting is a composite of the artist's past experience."

In the world of bird painting, as in all other aspects of the visual arts, Roger understands that there can be remarkable differences of opinion.

Roger once asked an ornithologist what he thought of a certain bird artist's work and the answer was: "It might be good art, but it is not good ornithology." Putting the same question to an artist, Roger got the answer: "It might be good ornithology, but it is not good painting."

Nonetheless, Roger admits, artists have to worry about critics. "You may do what seems to one person to be one of the most painstakingly executed paintings of a roadrunner, for example, and yet there will always be someone, somewhere, who may catch you up if you are not dead right.

"Several of the world's bird artists whose paintings demand the highest prices today are not by critical standards the best draftsmen or the most innovative or evocative painters. The thing they seem to have in common is extreme detail; one can put their work under a hand glass, and for that reason their buyers insist they are supreme. One hears the comment 'Can't you just feel those feathers?' These finicky portraits often lack the subtleties of form and pterylography in which Fuertes excelled."

Asked at what level Roger attempts to re-create detail, he says, "I don't go as far as Armachastegui or several others whose work you can literally put under a hand glass. The trouble with that approach is it tends to harden it up almost like horny, shell-like chitin. I think a bird has to have a little zip to it. A little informality isn't bad. You're looking at it. Theoretically, you're looking at it from about three times the width of the painting away and you're not going to see all that extremely fine detail if you look at it from the proper distance where you get the whole concept. If you're just going to put your nose up against it and just see one square inch, which isn't the idea at all, then you could perhaps play around with infinite detail. But I think it's rather pointless beyond a certain degree. People seem to like detail, and this is one of the things that irritates me about some of the noodlers who really bear down, and I can name several."

One bird artist was so attentive to detail that he copied the dust from the museum from which he had borrowed his specimen.

Comparing other wildlife artists, Roger says there are some, such as Don Eckelberry and Al Gilbert, who are fine draftsmen with distinctive styles "who do not fiddle, but paint with the sure touch Fuertes would have praised."

Roger was much influenced by Fuertes' approach. He has been fascinated by Fuertes' early development and particularly by his artistic dilemma, one which has also confounded Roger—whether

225

to paint birds impressionistically, as the eye sees them, bathed in light and shadow, or to paint them as detailed feather maps devoid of modifying atmosphere.

"The lay artists," says Roger, "unschooled in a field knowledge of birds, will insist they see more life in an Audubon bird, but this is because Audubon strongly reflected Audubon in everything he did, whereas Fuertes selected more the character of the bird, less of himself. The name of Audubon will always live in the minds of the American public. The name has become a myth and deservedly so. But Fuertes' name will be remembered longer. To the strictly ornithological clan, he stands without peer, placed way ahead of Audubon. To one who knows birds, there is far more latent life in a Fuertes bird, composed and at rest, than there is in an Audubon bird wildly animated."

The personality of Fuertes, too, may have had something to do with the character of his painting. Anyone who knew him spoke of his animation, his splendid sense of humor, and his very tender heart. Paul Howes, former curator of the Bruce Museum in Greenwich, Connecticut, had gone on a collection expedition to the rain forests in the Andes when Fuertes was painting for the American Museum. Howes wrote in *Photographing in the Rain-Forests:*

> Fuertes had a way of making odd sounds, sort of 'purrings and croonings,' when he was definitely conveying delight or deep appreciation of beauty and color, or the regret and pity or horror he felt at the sight of an injured animal or poor beggar or diseased person he saw on his expeditions. He was part bald, with most of his hair at the back of his head. He had a thick mushtache. Fuertes painted so rapidly and so expertly that I could not keep track of his methods. To me it was fascinating to observe this genius working with watercolors, how deftly and how confidently he made each stroke. It was amazing to see him create gloss and shading in plumage . . . and that subtle allowance of brilliant highlight left in the painted eye, a secret which if understood and properly attended to makes all the difference between good and bad bird or animal portraiture.

Fuertes continually pointed his brushes in his mouth. "I'se eats lots of paint," he would say smilingly when asked about it, not even looking up from his work. (It was one of these brushes that he gave to Roger.)

Roger, speaking of Fuertes, says that it must be remembered that Fuertes had predecessors to whose work he could refer, including Audubon. Audubon started more or less from scratch. His ideas were not influenced in any way by the uninspired men who had worked before him. The unborn art of photography had not schooled the eye or influenced the mind, as it has universally since then.

Even though an artist does not paint directly from a photograph, he is subconsciously influenced by the visual discipline imposed by this modern science, Roger explains. "One thing is certain: although Fuertes' birds are more truthfully like the birds they depict, they do not make as suitable wall decorations as the Audubon prints. Audubon had one great advantage over most of the other early bird painters—the benefit of artistic training. When in Paris, he studied drawing under the great French masters of the day. In that fortunate circumstance probably lies the background of his power. His works are not like the dull, documentary drawings of Alexander Wilson and his contemporaries." It has been said that Wilson was important only because he came before Audubon. Roger says "ornithologists might have other favorites, but artists universally recognize a genius in Audubon that has not dimmed in time. One of the things that sets Audubon's work apart is his success in dramatizing birds, although there are some who have condemned him for this. It is true that some of his paintings are overdone, as in the case of his barred owl plate with its grinning squirrel. Often he attempts to show as many details of plumage as possible which has resulted in distortion; in his catbird plate, for example, he has endeavored to show the brick-red undertail coverts."

There are two main sources for the inspiration of North American wildlife art, according to David Lank, that every artist almost unavoidably must reckon with before he decides what style is going to be employed. "First is Audubon. Second is Fuertes. If somebody who is painting or draws wildlife hasn't gone through a phase of mastering and then rejecting or modifying those two great masters, he has no business selling his stuff to the public."

THE WORLD OF ROGER TORY PETERSON

Roger says that he is most comfortable "frankly with the Fuertes approach, touched with a bit of the Audubon approach as well. Now if you look at some of my drawings such as the wood thrush, you might say that its open pattern, without background, places it in the Audubon tradition. At least, it is derived from the same approach as those Audubon plates in which he married the bird to some environmental elements, but in which he completely denied a full environmental and landscape background."

Today, Roger says there is more talent in bird and wildlife painting than we have ever had. And a growing number of these talented painters have, for the first time, been able to make a living painting. Among them are Guy Coheleach, Robert Verity Clem, Don Eckelberry, Arthur Singer, Maynard Reece, Al Gilbert, Terry Shortt, Robert Bateman, Keith Shackleton, Sir Peter Scott, Robert Gilmore, Fenwick Lansdowne, Owen Gromme, and others.

Guy Coheleach, Roger says, is one of the most professional of wildlife painters, his cats being outstanding and selling for $20,000 or more. The vibrant, brilliant leopard and tiger paintings are distinctive. Coheleach "can switch gears and paint in almost any style, from commercial art to wildlife 'gallery' art." Coheleach states unequivocally that he and the other practicing bird artists who are doing so well today "would not be in the business were it not for Roger Tory Peterson. His field guides created the climate and the audience which makes it possible to sell bird paintings and prints."

Although Coheleach does paint birds, he says that animal painting is his most important interest. There is no doubt that the "mystique" in his cats and elephants has terrific appeal to the public. Owls also have this mystique, and Roger went on a real owl "binge" in 1975, painting the great horned, the barn, and the snowy.

Audubon, in his 435 plates, drew all the owls, among them the snowy and the barn owls. Comparing them with Roger's has become a critic's pastime. Lank says Audubon made a decision. He could have done the snowy a different way, but he didn't choose to. Here are two manifestations of genius—Roger and Audubon. They looked at the same bird; each came to a conclusion as to the best way to do it. "You can't say one is better."

Another outstanding contemporary painter for whom Roger has

enormous respect is Robert Verity Clem. Clem lives on Cape Cod, and Roger says "excels in a very different way from Coheleach and some of the other modern bird painters. Clem," he says, is especially "glamorous" in his portrayal of the environment of his birds. But, Roger says, a bird is a lovely creature in its own right, independent of whether or not it is in a landscape.

Many years ago when Clem lived in Naples, Florida, in a two-apartment building, Alexander Sprunt, Jr., and his wife were caretakers and lived in the other apartment.

Roger visited the Sprunts there, and asked to see Clem's work, which interested him intensely. Mr. Sprunt recalled that when Clem left the room briefly, Roger turned to Sprunt and said, "How I wish I could paint like that."

Never envious (just competitive!), Roger has always respected the talent of his fellow bird artist. He has said of Don Eckelberry, one of the most prolific and successful of them all, both as an illustrator and as an accomplished creator of fine paintings: "Eckelberry is the most inventive and original of the various successful popular bird artists. I would give my soul to have what he has."

Eckelberry's work shows the academic "proper" art training in his work, according to Roger, as do the works of Coheleach and Singer.

Eckelberry, of course, has not hesitated to do illustrations for magazines, books, field guides and has written on the philosophy of natural history art.

Today Eckelberry says there are not enough paintings to fill the enormous demands, so prints are the answer. Guaranteed high quality, limited edition printing, signed by the artist, can permit hundreds of people to enjoy the art at a fraction of the cost of the original painting.

Arthur Singer, an excellent bird painter, is also, says Roger, "the greatest workhorse. He gets things done when he says he will." Roger doesn't, partly because he bites off more than he can chew.

Singer, a Cooper Union graduate, spent several years in general commercial art before gaining recognition as a wildlife artist. He is noted for his monumental series of illustrations of world birds for many books.

Singer's *Birds of North America, a Guide to Field Identification* is Roger's first real competition in bird field guides. The book by Chandler S. Robbins, Bertel Bruun, and Herbert S. Zim has not only Singer's admirable bird pictures, colorful and accurate, but also maps of the birds' habitats and the birds' descriptions on the same page. It does not, of course, have Roger's Peterson System of identification—the arrows—which makes him exclusive.

The bird artists, though competitive, are good friends. "Every summer," Roger says, "several of us who paint—Arthur Singer, Guy Coheleach, Don Eckelberry, and I—get together to have a party and to catch up on all the gossip of our occupation. At one of these parties, I looked at my three friends and thought that if the virtues of all three could be combined, we would have the *super-artist*."

When Roger Caras, the radio and television commentator on wildlife and pets, was showing modern bird and animal paintings recently on WABC-TV, paintings by Eckelberry, Coheleach, Singer, Reece, and Peterson, the name of Audubon came up. The interviewer asked for comparisons. Caras answered, "Peterson knows more about the anatomy of the bird than Audubon. And again, over here," he said, pointing to Eckelberry's tree duck painting, "it is far better than the painting done by Audubon of the same thing."

Then the interviewer asked, "If these people are better than Audubon, who are the critics that determine?" Caras answered, "The people who buy them and put them on their walls," and he added, "Nobody has ever delineated the small North American species better than Roger Tory Peterson." And when he showed the clouded leopard by Arthur Singer and a leopard by Coheleach, Caras said, "It is unlikely that at any other time five better wildlife artists were alive to paint."

Maynard Reece, the Iowa sportsman and conservationist, considered by many as the best of the waterfowl and game bird painters, is another highly respected colleague and close friend of Roger's.

George M. Sutton, of the University of Oklahoma, is another. Sutton, Roger says, has especially good feeling for feather texture and facial expression. Sutton feels the eyes are most important in bird painting. He starts with the eye and builds the rest of the bird around it. If the eyes have life, the rest of the bird should have life. Roger often does the head and eyes first.

Canada, too, has an extraordinary number of fine wildlife artists who are friends of Roger's. In addition to Terence Michael "Terry" Shortt at the Royal Ontario Museum, there are Robert Bateman and Fenwick Lansdowne, whose *Birds of the Eastern Forest* and *Birds of the Northern Forest* are painted in the deft, detailed Audubonesque tradition.

Others include Clarence Tillenius, who lost one arm while working on a construction project during the Depression and learned to paint with the other. Tillenius paints more in the manner of the late Bruno Liljefors (sometimes said to be *the* greatest of the bird artists), "tapping," says Roger, "the underlying rhythms of nature that have moved him deeply."

"Wildlife art has come of age," said Roger at the opening of the Royal Ontario Museum wildlife art show in Toronto in 1975 in which ten countries, four Canadian provinces, and twenty-one American states were represented. "Today, in the mid-seventies, there is far more talent and activity amongst wildlife artists than we have known previously—in direct proportion to the increased popular interest in these things."

Shortt is probably the best known of Roger's ornithological contemporaries in Canada. They say he can "produce a masterpiece on a table napkin." Shortt has traveled widely with Roger, and knows his foibles and his greatness. He retired in 1976 after forty-five years with the R. O. M., where, as chief of display biology, he reproduced more than a thousand exhibitions of wildlife dioramas. His watercolors are alive and full of humor, as delightful as the man himself. Terry, lean, with plenty of dark hair and many smile wrinkles in his rather narrow face, met Roger in 1945 at an A.O.U. meeting in Toronto and says Roger has never changed. "Roger is still as absorbed in his love of nature, and contributing to the greater understanding of others about nature. It is an obsession with Roger," he says, "and he is a perfectionist. He will never rest, never admit that he has done something that satisfies him."

Terry, who has a way with words as effective as he has with a paint brush, writes in his journal of one night he and Roger were in the Galápagos, talking about painting:

> We were sitting out of doors on an almost fanciful, dreamy sort of evening, looking at the weird landscape of stark, skeleton-like *Maytenus* and *Burseras* and the macabre forms of tree *Opuntias* and crumbling old candelabra cacti before us. Flitting about were *Geospizas* and *Nesonimus*. Both Roger and I were a bit disheartened about the way we had been forced to paint our beloved birds by commercial requirements. I think we agreed that a more eloquent interpretation of nature in art was highly desirable.

Roger, sitting on a boulder beside Terry, said he had three ambitions: "To write a really fine book, to take a really fine nature photo, and to paint a really fine bird picture."

Roger has done all three—many times.

Several British painters of birds have been very close to Roger, especially Keith Shackleton and Sir Peter Scott.

Shackleton, who excels in the portrayal of pelagic and Antarctic birds, is an aircraft pilot and sailor, and has an appropriate affinity with sky and sea in his paintings. "Shackleton has the best cloud effects of all," says Roger, who has known this handsome, popular painter for many years.

The other British painter, whom Roger has known since 1933 when they first met at the A.O.U. meeting at the American Museum and both exhibited, is Sir Peter Scott, who is well known to Americans. Son of the famous Antarctic explorer, he is, according to Roger, "the most spirited bird painter in Europe. He almost gets the smell of the marsh and the sea into his work."

Scott, "a sophisticated artist, and a true English Renaissance man," says Roger, went to art school in Munich, and his training shows in his work. Scott has written thirteen books, among them *Wild Chorus* and *Morning Flight*, and has illustrated fourteen others.

Sir Peter feels that there will be a similarity between his and Roger's ultimate recognition as "naturalists." "In spite of Roger's 'straight' painting, very fine, very polished, I think his 'contribution' is more likely to be for the concept and extraordinary meticulousness of the field guide type of paintings rather than for the more so-called free paintings. Beautiful as they are, my feeling is that it is the exciting discovery of the field guide concept that will make history."

Inevitably again the comparison of Roger's "so-called free painting" with Audubon's comes into the conversation.

"I think Roger is quite as good," Scott says. "I think Audubon is a cult. I think he was influenced to a large extent by the thinking of his day. I think Audubon's paintings are marvelous designs, but I think when it comes to actually *painting* birds, I think Roger—and Clem—excel."

Another Britisher, more writer than artist, Guy Mountfort, has a somewhat similar opinion about Roger's work, and explains why his art has been slow in being recognized:

"In one respect Roger's genius for diagnostic portraiture of birds has been a disadvantage to his artistic career. The insatiable demand by the publisher for this type of work has allowed him no time to develop his undoubted ability for wider artistic expression. Only occasionally are we permitted to see hints of this, for example, in the splendidly decorative treatment of his pictures [the whooping cranes] for the National Audubon Society, which immediately became collector's items. But even this, being painted for a definite purpose, did not allow him full freedom of expression.

"I have in my study a small scraper-board drawing which Roger did for his own pleasure without any thought of selling it, or of any publisher's requirement. It is a study of sunlight filtering down through giant trees in a coniferous forest, where a grizzly bear is ambling along a track. It is a wholly delightful work, which I treasure. One sees here in full measure a quite remarkable artistic interpretation of the atmosphere of an ancient forest and a profound appreciation of the beauty of the natural world."

Roger has much to say about bird art: "There is more than one way of approaching bird painting. One is to have these highly meticulous finished backgrounds, which I call Audubonesque treatment. Another kind is 'bird in space,' where detail is not so important. This is best done by Keith Shackleton in his albatross paintings, and in oil.

"Usually a painter who paints well one way can't do well the other. They tend to condition themselves. They get used to one style, one tradition. There are bird painters who can do both. I like to think that *I* can do both."

Curiously, there is no way to study bird painting, "except on your own," says Roger. He, himself, did not learn bird painting at art school. There were not many artists painting birds at that time, in the late 1920s, and "even in 1949," according to Don Eckelberry, "it was nearly impossible to paint birds for a living."

As Kodachrome photography developed, publishers leaned toward the camera for color illustrations. But fortunately it did not replace original painting as illustration, and though Roger has said there are at least a hundred painters today in the wildlife field—not limited to illustration, of course—"only a fraction of the young artists can expect to make a living at it. I urge them to regard bird painting as a sideline or a profitable hobby. Coheleach, by raising his prices, has helped raise the prices for other wildlife painters."

Many ambitious young painters have come to Roger for advice, and some have become successful just by exposure to Roger's art.

One of the reasons for the growing interest in wildlife art is the growing public interest in nature itself and the deepening concern about environment and what man has been doing to it with industry and exploding population. Nature organizations, not only the Audubon Society, but many other environmental groups, have boomed. There is no doubt that regardless of the type of nature art being done today, people are buying it.

And why has Roger not mentioned women nature and bird painters? For some reason, he says, the field has attracted very few women artists. But Roger has also expressed another opinion, according to Hal Borland, the superb writer of nature essays for the editorial page of *The New York Sunday Times* and author of several books. "A few years ago," Borland recalls, "at a dinner meeting at Cornell, Roger spent much of his time telling anyone within hearing that women couldn't draw birds." Roger denies this. He admires the work of Colleen Nelson and Diane Pierce.

Bob Lewin probably knows more about Roger's painting during the transition period from field guides to museum art than any other person. He and his wife, Katie, have known and worked with him affectionately for over thirty years.

They first knew Roger when he was art director for the National Wildlife Federation stamp series, a project that has raised millions of dollars for conservation. During this period more than 1,400 designs have appeared on the stamp sheet, and many a child has learned his nature lesson from those stamps representing the work of truly great wildlife artists. (He resigned as art director only in 1976.)

Bob Lewin was then vice president of the lithographing company that produced the stamps and he worked with Roger in assembling the separate illustrations into a decorative unified sheet and in writing the text.

The federation was sparked originally by Ding Darling, the famous political cartoonist, with the idea of coordinating various conservation groups so that their voices could be heard in a massive, unified way in the halls of government. Many young natural history artists got their first real start in this way, like Guy Coheleach, who had sent Roger several examples of his work on speculation. At first the stamps were directed more to hunters and sportsmen, but later to all people who realized that environment is the most important thing in saving wildlife, whether it be for the sportsman, the bird watcher's pleasure, or the person who simply loves the outdoors.

Roger's birds also appear on little packets of sugar that one finds on restaurant tables, another project of the National Wildlife Federation. Spreading the word of bird knowledge and conservation is justified no matter how it is done, Roger believes. On the back of the little packages is a description of the bird and there is a Wildlife Federation message: "Want to help save endangered animals and birds? Conserve and protect the natural environment. Clean air and water are needed by both wildlife and you. Tax-deductible contributions aid our vital conservation work."

Roger, at one time, contributed similar bird paintings to the Brooke Bond tea cards, small give-away pictures contained in the packages of tea.

There was also the Lewins' jigsaw puzzle company, Springbok Editions, for which Roger painted all seventeen species of penguins. When Roger discovered that Coheleach, Singer, Reece, and Eckelberry did paintings for these puzzles, Lewin says Roger decided that he, too, wanted to be represented. So the Lewins have followed—and stimulated—Roger's painting career from the beginning.

The Peterson limited-edition prints that the Mill Pond Press publishes are either lithographic or continuous tone prints or a combination of both processes. Museum quality all-rag paper is used, either French B.F.K. Rives, Arches, or other superb imported papers. The prints have a depth of color and richness that is extremely faithful to the original paintings.

Roger, never forgetting his childhood days when money was so scarce, worried about the prices being asked for the signed, limited edition prints—$150, $175, $225. But some of the first, the cardinal, for instance, are being purchased for $750; the great horned owl for $1,000.

In order that more people could have Roger's bird pictures at less expense, Lewin launched "Unlimited Edition Decorator Prints." These are small prints that sell for $15. Of course they are not signed or numbered so have no value as collector's items. They are, however, identical reproductions of the originals and many people can enrich their walls with a Peterson bird print.

Audubon had had similar problems about distribution of his work and had agreed to smaller prints, book-size for audiences having less money or wanting smaller prints.

As a matter of fact, about thirty-five years ago Roger did thirty or more paintings for the Quaker State Lithograph Company that were printed in Switzerland and sold for $5 to $15, unsigned, of course. They would have no intrinsic value today. These were in the open-pattern, Audubonesque tradition, Roger says, and adds that "they still stand up very well even today, especially the mocking bird, the cardinal, and the bluejay."

Most of the originals of these prints Roger gave to friends and there is no telling where they are now. These originals would have special interest as Roger's reputation soars as a painter, though the prints themselves, without Roger's penciled signature, are not of collector value.

With almost fanatic energy, Roger is determined to improve, to excel. Lewin says that "every time he finishes a new painting and we tell him how great it is, Roger will say, 'Is it better than anything I've done?'" And when Bob or Katie will say it is, Roger will ask, "Isn't that the thing—to make it better, to improve? It's the challenge."

Lewin says Roger has many years of great painting ahead of him, and Roger hopes to be painting when he's ninety.

And what determines whether an artist's work will last? "Only history determines this. Not the art critic," says Lewin. "An art critic of today can make many mistakes, say something is great, but in ten years it may be valueless. Time is the only judge."

Roger says he paints or writes because "I have something to say, or because I want to do it. If it does economically well, then that's pure gravy. If it doesn't, why, I've done what I want to do. I don't think it would be done on the basis that I'm going to get so many dollars out of something." Then he grins. "It's wonderful if it brings in dollars, though."

He has lost track of the number of paintings he has done, and doesn't know what has happened to many of them. "Mostly dispersed, given away." Many of the originals that appeared in the field guides are safe in the fireproof vault at his studio.

It takes about two days for Roger to sign and number an edition of 950 prints. The Lewins bring the prints up from Florida to Old Lyme, stay until he signs them, and take them back. Roger signs at an average rate of 120 an hour, but of course there is time out for tea and relaxation.

One day when Roger was signing prints, he said to Bob Lewin, "This is the only mindless, brainless activity that I do—where I don't feel that I am wasting time, that I am accomplishing something."

Bob says that in a way the signing of the prints is therapeutic for Roger. He signs every print carefully, neatly, and with a nice signature, says Lewin. He feels that people should have a good signature. "Sometimes when he has not closed an *o*, I have said, 'Roger, will you please close that *o*?' And he'll look up at me and say, 'Yes, people are entitled, at $225 a print, to have me close the *o*.'

"One day," says Bob Lewin, "when I was in Roger's studio, I noticed, on the edge of a painting he was doing, some cryptic symbols—T-30, W-60, and so on." I asked what these symbols meant.

"Roger smiled. 'I play a game with myself. You know I may work on a book for, say, four or five hours a day. If I get tired, I may go to a painting. I may go to the tail. T-30 means that I plan to work thirty minutes on the tail at that time. Then I may go back to writing. And I may go back to the wing of the painting—W-60—and work for an hour on the wing.' Roger knows just how much time he will allot to work on a certain portion of a painting during that session."

Roger weighs his energy. If he needs a break, he'll go to another project or shift to the flowers in the background of the painting or go jogging in the nearby state park.

The Lewins, who for so many years have respected his multi-faceted talents, pay tremendous tribute to Barbara for contributing to Roger's accomplishments.

Barbara was truly interested in Roger's painting. She knew that he could do it, and she knew he *should*, says Bob Lewin. "She knew he needed to come back into painting. And Roger has come back. Full circle. Back where he's always wanted to be, an artist. He might not have been if it hadn't been for Barbara's coaching us about *pushing* Roger. She opened up his time so we could come up to Old Lyme. She kept saying 'the squeaky wheel gets the grease. Come on up here.' She coached us on how to push Roger. And without Barbara this whole project would never have developed, never have been done."

Now, is Roger going to be a "second Audubon" or a "first Roger Tory Peterson?"

There is the comment of the outstanding Canadian critic and painter Terry Shortt: "An artist's work stands by itself even as he as an individual stands, a complete and separate entity from all the others. It remains only for the viewer to react and respond to the art as he might to a person. It is, of course, an individual preroga-tive and shouldn't necessarily influence anyone else. The response to Roger's painting speaks for itself.

"I recall Frank Chapman squelching a criticism of Audubon's efforts with the remark that 'Audubon was Audubon and the book is closed.' I think time will say the same of Roger Tory Peterson."

Epilogue

CHAPTER XIX

Ginny—and the Blue Canoe

1976: Bicentennial Year.

February 1: Roger and Barbara's New Year's letter:
  Barbara and Roger going their separate ways.

March 11: Roger and Barbara divorced.

April 8: Virginia and Robert Westervelt divorced.

April 12: Roger and Virginia married. Civil service.

May 15: Roger and Virginia married. Religious service.

  And who *is* Virginia?

Mrs. Virginia Quinlan Westervelt Peterson is an attractive blonde. She was forty-nine when she married Roger. Living in Old Lyme for some time, she had known Roger and Barbara socially for about twenty years.

Love did not materialize until August 1975 when Roger and Ginny had a boating accident on the Blackhall River, in view of the Saybrook Lighthouse. The blue canoe they were in upset. Ginny had reached for her paddle when the canoe tipped over. Nobody was hurt, though the cameras were soaked. Roger and Ginny had been photographing and birding in the marshes. Barbara was with her ninety-seven-year-old mother in Seattle, where she had been spending more and more time as the marriage had been deteriorating. ("I should have gotten a divorce ten years earlier," the fifty-seven-year-old Barbara told friends in January 1976, at the time she was presented with the New York Zoological Society Vera Award for her own achievements as a naturalist and conservationist.)

When the canoe upset, a resident of a nearby estate, young Matt Griswold, came out to help. Fortunately the water was not deep—Roger doesn't care much for swimming—but it was chilly. The "rescuer" threw a warm coat over Ginny when the canoe was righted.

Barbara came back from Seattle in October to learn of Roger's intention to marry Ginny. Only a few close friends knew that Barbara and Roger were getting a divorce. The ornithological world and others would have to wait to learn of the crucial changing pattern of Roger's life until the annual New Year's letter. It usually went out early in January to nearly a thousand friends on their list. But in 1976 it was not ready until February.

Reaction varied. "To us," said one couple, "it was like hearing of the disjunction of ham and eggs." Another friend said, "All I can say is that I envy Roger his evergreen outlook." Said Devin Garrity, the publisher, "Geniuses make their own rules." It was more than a bit of a shock to some, but "high time" to others who knew of Barbara's growing unhappiness with Roger. "You can't put the bloom back on a peach when it has rubbed off," said one of their mutual friends. "It's best for both of them."

On April 23, when Roger went to his old home town of Jamestown to receive the Linnaean Gold Medal, the highest award of the Royal Swedish Academy of Sciences, from King Carl Gustaf XVI, Ginny was at Roger's side.

It was inevitable that some local people of Old Lyme gossiped about the new marriage, but the community was soon to accept it as a fact of life. Invitations were readily accepted to the Petersons, and though Lee, Roger's son who had been living at home writing his edible-plant book, took a room over in the office, he was in and out of his father's house as constantly as ever, and working in Roger's studio on his book.

Ginny is a lively, spirited, personable, capable, and amazingly energetic woman. She had walls ripped out to make larger rooms here and there, including a massive bath. Roger's office equipment was moved down to the newly purchased Colonial house on the main road, called the York House for its original owner.

Roger's paintings were hung in the halls and living room of the main house. A gardener transformed the area outside the sliding glass-wall panels into a brilliant display of color. Soft music permeates the house and office and studio. There is a color television set for the first time. Fresh flowers grace every room. Ginny wants "everything to be glowing and warm and cheerful," and she holds out her arms in an open gesture of welcome.

Roger's white hair lost all of its blondish streaks. Ginny, knowledgeable in the ways of caring for hair, has brought out the highlights of the handsome husband's plentiful locks, clipping them here and there to flatter his profile. Femininity and soft fragrances flow pleasantly through the rooms. If Roger had ever feared getting old, he no longer has any pangs. New life surges through his bones. "The last years of my life," he said, "I intend to indulge myself."

Their honeymoon was a "working" trip—off to Wyoming to photograph the golden eagle and to Arizona to photograph a roadrunner for a new painting. A visit to Roger's sister, Margaret, in California was included, and plans made for a memorial to their devoted mother, who had died following a fall at the age of ninety-seven during the winter. Barbara, on her way to Seattle to live, had seen Mrs. Saxton just before her death.

In spite of her femininity, Ginny is anything but a butterfly, though perhaps she personifies some of Roger's enthusiasm for butterflies and luna moths whose gossamer wings Roger has pursued into the woods and fields and the Lakeview Cemetery in Jamestown.

Ginny is an expert manager and helps Roger in many ways. Way back in the 1920s, Florence Page Jaques wrote of Roger in the biography of her husband that there was something about Roger that made women want to help him. Many women have "mothered" Roger—Evelyn Allen, Kate Allen, and Barbara. There has always been a woman ready and willing to carry his cameras or pick up his clothes. It is doubtful that Ginny will pick up Roger's clothes where he has dropped them indifferently. "We will pick up together," Ginny has said. "We even make our *bed*—king-size—together." The habits of Roger's lifetime may be changed by the ways of a new mate.

Moreover, Ginny works with Roger in his studio. She is an organizer and a prodder, but in a way that is not pushy. Ginny will drive the car for the most part, though Roger still insists that he "really doesn't drive badly." Ginny will care for Roger. He likes having her plan his meals and order them in a restaurant, where they eat more frequently now. She understands his need for proper food, not a hurried order of hot dogs and beans and ice-cream sodas.

And Ginny will learn about birds! She is not an experienced bird watcher, but she enjoys seeing and hearing them. Roger, a born teacher, enjoys teaching her, preferably at first by hearing the birds before sighting them.

Ginny likes to photograph, and in the winter of 1975–1976, before they were married, they were in the same photography class in New London. Roger, though a renowned wildlife photographer, wants to continue learning, never wanting to lose touch with photography.

She is an expert on nutrition. She has held positions in biochemical laboratories, evaluating the safety of food and drugs. She knows what foods Roger should eat. In 1975 he had been told by a doctor that he had a blood sugar problem—"not quite diabetic." Ginny thinks regular meals are important. And vitamins and minerals. White wine is his only alcoholic drink—and that for dinner. No smoking.

Roger began their marriage by bringing breakfast to Ginny in bed. Roger's all-night painting and writing hours have been switched to a more conventional schedule.

As for exercise, Roger's jogging continues with discretion, and Ginny joins him jogging and on brisk walks and other exercises in the morning, sometimes using special weights.

Ginny is Irish, a Boston Catholic Irishwoman. She is the daughter of Ellen Theresa Quinlan of Marshfield, Massachusetts, and the late Daniel J. Quinlan of Boston. She attended Connecticut College in New London, majoring in chemistry. When her first husband, Robert Westervelt, was a scientist with NATO in Italy, Ginny learned Italian at a Berlitz school.

Ginny's jobs have ranged from raising two talented daughters, Miriam and Linda Westervelt, to selling real estate and leading and training the leaders of four hundred Girl Scouts. Active in the Nature Conservancy and other local civic affairs, Ginny is a charter member of the National Organization for Women. She is a stout advocate of equal rights for women.

Professionally, Ginny has worked as a biochemical research assistant at the Pfizer Inc. Medical Research Laboratories at nearby Groton, Connecticut. Here Ginny participated in biochemical experiments, performing complex animal surgery and operating delicate laboratory equipment. She left Pfizer to go with her first husband to Naples, where he was a science advisor to the U.S. Naval Sixth Fleet.

On returning to the United States, Ginny went to the U.S. Coast Guard Research and Development Center in Groton. It was here that she made her contribution to the use of infrared spectroscopy to identify oil spills and to solve the mystery of their source. Oil "fingerprinting" is being used with increased frequency to identity the source of pollution. Any ship spilling oil leaves a mark as damning as a fingerprint at the scene of a crime.

Ginny not only assisted in the creation of the methods and techniques of oil-spill identification, but wrote an intricate and detailed guide book for the Coast Guard. It bears the name of "V. Q. Peterson," which pleases Roger. In June 1976 the chief of the U.S. Coast Guard Research and Development Center sent Ginny a commendation for her exceptional achievement leading to the apprehension of the alleged perpetrator of a major oil spill in the Florida Keys.

Ginny resigned from her position when she married Roger. But she has no intention of retiring from active participation in creative work. She longs to add her qualifications to Roger's genius and yet retain her own identity. Living with a genius may not be easy, but it should not be dull for Ginny.

Unlike George Bernard Shaw, who said of himself, "I am a genius," Roger has not admitted he is a genius in so many words, but there is no doubt that he senses his own worth. He said recently, "I am beginning to be recognized now, not only as a naturalist of the old school, but as an artist." The Peterson System of bird identification alone assures him a place in history. His field guides, his books, his teaching and lecturing, and now his gallery painting further establish his permanence in the archives of great men.

"Say, isn't that Roger Tory Peterson?"

Henry Martin in *The Christian Science Monitor,* © 1965 TCSPS.

Works by Roger Tory Peterson

THE PETERSON FIELD GUIDE SERIES, HOUGHTON
MIFFLIN COMPANY

The "Peterson System" of field identification is used in all twenty-one
volumes of The Peterson Field Guide Series. Twelve additional field
guides for this series are now in preparation under Peterson's editorship.
The basic component of the "Peterson System" is used by other
authors and illustrators of field guides on a wide variety of natural
history subjects in this series.

Editor/Author/Artist

A Field Guide to the Birds, 1934, 1939, 1947
A Field Guide to Western Birds, 1941, 1961
A Field Guide to the Birds of Texas and Adjacent States, 1960, 1963
A Field Guide to the Birds of Britain and Europe, Roger Tory Peter-
   son, Guy Mountfort, and P. A. D. Hollom, 1954, 1959
*A Field Guide to Wildflowers (Northeastern and North-central North
   America),* Roger Tory Peterson and Margaret McKenny, 1968
A Field Guide to Mexican Birds, Roger Tory Peterson and Edward L.
   Chalif, 1973

Editor

*A Field Guide to Shells of the Atlantic and Gulf Coasts and the West
   Indies,* Percy A. Morris, 1947, 1951, 1973
A Field Guide to the Butterflies, Alexander B. Klots, 1951
A Field Guide to the Mammals, William H. Burt and Richard P. Gros-
   senheider, 1952
*A Field Guide to Pacific Coast Shells (Including Shells of Hawaii and
   the Gulf of California),* Percy A. Morris, 1952, 1966
A Field Guide to Rocks and Minerals, Frederick H. Pough, 1953, 1955,
   1960

Works by Roger Tory Peterson

Editor (cont.)

A Field Guide to Animal Tracks, Olaus J. Murie, 1954
A Field Guide to the Ferns and Their Related Families (Northeastern and Central North America), Boughton Cobb, 1956
A Field Guide to Trees and Shrubs (Northeastern and Central North America), George A. Petrides, 1958
A Field Guide to Reptiles and Amphibians (Eastern North America), Roger Conant, 1958
A Field Guide to Rocky Mountain Wildflowers, John J. Craighead, Frank C. Craighead, Jr., and Ray J. Davis, 1963
A Field Guide to the Stars and Planets, Donald H. Menzel, 1964
A Field Guide to Western Reptiles and Amphibians, Robert C. Stebbins, 1966
A Field Guide to the Mammals of Britain and Europe, F. H. van den Brink, 1968
A Field Guide to the Insects (America North of Mexico), Donald J. Borror and Richard E. White, 1970
A Field Guide to Birds' Nests (Found East of Mississippi River), Hal H. Harrison, 1975

OTHER BOOKS

Co-editor, The Naturalist America Series, with John A. Livingston, Houghton Mifflin Company

The Appalachians, Maurice Brooks, 1965
Sierra Nevada, Verna R. Johnston, 1970
Desert, Ruth Kirk, 1973
Shaping America's Heartland, Betty Flanders Thompson, 1977

Author/Artist

The Junior Book of Birds, Houghton Mifflin, 1939
Birds Over America, Dodd, Mead, 1948, 1964
How to Know the Birds, Houghton Mifflin, 1949, 1957, 1962
Wildlife in Color, Houghton Mifflin, 1951
The Bird Watcher's Anthology, Harcourt, Brace, 1957

Co-author/Artist

Wild America, with James Fisher, Houghton Mifflin, 1955

The World of Birds, with James Fisher, Doubleday, 1964 (translated into five languages)

The Audubon Guide to Attracting Birds, with John H. Baker, Doubleday, 1941

The Birds, with the editors of *Life*, *Life* Nature Library, Time, Inc., 1963, 1968 (translated into eight languages)

The Birds, Young Readers' Edition, with the editors of *Life*, *Life* Nature Library, Time, Inc., 1967 (translated into three languages)

CONTRIBUTING AUTHOR (1963–76)

Introductions (A partial list)

A Field Guide to the Birds of East and Central Africa, John G. Williams, Houghton Mifflin, 1963

Birds of New York City, John Bull, 1963

Birds Studies at Old Cape May, Witmer Stone, 1964

Birds of Cape Cod, Norman Hills, 1965

This Good Earth, National Audubon Society, Crown, 1968

North America (World Wildlife Guide), Viking, 1971

Louis Agassiz Fuertes and the Singular Beauty of Birds, Frederick George Marcham, Harper and Row, 1971

Connecticut River, Wesleyan University, 1972

Stacey Wildlife Yearbook, 1973

Birds—An Illustrated Survey of the Bird Families of the World, John Gooders, 1974

Roger Tory Peterson's Dozen Birding Hot Spots in North America, George Harrison, Simon and Schuster, 1976

Outdoorsman Guide to Birds of Canada and Eastern North America, John MacKenzie, 1976

Francis Lee Jaques, Artist of the Wilderness, Doubleday

Forewords (A partial list)

Nature Study for Conservation, John Brainard, 1970

Animal Architecture, Roger Caras, Westover, 1971

Birds and Flight, Roger Caras, Westover, 1971

Works by Roger Tory Peterson

Birds of Wisconsin, Owen Gromme, 1971
Animal Courtships, Roger Caras, Westover, 1972
Protective Coloration and Mimicry, Roger Caras, Westover, 1972
The Bizarre Animals, Roger Caras, Barre/Westover Books, 1974
The World Atlas of Birds, Sir Peter Scott, Random House, 1974
Wildlife Paradises, John Gooders, Praeger, 1975
National Parks of East Africa, Houghton Mifflin

ARTIST

Birds of South Carolina, 1949
Birds of Newfoundland, Harold Seymour Peters, Houghton Mifflin, 1951
Arizona and Its Bird Life, 1952
Birds of Nova Scotia, 1961
Birds of Colorado, 1965
Birds of New York State, 1973

Contributing Artist

The Hawks of North America, John Bichard May, National Association of Audubon Societies, 1935
Beautiful Birds of Southern Audubon Sanctuaries, Alexander Sprunt, Jr., (illustrations reproduced from paintings by R. T. Peterson), National Association of Audubon Societies, 1938
A Natural History of the Birds of Eastern and Central North America, Edward Howe Forbush, Houghton Mifflin, 1939
Birds of North Carolina, Thomas Gilbert Pearson, Bynum Printing Co., 1942
The History of Wildlife in America, Hal Borland, National Wildlife Federation, 1975
A Watcher at the Nest, Macmillan
Birds of the Connecticut Valley
Field Book of Animals in Winter, Putnam
The Roseate Spoonbill, National Audubon Society
Wings at Dusk
Numerous covers, ornithological maps, and illustrations in *Audubon* magazine

248

NATIONAL PUBLICATIONS

Articles by Roger Tory Peterson have appeared in:

Animals	*Life*
Audubon	*National Geographic*
Bird Lore	*National Wildlife*
Carnegie	*Nature*
Christian Science Monitor	*New York Times Magazine*
Field and Stream	*Ranger Rick*
International Wildlife	*Reader's Digest*
Intrepids	*Texas Game and Fish*

EDUCATIONAL MATERIALS

More than 100 educational leaflets for National Audubon Society
Bird Study Merit Badge booklet, Boy Scouts of America

MOTION PICTURES

Filmed and narrated by Roger Tory Peterson

Galápagos—Wild Eden	*Wild America*
Wild Africa Today	*Wild Europe*

COMMISSIONS

Numerous paintings and natural history feature articles, *Life*, 1938–1945
Numerous paintings, National Wildlife Federation, 1940–1960
Numerous paintings, Morell and Co., Ottumwa, Iowa
Bird prints, Quaker State Publishing Company, 1940–1945
Limited edition prints, Mill Pond Press, Inc., 1973–present
Audubon magazine

EXHIBITIONS (A partial list)

American Museum of Natural History, New York, New York, 1974
Explorers Club, New York, New York, 1974
Cornell Laboratory of Ornithology, Ithaca, New York, 1975
Florida Audubon Society, Annual Convention, Orlando, Florida, 1975
Mt. Holyoke College, FOCUS: Outdoors Weekend, South Hadley, Massachusetts, August 1–3, 1975

Works by Roger Tory Peterson

National Audubon Society, Biennial Convention, New Orleans, Louisiana, 1975
National Wildlife Federation, Pittsburgh, Pennsylvania, 1975
Royal Ontario Museum, Toronto, Canada, 1975
Cosmos Club, Washington, D.C., 1976
Griswold Communications Center, Northwood Institute, Midland, Michigan, 1976
Hamilton College, Clinton, New York, 1976
Jamestown Community College, Jamestown, New York, 1976
Leigh Yawkey Woodson Art Museum, Wausau, Wisconsin, 1976
Amherst College, Amherst, Massachusetts, 1977
Cincinnati Nature Center, Milford, Ohio, 1977
Glenbow–Alberta Institute, Calgary, Alberta, Canada, 1977

WORK IN PUBLIC COLLECTIONS (A partial list)

American Museum of Natural History, New York, New York
Amon Carter Museum, Fort Worth, Texas
Bell Museum of Natural History, Minneapolis, Minnesota
California Academy of Arts and Sciences, San Francisco, California
Carnegie Museum of Natural History, Pittsburgh, Pennsylvania
Chicago Academy of Sciences, Chicago, Illinois
Cincinnati Nature Center, Milford, Ohio
Colby College Art Museum, Waterville, Maine
Hamilton College, Clinton, New York
Hawk Mountain Sanctuary Association, Kempton, Pennsylvania
Jamestown Nature Center, Jamestown, New York
Laboratory of Ornithology, Cornell University, Ithaca, New York
The Metropolitan Museum of Art, New York, New York
Minneapolis Institute of Art, Minneapolis, Minnesota
Munson-Williams-Proctor Institute, Utica, New York
Museum of Natural Science, Louisiana State University, Baton Rouge, Louisiana
Museum of Science, Boston, Massachusetts
New Britain Museum of American Art, New Britain, Connecticut
Northwoods Institute, Midland, Michigan
Rochester Museum & Science Center, Rochester, New York
Smithsonian Institution, Washington, D.C.
Taft Museum, Cincinnati, Ohio

Activities and Professional Affiliations

ART

Art Editor, *Audubon*, 1934–1943
Art Director, National Wildlife Federation, 1946–1975
Vice President, Society of Wildlife Artists (England)
Member, Society of Animal Artists (United States)

BIOLOGY

Member, Biologists Field Club
Member, Washington Biological Society

CONSERVATION

Board of Directors, National Audubon Society, 1958–1960, 1965–1967, 1968–1970
Secretary, National Audubon Society, 1960–1964
Special Consultant, National Audubon Society, 1970–present
Board of Directors, World Wildlife Fund, 1962–1976
Board of Directors, Hawk Mountain Sanctuary Association, 1962–1967
Board of Sponsors, Hawk Mountain Sanctuary Association, 1967–1974
Chairman, American Section, International Committee for Bird Protection, 1965–1970
Board of Directors, Baharini Foundation (Kenya, Africa), 1970–present
Dean, Conservation Summit, National Wildlife Federation, 1970
Delegate, International Bird Protection Conferences in:
    Tokyo, Japan, 1960
    Cambridge, England, 1966
    Amsterdam, Netherlands, 1970
Chairman, Flamingo Group, International Committee for Bird Protection, 1973
Keynote Address, Earth Care Conference at the United Nations, New York, 1975

Panelist, International Advisory Committee, Earth Care Conference at the United Nations, New York, 1975

Chairman, Policy Committee, Audubon Society of the District of Columbia (formerly)

Board of Directors, American Committee for International Wildlife Protection (formerly)

Consultant, Survival Service Commission, International Union for Conservation of Nature and Natural Resources

Member, National Parks Association

EDUCATION

Education Director, National Audubon Society, 1934–1943

Audubon Screen Tour Lecturer, National Audubon Society, 1946–1972

Fellow, Davenport College (Yale University), 1966–present

Keynote Address, Annual Convention, National Association of Biology Teachers, 1974

Commencement Address, University of Arizona, 1974

Commencement Address, Amherst College, 1977

LITERARY

Roving Reporter, *International Wildlife* magazine, 1970–present

NATURAL HISTORY

President, American Nature Study Society, 1952–1953

Member, Association of Interpretive Naturalists, 1968–present

Fellow, Rochester Museum and Science Center, 1972–present

ORNITHOLOGY

Associate, American Ornithologist's Union, 1925

Elected Member, American Ornithologist's Union, 1935

Fellow, American Ornithologist's Union, 1948

Delegate, International Ornithological Congresses in:
>   Uppsala, Sweden, 1950; Basel, Switzerland, 1954; Helsinki, Finland, 1958; Ithaca, New York, 1962; Oxford, England, 1966; Amsterdam, Netherlands, 1970

Patron, American Ornithologists' Union, 1958–present

First Vice President, American Ornithologists' Union, 1962–1963
President, Wilson Ornithological Society, 1964–1965
Keynote Speaker, Annual Convention, American Birding Association, June, 1973
Chairman, Birds of Prey Group, International Committee for Bird Protection
Fellow, New York Zoological Society
Life Member, Wilson Ornithological Club
Member, Baird Club
Member, British Trust for Ornithology
Member, Brooks Bird Club
Member, Cooper Ornithological Society
Member, Council of Cornell Laboratory of Ornithology
Member, Maryland Ornithological Society
Member, Nuttall Club (Cambridge, Massachusetts)
Member, Severn Waterfowl Trust (England)
Member, South Dakota Ornithologist's Union

RESEARCH

Galápagos International Scientific Project, 1964
United States Antarctic Research Program—Operation Deepfreeze, 1965
Yale University Patagonian Expedition, 1960

SCIENCE

Fellow, American Association for the Advancement of Science, 1963
Keynote Speaker, Annual Convention, American Association for the Advancement of Science, 1974

SOCIAL

Century Club, New York, New York
Cosmos Club, Washington, D.C.
Savile Club, London, England

WORLD TRAVEL

Explorers Club, member and medalist, 1972–present
Intrepids Club, president, 1974–present

253

Honors and Awards

HONORARY DEGREES

Doctor of Science, Franklin and Marshall College, 1952
*One of America's greatest naturalists, one of America's greatest painters
of birds. Mr. Peterson has by illustration and text added immeasurably
to the common knowledge of wildlife about us . . . and has been
able to influence a generation of students of nature's lore.*

Doctor of Science, Ohio State University, 1962
*Largely because of this man, the study of nature has become the pur-
suit and hobby of millions of persons in many countries. His distinguished work has been a major force in bringing diverse peoples
more closely together in a mutual appreciation of nature and of each
other.*

Doctor of Science, Fairfield University, 1967
*Roger Tory Peterson is one of the world's truly great and truly inter-
esting ornithologists. He has combined the tireless observation of the
scientist with the imaginative skills of an artist, photographer, and
writer to illuminate for millions the birds of Europe and the Americas.*

Doctor of Science, Allegheny College, 1967
*Roger Tory Peterson . . . honored because . . . you have helped
to open the eyes of millions to a beauty which would otherwise have
gone unseen.*

Doctor of Science, Wesleyan University, 1970
*Roger Tory Peterson, ornithologist and naturalist, in a threatened
world suddenly aware of its own mortality, you have long been a
prophet of the interrelatedness of all living things. As author, illustrator, editor, and incomparable guide to our wildlife, you have opened
our eyes to the beauty, the wonder, and the sanctity of life itself.*

Doctor of Science, Colby College, 1974
No person has done more to make the beauty and diversity of nature

both apparent and accessible to the layman than Dr. Peterson. . . . .
Colby is privileged to honor Dr. Peterson for his unique and spectacu-
lar contribution to our understanding of the world we live in.

Doctor of Humanities, Hamilton College, 1976
We recognize you for your contributions as an artist, writer, and
lecturer. . . . While not disagreeing with our many colleagues who
have honored you as a scientist, Hamilton is proud to recognize you as
a humanist and artist.

Doctor of Humane Letters, Amherst College, 1977
In teaching us how to see, you have taught us also to see the human need
for a balanced and harmonious environment.

CONSERVATION

Honorary Trustee. Uganda National Parks (Uganda, Africa), 1958–62.
Honorary Member. *For the continued and unselfish efforts in the field*
   of bird conservation, National Wildlife Society, 1966.
First Distinguished Scholar in Residence at Fallingwater. *In recognition*
   of his outstanding contribution to the promotion of conservation
   through interpretation, inspiration, and scholarship, Western Penn-
   sylvania Conservancy, 1968.
Gold Medal. *For his devotion to the conservation of wildlife*, African
   Safari Club of Philadelphia, 1968.
Conservation Award. *To America's most distinguished teacher in the*
   field of ornithology and conservation, The White Memorial Founda-
   tion, 1968.
Frances K. Hutchinson Medal. *For an internationally eminent con-*
   servationist, ornithologist, artist and author, The Garden Club of
   America, 1970.
Honorary Vice President. New Jersey Audubon Society, 1970–71.
Audubon Medal. *For distinguished service to conservation*, National
   Audubon Society, 1971.
Gold Medal. *In recognition of his outstanding contribution to the*
   promotion of conservation as an artist and ornithologist, World
   Wildlife Fund, 1972.
Joseph Wood Krutch Medal. *For significant contribution towards the*
   improvement of life and environment, The Humane Society of the
   United States, 1973.
Special 75th Anniversary Award. *In recognition of his willingness to*

share his knowledge and talents with millions throughout the world and his everlasting contribution to the cause of conservation, Florida Audubon Society, 1975.

Conservation Achievement Award. *Today he continues to blaze new paths which create a deeper awareness of nature for millions of Americans,* National Wildlife Federation, 1975.

Honorary Vice President. Audubon Naturalist Society.

Honorary Vice President. Massachusetts Audubon Society.

EDUCATION

Golden Key Award, Outstanding Teacher of the Year. *Selected by Elliot L. Richardson as the teacher who was most influential in shaping his formative years,* 1974.

Sponsored by:
American Association of School Administrations
Council of Chief State School Officers
Education Industries Association
National Council of State Education Associations
National Congress of Parents and Teachers
National School Boards Association
National School Public Relations Association

Honorary Member. *For outstanding contributions in biology and biological science education,* National Association of Biology Teachers, 1965.

Dedication, *Roger Tory Peterson Nature Interpretive Building,* at the Burgeson Sanctuary of the Jamestown Audubon Society, October 16, 1976.

LITERATURE

John Burroughs Medal. *For exemplary nature writing of* Birds Over America, John Burroughs Memorial Association, 1950.

Carey–Thomas Award Honorable Mention for creative publishing in 1959, presented to Houghton Mifflin Company for the publication of *A Field Guide to the Birds,* by Roger Tory Peterson, and *A Field Guide to the Bird Songs,* by Dr. Peter Paul Kellogg and Dr. Arthur A. Allen.

Special Award. *For his excellent contribution to* Birds in Our Lives, *a* publication of the Bureau of Sport Fisheries and Wildlife, Secretary of the Interior, 1966.

Sarah Josepha Hale Award. Richards Library (New Hampshire), 1977.

NATURAL HISTORY

Honorary Fellow. Linnaean Society of New York, 1927.

Certificate of Recognition. *In grateful appreciation for services rendered as President 1952–1953,* American Nature Study Society, 1953.

Geoffrey St. Hilaire Gold Medal. French Natural History Society (Paris), 1958.

Certificate of Appreciation. *For valued contribution to the program success of the 3rd Annual Conference as a Featured Speaker,* FOCUS: Outdoors, University of Massachusetts, 1969.

Paul Bartsch Award. *For dedicating an exceptional range of abilities and knowledge to the education of the public in the understanding of the beauties and wonders of the natural world,* Audubon Naturalist Society, 1969.

Oak Leaf Cluster Award. Audubon Naturalist Society, 1974.

Jamestown Hall of Fame. *In recognition of the pride and honor he has brought to Jamestown High School through his lifetime achievements,* Jamestown, New York, 1972.

Explorers Medal. *Presented to Roger Tory Peterson, artist, naturalist, explorer, whose own ethic has helped develop our new environmental consciousness,* Explorers Club, 1974.

Roger Tory Peterson Week. *To honor and recognize an outstanding talent who has created renewed appreciation of the world around each of us,* Robert D. Goodenough, Mayor of Midland, Michigan, January 17–25, 1976.

Linnaeus Gold Medal. Awarded by the Swedish Academy of Sciences, presented by King Carl XVI Gustav of Sweden at Jamestown, New York, 1976.

ORNITHOLOGY

William Brewster Award, for second (1939) edition of *A Field Guide to the Birds,* American Ornithologists' Union, 1944.

Gold Medal. *Inspired interpreter of birds for the benefit of man,* New York Zoological Society, 1961.

Recognition of contribution to ornithology and conservation. Detroit Audubon Society, 1961.

Certificate of Recognition. *For significant and outstanding service to the cause of Wisconsin wild bird conservation through leadership resulting in appreciation and action by the public,* Wisconsin Society of Ornithology, 1964.

Arthur A. Allen Award. *For outstanding service to ornithology,* Cornell Laboratory of Ornithology, 1967.

Gold Medal. *For ornithological, literary, and artistic achievement, leadership, and inspiration,* Garden Club of New Jersey, 1970.

Honorary Member. British Ornithologist's Union, 1973.

Honorary Fellow. *To recognize your services to ornithology,* Zoological Society of London, elected in 1974, installed in 1975.

Honorary Fellow. Texas Ornithological Society, 1977.

PUBLIC SERVICE

Distinguished Public Service Award. *In acknowledgment of his scholarship, for his vast contribution to our knowledge and enjoyment of the wonders of nature, for the recognition he has brought to our state, for his talent as an incomparable and painstaking artist,* Connecticut Bar Association, 1974.

Green World Award. *For outstanding public leadership in the preservation and protection of the natural environment,* New York Botanical Garden, 1976.

Horatio Alger Award, 1977.

SCIENCE (General)

1976 Cosmos Club Award. *In recognition of his successful career in popularizing this important field of natural science,* Cosmos Club, 1976.

Index

Index

Hammerstrom, Carl, 6, 8, 9, 13, 15
Hammond, Victor, 76
Handbook of Birds of Eastern North America (Chapman), 18
Harty, Marcia, 22
Harvard Bird Club, 64
Hawaiian Islands, 201–202
Heflin, Van, 76
Herald, Earl, 108
Herbert, Richard, 43, 44, 45
Hernandez, Robert, 171
Hickey, Joseph J., 32, 33, 43, 44, 45, 46, 49, 95, 151, 190
Hiss, Alger, 111–112
Hog Island, Muscongus Bay, Maine, 80–89
Hollan, W. J., 21
Hollom, Philip A. D., xv, 121–122, 130, 133
Holton, George, 175–176
Hornbeck, Blanche, 6, 7, 27
Horsfall, Bruce, 6, 31
Hosking, Eric, 133–134
Houghton Mifflin Company, xvii, 61, 62–63, 64, 108, 121, 128, 135
House at Nauset Marsh, The (Richardson), 58
"How We Counted Forty Million Blackbirds" (Halberg), 164
Howes, Paul, 226
Hudson, W. H., 152
Humphrey, Dr. Philip, 205
Hurst, Barbara, 174, 208
Huxley, Sir Julian, 133

International Committee for Bird Protection, 196
International Ornithological Congress (Sweden, 1950), 200
International Union for the Conservation of Nature, 188, 202–203
"Intrepids, The," 213–214

Jacobs, Charles Tenno, 76, 81–82
James Fisher Memorial Conservation Island, 138
James's flamingo, 177–178, 201
Jamestown Audubon Society, 17
Jaques, Francis Lee, 27–28, 91

Johnson, F., 21
Jones, Allan, 12, 24
Juan Carlos, 186
Junior Audubon Clubs, 72–74, 115

Kassoy, Irving, 42, 43, 44, 104, 121
Kastner, Barbara, 76, 77
Kastner, Joseph, 76, 77, 81, 106, 117–118
Keith, Anthony, 160
Keith, G. Stuart, 151, 155, 160–161, 174
Kessler, Phillip, 43, 44
Kieran, John, 45–46, 67
Kifner, John, 167
King Ranch, 161–162
Kinne, Jane, 140–141, 143–144, 171, 173–174, 175
Klots, Alexander, 108
Kuerzi, John F., 43, 44
Kuerzi, Richard, 44

Lager, Mrs. Edwin. *See* Peterson, Margaret
Langereis, Willem Dieperink Von, 25, 30
Lank, David M., 68, 177, 218, 220, 221, 227
Lank, Ellen, 177
Lansdowne, Fenwick, 228, 231
Lemar, Charles, 76
Leopold, Aldo, 176
Lewin, Katie, 234–238
Lewin, Robert, xv, 141, 144, 219, 220, 234–238
Lichtenstein, Prince of, 66
Life magazine, 76, 81, 106, 117–120, 177, 217, 222
Liljefors, Bruno, 29, 231
Lindbergh, Charles A., 192, 193
Lindblad, Lars–Eric, 206–207, 209, 210, 211, 213, 221
Lindblad Explorer, xvi, xix, 145, 165, 174, 176–177, 184, 196, 200, 206–213
Linnaean Gold Medal, 240
Linnaean Society, 42, 44, 45, 84
Linné, Carl von, 201

Index